POCKET

Factfile of 20TH CENTURY PEOPLE

Vanwell Publishing Limited

St Catharines, Ontario

Project Editors: Fiona Gold,
Simon Kooter
Editor: Helen McCurdy
Designer: Frankie Wood
Production Manager: Clive Sparling
Picture Manager: Claire Turner

Planned and produced by
Andromeda Oxford Ltd
11–15 The Vineyard
Abingdon
Oxfordshire OX14 3PX

Published in Canada by
Vanwell Publishing Ltd
1 Northrup Crescent, Box 2131
St. Catharines, Ontario
Canada L2R 7S2

Canadian Cataloguing in Publication Data

Main entry under title:

The pocket factfile of 20th century people

(The pocket factfile series)
1st Canadian ed.
ISBN 1-55068-083-8

1. Biography – 20th century. I. Gold, Fiona.
II. Kooter, Simon. III. Series

CT120.P63 1996 920'.009'04 C96-931205-9

Origination by Perdana Grafik, Malaysia

Printed by Tien Wah Press, Singapore

INTRODUCTION

In making this selection of 500 key figures of the 20th century we have tried to present as rounded a picture of recent times as possible. We make no apology that **political leaders** form by far the largest group – after all, they shape, for better or worse, the world we live in. The 20th century, which has seen two world wars and the rise and fall of totalitarian states of both left and right, has had more than its share of rogues and villains, but it has thrown up plenty of men and women who have offered a higher vision of humanity – people such as Mother Teresa or Raoul Wallenberg – and politicians who have worked to end poverty and inequality, lift oppression, or solve some of the world's more intractable conflicts.

The next largest group consists of **entertainers** – filmmakers, movie stars, songwriters and performers – for the 20th century has seen the emergence of a vast global entertainment industry, fostered first by Hollywood and more recently by the media giants of the television and recording industries. Then there are the **scientists**: men like Einstein at the beginning of the century and Stephen Hawking at the end who have changed the way we think about the Universe; researchers who have discovered viruses or explained the structure of the human body; psychoanalysts who have explored the human mind. **Business and industrial tycoons** are here as well, balanced by the **writers, artists and musicians** who form our ideas, charge our imaginations and enrich our inner lives. Finally there are the **sportsmen and women** whose outstanding physical achievements lift our spirits and give us a goal to aim at.

The book is arranged by alphabetical entry. It can be used as a straightforward work of reference or as a book to be dipped into for pleasure and enlightenment, providing a fascinating commentary on the history of the 20th century.

The Russian poet, Anna Akhmatova, whose work was banned during the Stalinist era.

Acheson, Dean (1893–1971) US secretary of state. A lawyer, Acheson was under secretary of state in the treasury and state departments (1945–47), where he helped shape the Marshall Plan for postwar economic recovery in Europe and formulate the policy of Soviet containment (the Truman Doctrine), before serving as President Harry S. Truman's secretary of state (1949–53). He played a key role in the formation of NATO but despite his firm stand against communism was blamed by for Cold War defeats in China and Korea. After his retirement from the state department he continued to serve as a valued foreign-policy adviser.

Adenauer, Konrad (1876–1967) West German chancellor. A member of the Catholic Center Party, Adenauer was mayor of Cologne (1917–33) but was dismissed from office by the Nazis and eventually sent to a concentration camp in 1944. As leader of the Christian Democratic Union party, he was prominent in rebuilding politics in the postwar period of occupation and in 1949 became the first chancellor of the Federal Republic of West Germany. In working for his country's reconstruction, Adenauer aligned it firmly with the West and steadfastly refused to recognize the German Democratic Republic. Combining his role as chancellor with that of foreign minister, he negotiated West Germany's full membership of the Council of Europe and of the European Coal and Steel Community in 1951 (transmuted into membership of the EEC in 1957), secured its recognition as a sovereign state and brought it into NATO in 1954. By the time of his retirement in 1963 he had achieved postwar reconciliation with France.

Agnelli, Giovanni (1866–1945) Italian industrialist. A founder and chairman of the Turin automobile manufacturing company Fiat (Fabbrica Italiana Automobili Torino), Agnelli helped turn it into Italy's largest industrial enterprise, producing airplanes, buses, tractors, diesel engines and ball-bearings as well as automobiles: its Turin plants were at full capacity during World War I manufacturing arms for the Italian government. Agnelli became president of Fiat in 1920. He employed over 30,000 people and favored a paternalistic form of management with an emphasis on workers' welfare. He supported Mussolini, who made him a senator in 1923. Fiat was again the chief military supplier in World War II, and in April 1945 the Italian Committee of National Liberation removed Agnelli and his top executives from control of the company. His family regained a role in the running of the company in the 1960s.

Akhmatova, Anna (1889–1966) Russian poet. With the poets Nikolai Gumilev (her husband) and Osip Mandelstam, Akhmatova founded Acmeism, a literary movement that called for a return to direct poetic expression and concrete clarity, away from the fuzzy mysticism of the Symbolists. Her first collection, *Evening* (1912), dealt mostly with the pain of love. Gumilev, to whom she was no longer married, was executed in 1921, and she suffered increasing political oppression; her son Lev was exiled to Siberia and she was banned from publishing from 1923–40, and 1946–56. Though she was denounced by the Soviet authorities for her bourgeois individualism, her poems remained popular. She continued to write, and works like *Poem Without a Hero* (1940–62), for long unpublished, which deals powerfully with the dilemma of being a poet during the Stalinist era, and *Requiem* (1963) exemplify the responsibility she felt to bear witness to the truth.

Ali, Muhammad (1942–) US boxer. Born Cassius Clay, he began boxing at the age of 12 and turned professional after winning the Olympic heavyweight championship in 1960. In 1964 he knocked out Sonny Liston to become world heavyweight champion. On becoming a Black Muslim he changed his name to Muhammad Ali. After refusing to join the army on religious grounds, he was stripped of his title in 1967 and given a five-year prison sentence, but the Supreme Court quashed his conviction in 1970. In 1974 Ali beat Joe Frazier and George Foreman to regain his title. He lost it to Leon Spinks in 1978 but beat him the same year to become the first heavyweight boxer to win the world title three times. He retired in 1979, but attempted a comeback a year later. Ali was noted

The Philippines president, Corazón Aquino, who brought down Ferdinand Marcos.

for his lightning reflexes and great coordination, as well as his humorous showmanship and gift as a self-publicist. In 1984 he was found to have brain damage, sustained through heavy punishment in the ring.

Allen, Woody (1935–) US film actor, director, writer and jazz clarinetist. Born Allen Stewart Konigsberg in Brooklyn, his cynical, self-deprecating style colored 1970s American humor. *What's New Pussycat?* (1965) was his first screen credit (writer/actor), followed by other parodies, including *Love and Death* (1975). Greater success came with *Annie Hall* (1977) and *Manhattan* (1979). During the 1980s his subject matter broadened and he made several successful movies, including *Midsummer Night's Sex Comedy* (1982), *Broadway Danny Rose* (1984) and *Hannah and Her Sisters* (1986) with his then partner, Mia Farrow. In 1992 Allen endured a highly publicized legal battle with Farrow after he left her for her adopted daughter.

Allende (Gossens), Salvador (1908–73) Chilean president. Allende was arrested while at medical school for "revolutionary activities". In 1933 he helped found the Chilean Socialist party which broke away from the Soviet-orientated Communist party. A long-time politician in the Chilean parliament, Allende contested the presidential elections for the fourth time in 1970, as Popular Unity candidate, a Socialist-Communist-radical coalition. He won narrowly and set out to create a socialist society in an undeveloped country while maintaining a liberal form of parliamentary agreement. Chile's large copper mines, previously part US-owned, were nationalized without compensation, most industry brought under state control and land reforms put into effect. Higher wages and price freezes led to soaring inflation. Though Allende increased his majority slightly in the 1972 elections, middle-class opposition to his policies was growing. The threat of further nationalization caused strikes, inflation continued, food was short and street violence spread. The US government voiced criticism of his regime and there was internal interference from US agencies. In September 1973 Allende was killed in a military coup.

Alpher, Ralph Asher (1921–) US physicist. With George Gamow and Hans Bethe he formulated the "hot big bang" theory of the origin of the Universe, based on interpretation of the relative distribution of its known elements, and involving thermonuclear process. This convincingly explained the universal abundance of helium, resulting from the fusion of four hydrogen nuclei, with intense emission of energy. A corollary of this theory (known as the alpha, beta, gamma theory) was that there should be a background of radio "noise" throughout space corresponding to a temperature of 5°K. Such radiation was detected in 1965.

Amin (Dada), Idi (1925–) Ugandan dictator. An army officer, in 1971, Amin led a coup against prime minister Milton Obote, who had previously appointed him commander in chief of the army, installed himself as president and dissolved parliament. He instigated a reign of terror in Uganda, expelling all Asian citizens and persecuting tribes other than his own, the Kakwa. It is estimated that 100,000–300,000 people were tortured and killed during his rule. Border disputes strained relations with Tanzania and Kenya. In 1978 he attacked Tanzania, and Tanzanian troops invaded Uganda. Amin escaped abroad and eventually found refuge in Saudi Arabia.

Aquino, Corazón (1933–) Philippines president. The daughter of a wealthy landowning family, Aquino was thrown into the political arena when her husband, the political activist Benigno Aquino, was assassinated as he stepped off his plane on returning to the Philippines from exile in the US in 1983. Corazón Aquino took up the political baton and threw herself into a turbulent and emotional campaign to oust Ferdinand Marcos from power. The strength of the "People's Power" opposition forced Marcos to flight after he had tried to rig the presidential elections in 1986, and Aquino took over. The volatile political situation in the Philippines made her presidency an uneasy one. Though popular with the public she had to face the constant threat of assassination and chose not to stand for reelection in 1992.

Leader of the PLO, Yasir Arafat has played a key role in Middle Eastern politics.

Arafat, Yasir (1929–) chairman of the Palestine Liberation Organization. Born in Jerusalem, Arafat studied engineering at the university of Cairo. From 1957–65 he was head of the Palestinian resistance group, al-Fatah. When al-Fatah assumed control of the recently established Palestine Liberation Organization (PLO) in 1969, Arafat became chairman. He succeeded in gaining Arab support for the PLO's claim to be the legitimate representative of the Palestinian people, and it was formally recognized by the UN in 1974. Arafat temporarily lost overall control of the PLO in 1982 when Israel invaded Lebanon. In 1988 Jordan surrendered its claim over the West Bank to allow the PLO to take over responsibility. Arafat's condemnation of terrorism increased his standing in world opinion, as did his apparent acknowledgment of Israel's right to coexistence with a Palestinian state, though this lost him support among extremist Arabs. He entered into peace negotiations with the Israeli prime minister Yitzhak Rabin, sharing the Nobel peace prize in 1994 with him and Shimon Peres, the Israeli foreign minister. In the first free elections to be held on the Palestinian West Bank in January 1996, Arafat was elected president of the legislative council.

Arbuckle, Roscoe ("Fatty") (1887–1933) US film actor. Arbuckle played in vaudeville before joining the early movie industry, performing in comedy one-reelers for Selig Polyscope. In 1913 he became part of Mack Sennett's Keystone Cops, starring with Charlie Chaplin, Chester Conklin and Mabel Normand. He turned to screenwriting and directing, forming his own production company in 1917. A large, baby-faced, remarkably agile man, Arbuckle was one of Hollywood's most popular stars until his career ended suddenly in a notorious sex scandal (1921). He later directed under the name of William B. Goodrich but failed to reestablish his acting career.

Arden, Elizabeth (1878–1966)
Canadian-born US businesswoman. Born Florence Nightingale Graham, she studied nursing before opening her first beauty salon on New York's Fifth Avenue in 1909. A pioneer in the advertising and marketing of cosmetics, Arden became one of the world's leading producers of beauty aids, selling over 450 different preparations. She owned over 100 salons and two luxury beauty resorts at the time of her death.

Armstrong, Louis ("Satchmo") (1900–71) US jazz trumpeter, vocalist and composer. Regarded by most people as the greatest jazz trumpeter ever, Armstrong was born in New Orleans and learned to play the cornet in the city's Colored Waifs Home for Boys. His talent was encouraged by the cornetist Joe "King" Oliver. In 1922 Armstrong left New Orleans to join Oliver's band in Chicago and then moved to New York, where he played with Fletcher Henderson's Orchestra before forming his own band, the Hot Five (1925). Recordings such as "Potato Head Blues" and "West End Blues" established him as a virtuoso instrumentalist and vocalist: he invented scat singing in which nonsense syllables are used to imitate instrumental sounds. Until 1947 Armstrong played with big bands, his final line-up being the six-piece All Stars, which produced classic albums such as *Plays Fats* and *At the Crescendo*. His friendly and cheerful personality helped popularize jazz throughout the world, and he later appeared in several hit movies including *Hello Dolly* (1969). At the end of his career he scored a popular hit with "What a Wonderful World".

Ashrawi, Hanan (1946–)
Palestinian politician. Ashrawi was Professor of English Literature at the Bir Zeit University on Israel's West Bank, before becoming plunged into the world of Palestinian politics. After Israel's invasion of Lebanon in 1982 and the Israeli-backed raids on refugee camps she formally espoused the Intifada (the call for a Palestinian uprising) and became a well-known figure through numerous TV appearances, particularly in the US. Her reasoned arguments presented the intelligent and compassionate face of the Palestinian cause to the public. She gained US backing for her inclusion on the advisory committee to the Palestinian delegation to the US-led peace talks in the fall of 1991. In the first free elections to be held in the newly autonomous Palestinian West Bank and Gaza in 1996, Ashrawi was elected to the legislative council as a member for Jerusalem.

Mustafa Kemal Atatürk, the founder and first president of modern Turkey.

Asquith, Herbert (1852–1928) British prime minister. The son of a Yorkshire cloth manufacturer, Asquith had a brilliant career at Oxford and was an accomplished barrister who moved easily from the courtroom to the political debating chamber. He served as Liberal MP for East Fife (1886–1918), gaining his first cabinet post as home secretary (1892–95) in Gladstone's last government. In opposition, he championed free trade, the issue that returned the Liberals to power in 1906. He served as chancellor of the exchequer (1906–08) before succeeding as prime minister (1908–16). Asquith's administration put through a program of social reform that included the introduction of old age pensions and reform of the House of Lords. He came under pressure over the question of Irish home rule and from the suffragette movement, and his government was criticized for its early handling of World War I. In May 1915 he formed a coalition government but this undermined Asquith's position still further and in December 1916 he was ousted from the premiership.

Assad, Hafiz al- (1928–) Syrian president. Assad joined the Arab nationalist and socialist Ba'ath party at the age of 16. He trained as an air pilot and in 1955 was sent to the Soviet Union to learn night flying. From 1958–61 he served with the United Arab Republic airforce in Cairo, returning to Syria when the political union with Egypt was dissolved. In 1963 the Ba'ath party assumed power and Assad was made a general and airforce commander. He became airforce chief and defense minister in 1966 and, despite presiding over Syria's decisive defeat in the 1967 Arab–Israeli war, used the position to build up his personal power base. In 1970 he led a bloodless coup to assume the presidency. Repeatedly clashing with Israel over Lebanon, he sought to dominate the Palestinian Liberation Organization (PLO) and denounced the 1980 Egypt–Israel peace treaty, signing a 20-year friendship treaty with the Soviet Union. He supported Iran in the Iran–Iraq war (1980–88) and in 1982 closed Syria's border with Iraq, cutting off an Iraqi pipeline. Political opposition at home was dealt with ruthlessly: in 1982 some 20,000 rebels were killed. After the collapse of the Soviet bloc in 1989, Syria was without international allies, and in the crisis precipitated by Iraq's invasion of Kuwait in 1990, Assad added his support to the UN force.

Astaire, Fred (1899–1987) US actor, dancer, singer and choreographer. Born Frederick Austerlitz, he pursued a successful stage career with his sister Adele before turning to films in 1933. He formed a famous dance partnership with Ginger Rogers which lasted through 10 movies, including *Roberta* and *Top Hat* (both 1935), *Swing Time* (1936) and *Carefree* (1938). His sophisticated, yet apparently casual style was based on matchless technique and elaborate rehearsal and preparation. Later partners included Rita Hayworth, Eleanor Powell and Cyd Charisse. Astaire had a light, charming singing voice which he used to good effect. In one of his last great musical roles he starred opposite Audrey Hepburn in *Funny Face* (1957).

Atatürk, Mustafa Kemal
(1881–1938) Founder and first president of modern Turkey. During World War I, Mustafa Kemal (the name Atatürk, meaning "father of the Turks", was assumed later) was the general in command of the Turkish forces at the Dardanelles. After the defeat of the Ottoman empire he led the nationalist movement that sought to establish Turkey as a modern state. He was fiercely opposed to the Allied plan to partition Turkey with Greece and organized the expulsion of the Greek population from Asia Minor in 1922. On the abolition of the sultanate he became the first president (1923–38) of the new Turkish republic. Determined to bring Turkey into the modern western world, Atatürk ruled as a benevolent dictator. Turkish script was replaced by the Latin alphabet, western-style surnames and western dress imposed, the legal and educational systems reformed, and women were given the vote. He promoted nationalism over religion, nationalized foreign industry and created a national bank.

Atlas, Charles (1893–1972) Italian-born body builder. Atlas was a young, skinny immigrant named Angelico Siciliano when a lifeguard kicked sand in his face and stole his girl at Coney Island. The humiliation he felt

The British poet W. H. Auden on his way to observe the war in China in 1938.

impelled him on a course of bodybuilding. He changed his name to Charles Atlas and by 1922 had improved his physique so much he was described as "America's Most Perfectly Developed Man". In 1929, with a young advertising man, Charles Ronan, Atlas began marketing a program of isotonic exercises and advice on nutrition. Advertisements proclaiming "You too can have a body like mine!" became a familiar feature of popular magazines.

Attlee, Clement (1883–1967)
British prime minister. An Oxford-educated lawyer, Attlee was converted to socialism as a social worker in London's East End. He was a lecturer at the newly-founded London School of Economics (1913–23) and in 1919 was elected mayor of Stepney. He became a member of parliament for Stepney in 1922 and rose through the Labor party ranks to become leader in 1935. On the outbreak of war in 1939 he refused to form a coalition with the Conservatives under Chamberlain, but gave his support to Churchill's premiership. He served in the wartime cabinet and was deputy prime minister (1942–45). In the immediate postwar parliamentary elections, Attlee led the Labor party to decisive victory. During his premiership (1945–51), Britain joined NATO and the Council of Europe, granted independence to India and the newly-formed states of Pakistan, Ceylon and Burma, and ceded control of Palestine and Egypt. At home the Labor government nationalized industries and set up the welfare state system of social security, including a free National Health Service. Attlee continued as leader of the opposition after the Labor defeat of 1951 and was created an earl in 1955.

Auden, Wystan Hugh (1907–73)
British-born US poet. Influenced by Marx and Freud, Auden was the intellectual leader of a group of poets, including Christopher Isherwood,

Stephen Spender and Cecil Day-Lewis, who dominated the literary left in 1930s Britain. His collection *Look, Stranger!* was published in 1936. He went to Spain and wrote about the Spanish civil war in *Spain* (1937), a poem he repudiated in later life, and wrote a verse commentary on the Sino-Japanese war in *Journey to a War* (1938). This included prose reports by Isherwood, with whom Auden had earlier collaborated in three verse plays including *The Ascent of F6* (1936). Auden emigrated to the US in 1939 and became a naturalized citizen in 1946 but continued to spend half the year in Europe. Two long poems, *For the Time Being* and *The Sea and The Mirror* (both 1944), were influenced by his conversion to Anglicanism, and *The Age of Anxiety* (1947) won the 1948 Pulitzer Prize. He collaborated with his companion Chester Kallman on libretti, including Stravinsky's *The Rake's Progress* (1951). His later works include *Homage to Clio* (1960) and *City Without Walls* (1969).

Bacon, Francis (1909–92) Irish-born British painter. A self-taught painter, Bacon began his career as an interior designer. He won acclaim and notoriety for *Three Studies for Figures at the Base of a Crucifixion* (1945) and retained a reputation for sinister, emotionally and physically shocking and distorted work. Many of his paintings had religious themes, like the intense series of *Screaming Popes* (1949–1950s). His work shed some of its weird imagery during the 1950s, and the portraits he painted thereafter had simplified settings but displayed violently intensified emotion in faces and figures.

Baekeland, Leo Hendrik (1863–1944) Belgian-born US chemist. Baekeland emigrated to the US in 1889 hoping to find greater outlet for his interest in technological chemical research than he had in his home-town of Ghent. Working for a photographic manufacturer, he invented a fast-printing photographic printing paper and set up his own company to market it. This he sold to Kodak for $1 million in 1899 and he then turned his attention to electrochemistry. In 1909, while seeking a substitute for shellac, widely used as an insulator, Baekeland discovered the first synthetic phenolic resin, or plastic, which he called Bakelite.

Baird, John Logie (1888–1946) British television pioneer. Born in Scotland, ill health forced him to abandon his career as an electrical engineer and he retired to the south

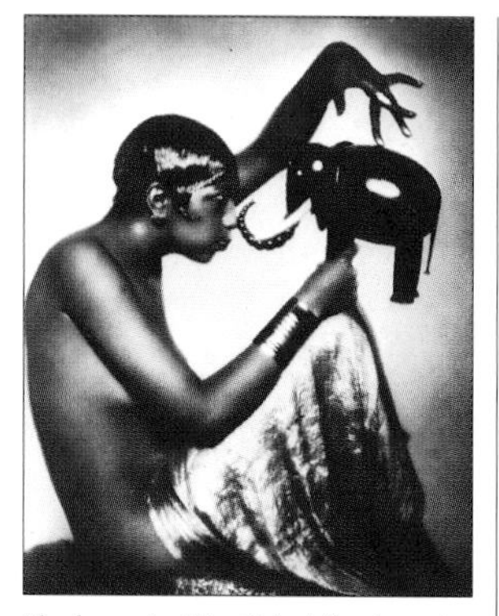

The dancer Josephine Baker's flamboyant style delighted Parisian audiences.

coast. He became interested in the possibilities of television and on 26 January 1926 gave the world's first public demonstration of a television image, using a crude electromechanical system. In 1927 he transmitted pictures from London to Glasgow, and in the following year to New York. His system was used by the British Broadcasting Corporation (BBC) from 1929–35, but it was superseded by the Marconi-EMI system.

Baker, Josephine (1906–75) US-born dancer and singer. Daughter of a Black washer-woman in St Louis, Baker was a flamboyant entertainer whose beauty and vivacious personality made her the toast of Paris in the late 1920s and 1930s. She joined a touring company at 16 and made it to Broadway, but her greatest successes were reserved for Paris, where she joined La Revue Nègre in 1925. The Parisian audiences adored her exotic dancing, daring costumes and astonishing entrances and she took French citizenship in 1937. At the height of her success she was the highest-paid entertainer in Europe. She was famed for her many eccentricities, which included walking a pet cheetah in public. During World War II she joined the French resistance and was later awarded the Croix de Guerre and the Legion of Honor. Toward the end of her life she marched alongside Martin Luther King in the civil rights demonstrations of the 1960s.

Baldwin, James (1924–87) US writer. Raised in Harlem's Black ghettoes, Baldwin became a revivalist preacher at the age of 14 but soon lost his faith. In 1948 he won a major literary fellowship and moved to Paris, where he lived until 1956. *Go Tell it on the Mountain* (1953), based on his experience of revivalism, brought him fame. In *Giovanni's Room* (1956) he wrote about homosexuality which, along with racism, was a lifelong theme in his novels and essays. From

1957 he was active in the civil rights movement, and focused more and more of his writing on the racial issue; he was recognized as the literary voice of Black America. Martin Luther King's assassination shattered Baldwin's hopes of a peaceful resolution to the problem of racism, and he became bitterly resigned to violence, a bitterness that shows in his best-seller *The Fire Next Time* (1963).

Balfour, Arthur J. (1848–1930) British prime minister. Born into a well-connected Scottish family (his mother was sister to Lord Salisbury), Balfour was educated at Eton and Cambridge. From 1878–80 he was private secretary to his uncle, the then foreign secretary who soon succeeded Disraeli to leadership of the Conservative party. Balfour became an MP in 1885, serving as secretary for Scotland (1886–87) and Ireland (1887–91), in which post he was firmly opposed to Irish home rule. He was first lord of the treasury and leader of the Commons (1892–93), and succeeded to the premiership in 1902. The Conservative party split in 1903 over the question of tariff reform versus free trade, and this led to Balfour's resignation as prime minister in 1905, though he remained party leader until 1911. In 1915 he became first lord of the admiralty in Asquith's wartime coalition cabinet. As foreign secretary (1916–17), he issued the statement, later known as the Balfour Declaration, expressing British support for a Zionist homeland in Palestine.

Bandaranaike, Sirimavo (1916–) Sri Lankan prime minister. The daughter of wealthy parents, she married the politician S.W.R.D. Bandaranaike in 1940 and supported her husband's career, as well as working as a volunteer to improve the condition of women in Sri Lankan society. When her husband was assassinated in 1959, Mrs Bandaranaike succeeded him as leader of the Sri Lankan Freedom Party (SLFP) and, after winning national elections, became the world's first woman prime minister. She improved health and educational facilities, promoted Sinhalese culture, and brought private schools into the state sector. She lost power in 1965 after leading the SLFP into coalition with a Marxist group, but regained it in 1970 when the SLFP became the senior partner in the United Front coalition. Mrs Bandaranaike expelled the US Peace Corps, and announced more nationalization, but rising unemployment checked the pace of her program. In 1971 she withstood an attempted leftist coup. Her government's policies

Spotted at the age of 15, Brigitte Bardot became an international sex symbol.

favored the majority Sinhalese population at the expense of the minority Tamils, and in 1972 she introduced a new constitution and changed the name of the country from Ceylon to Sri Lanka. Defeated in the 1977 elections, Mrs Bandaranaike was excluded from political office by the United Nationalist Party, but her rights were restored in 1986.

Bannister, Roger (1929–) British athlete. Bannister ran a mile in a time of 3 minutes 59.4 seconds (6 May 1954) to became the first man to beat the 4-minute barrier, then regarded by many as an impossible feat. A medical student, Bannister had prepared himself physically and mentally for the challenge through systematic training. He later wrote several articles on the physiology of exercise and became a successful neurologist. He was knighted in 1975.

Banting, Frederick Grant (1891–1941) Canadian physiologist. Working at the University of Toronto, he succeeded in 1921, with his research student Charles Herbert Best (1899–1978), in isolating insulin (a pancreatic hormone) by preparing an extract from the pancreases of dogs. This proved effective in the treatment of diabetes in humans. With the aid of a colleague, J.B. Collip, and the professor of physiology, J.J.R. Macleod, Banting and Best succeeded in preparing much larger quantities of active extract. Clinical trials were highly successful and a pharmaceutical firm began manufacturing insulin in 1922. Banting and Macleod shared the Nobel prize for physiology or medicine in 1923. Believing that the contributions of Best and Collip had been gravely underestimated they insisted on sharing it with their younger colleagues.

Bardot, Brigitte (1934–) French film actress. In 1952, aged 15, she appeared on the cover of *Elle* magazine, and was spotted by Roger Vadim, an aspiring film director. She made her film debut in *Le Trou Normand* (1952), but it was her role in *And God Created Woman* (1956), directed by Vadim (by then her husband), that established her as an international sex symbol. Celebrated as the original "sex kitten", her private life excited as much interest as her films, which included *La Verité* (1960) and *Viva Maria* (1965). In the 1970s she ceased making films and withdrew from the public eye, devoting herself to campaigning for animal rights.

Barnard, Christiaan (1922–)
South African surgeon. After studying medicine at the Universities of Cape Town and Minnesota he became a specialist cardio-thoracic surgeon in the University of Cape Town (1958) and subsequently (1961) head of cardiothoracic surgery. He developed an interest in the possibility of replacing diseased hearts with healthy ones from accident victims and in 1967 successfully carried out the world's first heart transplant operation. It was a success, though unfortunately, the patient, Louis Washkansky, died 18 days later from complications. Barnard pioneered the replacement of diseased heart valves with artificial ones, but the onset of rheumatoid arthritis in his hands cut short his surgical career in 1983.

Bartók, Béla (1881–1945)
Hungarian composer. Taught piano by his mother from the age of five, Bartók began to compose at nine, and he went on to study at the Budapest Academy (1898–1903). In 1902 he heard a performance of Richard Strauss's *Also Sprach Zarathrustra*. It was a revelation to him and his earliest compositions were Straussian in flavor. He took an interest in Hungarian peasant music, and began to notate traditional folk songs. In 1905 his lifelong collaboration with fellow composer Zoltan Kodály began; together, they classified and recorded thousands of folk-songs from Europe and elsewhere. But Bartók's own music remained virtually unrecognized until 1917, when his ballet *The Wooden Prince*, followed by his opera *Duke Bluebeard's Castle* (1918), brought him fame and popularity. His ballet *The Miraculous Mandarin* (1924) initially offended audiences with its sexually explicit and farcical subject-matter. In 1927–28 Bartók toured the US, playing his own and Kodály's music. Utterly opposed to Nazism, it was only after his mother's death, which devastated him as his tragic Sixth Quartet shows, that he was able to leave Europe to settle in the US in 1940. He was given a post at Harvard University researching folk-music, but missed his homeland and

Count Basie, the jazz pianist and entertainer, had many bigtime hits.

the public acceptance he had received there. In 1942 an incurable blood disease was diagnosed, and Bartók died before he was able to complete his Third Piano Concerto.

Basie, Count (William) (1904–84) US jazz pianist and organist. Born in Red Bank, New Jersey, Basie played drums at school and later took piano lessons. Neglecting his studies for music, he was coached by Fats Waller in New York. He toured for several years before reaching Kansas City in 1927, which was at the time the center of a distinct style of orchestral jazz. He played with Bennie Moten's band (1929–33) before forming his own ensemble which grew from 9 to 12 players. By late 1936 Basie had won a record contract and moved to New York. His style relied on a uniquely cohesive rhythm section which functioned like a sextet. Through the 1940s the line-up changed a lot and the band shrank to an octet, but in 1952 he established a 16-piece line-up and in 1954 made the first of many European tours. His band's best-known numbers were "One O'Clock Jump" and "One, Two, Three O'Lairy". Basie's music remained a formative influence on most big bands throughout the 20th century.

Beaton, Cecil (1904–80) British photographer, socialite and stage designer. Beaton's decorative portraits of celebrities were his most important work, and he made his name when working as a staff photographer on *Vogue* and *Vanity Fair* in the 1920s. During World War II he served as an official war photographer. He later won great acclaim as a designer of costumes and sets for operas, ballets and Broadway shows, and gained Academy awards for his designs for the movies *Gigi* (1959) and *My Fair Lady* (1965). A great wit and conversationalist, Beaton wrote several books and published five volumes of diaries. He was knighted in 1972.

Beaverbrook, Lord (William Maxwell Aitken) (1879–1963) Canadian newspaper magnate and politician. Beaverbrook had already made a fortune on the Canadian stock-market before arriving in England in 1910. He entered parliament (1910), was given a peerage by Lloyd George and served in his cabinet as minister for information (1918). Having acquired a majority interest in the *Daily Express* in 1916, he quickly turned it into a leading national daily and went on to found the *Sunday Express* (1921) and take over the *Evening Standard* (1929). During World War II Churchill made Beaverbrook minister of aircraft production (1940–1) and minister of supply (1941–2). He performed these jobs ably and efficiently and made a significant contribution to aircraft production during a critical period of the war. As a newspaper proprietor, Beaverbrook frequently championed his own pet causes, in particular free trade. He never achieved his deeply held ambitions for personal political power.

Beckett, Samuel (1906–89) Irish writer. A graduate of Trinity College, Dublin, Beckett taught French before moving to Paris in 1933, where he became secretary and friend to the writer James Joyce. He wrote several novels, including the trilogy, originally written in French, *Molloy* (1951), *Malone Dies* (1951), and *The Unnameable* (1953). But his international reputation lies in his plays, also written in French, notably *Waiting for Godot* (1952), *Endgame* (1957), and *Krapp's Last Tape* (1958). Beckett wrote in the tradition of his fellow Irish writers Joyce and Flann O'Brien, with a sense of the absurdity and futility of life; his strangely comic characters are disabled or physically or psychologically trapped, remarkable chiefly for their persistence. His bleak poetic manner became increasingly austere, culminating in *Breath* (1969), a 15-second wordless piece. He won the Nobel prize for literature in 1969.

Begin, Menachem (1913–92) Polish-born Israeli prime minister. Begin was deeply involved in the Zionist youth movement as a student in Warsaw. When the Nazis invaded Poland in 1939 he fled to Lithuania, and was later deported by the Russians to Siberia. Upon his release in 1941 he joined the Free Polish Army, and in 1942 was sent to Palestine. He left the army in 1943 to become leader of the Jewish resistance group Irgun, known for its terrorist activities. In 1948 Begin founded the rightwing Herut party, which demanded Israeli sovereignty on

Ingrid Bergman found worldwide fame in the 1940s in films such as Casablanca.

both sides of the Jordan, no Palestinian state, and economic laissez-faire. He headed the opposition in the Knesset, the Israeli parliament (1948–67) and then served in a national unity government (1967–70) before becoming prime minister as head of the Likud coalition in 1977. Begin took a hard line on the return of the territories occupied during the Six-Day War of 1967, and began the Israeli colonization of the West Bank. He did, however, withdraw from the Sinai peninsula as part of the peace treaty signed in 1979 with President Sadat of Egypt, for which they were jointly awarded the Nobel peace prize in 1978. Begin retired from politics in 1983.

Ben-Gurion (Gruen), David (1886–1973) First prime minister of Israel. Ben-Gurion, an active Zionist, left Poland for Palestine and was expelled as a subversive by the ruling Turks at the outbreak of World War I. After the publication of the Balfour Declaration, he returned to Palestine in 1917 to fight for the Allies and during the British mandate was a keen advocate of massive Jewish immigration into the region. A founder member of the Zionist-Socialist party Mapai, and from 1935 head of the influential Jewish Agency, he played a leading role in the war of independence which ended in 1948 with the UN partition of Palestine and the creation of the state of Israel. Elected the country's first prime minister (1949–53; 1955–63), Ben-Gurion's greatest achievement was the unification of Jews from widely differing cultures in the new Israeli state. He encouraged the creation of settlements in desert areas, and founded a public education system. During the Suez crisis of 1956 Ben-Gurion ordered the Israeli army to occupy the Sinai peninsula, but withdrew after obtaining an assurance of peace along the Egyptian border and guaranteed access to the Strait of Tiran. In his later years he worked for peace in the Middle East, and came to be regarded as the embodiment of the Israeli state.

Bergman, Ingmar (1918–) Swedish film and TV director. Bergman started as a theater director and began writing filmscripts in 1941. The success of *Frenzy* (1944) led to his début in movie directing. It was with *Smiles of a Summer Night* (1955) and *The Seventh Seal* (1956) that his international reputation was established. Bergman's themes were metaphysical, agonizing examinations of his own inner world or the human predicament, or studies in human psychology with the interior life of women a dominant concern. He created a troupe of actors with whom he worked for many years. Among his greatest works are *Wild Strawberries* (1957), *The Silence* (1963), *Persona* (1966), *Cries and Whispers* (1972) and *Fanny and Alexander* (1982).

Bergman, Ingrid (1915–82) Swedish film actress. Bergman's radiant vitality brought rapid success in Swedish films and in 1939 she went to Hollywood to star in the movie *Intermezzo,* which brought her instant, worldwide fame. In 1949 her enormous popularity was shattered by revelations about her private life which destroyed her wholesome image. Her love affair with Italian director Roberto Rossellini forced her to find work in Europe and not until 1956 was she welcomed back in Hollywood, to star in *Anastasia.* Her most memorable movies include *Casablanca*, *For Whom the Bell Tolls* (both 1943), *Gaslight* (1944), *Notorious* (1946), *Joan of Arc* (1948), *Murder on the Orient Express* (1974) and *Autumn Sonata* (1978).

Berkeley, Busby (1895–1976) US choreographer and film director. One of Broadway's leading dance directors, Busby's break into movies came when Warner Brothers hired him to choreograph the musical *42nd Street* (1933). Lavish, erotic, vulgar, his set-pieces for massed girls delighted audiences during the Depression years, and his inventive camera shots, taken from above, below, diagonally or on the move, combined with rhythmical cutting, multiplied the pleasure. His other films include *Gold Diggers* (1933) and *Dames* (1934).

Berlin, Irving (1888–1989) US song writer. Born Israel Beline, the son of Russian immigrants, Berlin graduated from street singer and singing waiter to song plugger He began writing song lyrics, and later composed his own music for them. In a long career stretching from the jazz age to the 1950s he wrote Broadway revues, musical comedies, including the popular

The conductor Leonard Bernstein rehearses the Prague Spring concert, 1990.

Annie Get Your Gun (1946), and the film scores for his stage successes, notably *Top Hat* (1935), *Easter Parade* (1948) and *Call Me Madam* (1953). Among the best-known of the 800 and more songs he wrote are "Alexander's Ragtime Band", "God Bless America", "There's No Business Like Show Business" and "White Christmas".

Berlin, Sir Isaiah (1909–) Latvian-born British philosopher. One of the most human and accessible thinkers of his generation, Berlin's gift lay in his ability, both as public speaker and prolific essayist, to provide realistic rather than abstract commentary on the impact of ideas on people's lives. With his vivid and energetic style of lecturing, he established a reputation as an outstanding philosopher at Oxford before World War II but his interests later moved to the history of ideas. In his many books and essays he wrote penetratingly of the great philosophical and historical traditions of the 18th and 19th centuries.

Berlusconi, Silvio (1936–) Italian TV tycoon and politician. A successful property dealer by his early twenties, Berlusconi went on to create a business empire, Fininvest, the largest private company in Italy, with stakes in commercial TV, newspapers, advertising, insurance and financial services; by the early 1990s he headed Europe's largest commercial TV network. Turning to politics, he founded the rightwing Forza Italia political movement, relinquishing his executive posts in Fininvest to campaign in the Italian general election of 1994. Though lacking political experience, he became prime minister of a rightist coalition government, swept in on a wave of public support for its promises to clean up the corruption endemic in Italian politics. Forced to step down when allegations of illegal business practices were made against him, Berlusconi failed to win reelection in April 1996.

Bernhardt, Sarah (1844–1923) French actress. Educated at a convent school and for the stage at the Paris Conservatoire, Bernhardt made her debut with the Comédie Française in 1862 but was sacked after a row with a senior actress. She found work as a singer before joining the Odeon theater for 6 years: it was here that she began to establish a reputation with the Parisian audiences, praised especially for her beauty and the quality of her voice, which the playwright Victor Hugo described as golden. Bernhardt returned to the Comédie Française in 1872 and acted a number of minor parts before winning instant success playing the title roles in Racine's *Phèdre* and Voltaire's *Zaïre*. In 1880 she formed her own company and embarked upon a glittering international career as the leading tragedy actress of her day. Basing herself in London, over the next two decades she visited the US six times as well as South America and Australia. "The Divine Sarah" played almost all the great classic roles, including Hamlet. In 1905 she injured her leg jumping off the parapet in the famous suicide scene in *Tosca*. Gangrene later set in, and the leg was amputated in 1915, but she continued to act from a litter and was carried to the Front to entertain the troops in World War I.

Bernstein, Leonard (1918–90) US conductor and composer. Bernstein studied at Harvard, the Curtis Institute of Music, and at Tanglewood under Serge Koussevitsky, to whom he became assistant. Fame came at once when he conducted the New York Philharmonic in 1943 as a last-minute replacement for the great conductor Bruno Walter. Bernstein then worked with the New York City Center Orchestra and toured the world as a guest conductor. His first composition, the *Jeremiah Symphony* (1942), was followed by the ballet *Fancy Free* and the hit musical *On the Town* (both 1944). His musical *Candide* (1956), based on Voltaire's novel, had mixed notices but in 1957 came the outstandingly successful musical *West Side Story,* which bridged the gap between serious and popular music and was later made into a movie. From 1958–69 conductor of the New York Philharmonic, Bernstein's recordings were responsible for the 1960s' Mahler revival. His *Mass* (1971) aroused controversy on its first performance at the inaugural concert of the J. F. Kennedy Center for the Performing Arts. Bernstein was an eclectic artist, and his compositions, noted for their energetic rhythms, drew on many sources including the Jewish liturgy, jazz and Latin American music.

Steve Biko, the Black South African leader who was murdered in police custody.

Beveridge, William (1879–1963) British economist. As head of the employment department of the Board of Trade, Beveridge was instrumental in designing Britain's system of compulsory unemployment insurance in 1910. He then entered academic life, and was director of the London School of Economics (1919–37) which he helped build into an influential and respected institution. Called to the Ministry of Labor in 1940, he produced the famous Beveridge Report on Social Insurance in 1942. Its recommendations, which included the payment of unemployment benefits without means tests, the eradication of unemployment, the creation of a health service and a system of family allowances, formed the basis of the comprehensive welfare legislation that was introduced by the Labor government after 1945. Beveridge was elected a Liberal MP in 1945 and created a baron in 1946.

Bhutto, Benazir (1953–) Pakistani prime minister. The daughter of Z. Ali Bhutto, Benazir was educated at Oxford and Harvard Universities. After her father's trial and execution in 1979 she spent seven years under house arrest and two further years in exile as leader of the Pakistani People's Party. She returned to Pakistan after General Zia's downfall, and was elected prime minister in 1988 but soon fell foul of her coalition partners, and of the president, a former supporter of Zia. She had a difficult role to perform as the female leader of an Islamic country, and felt constrained to marry to satisfy her critics. Amid charges of corruption (she was accused of overlooking her husband's criminal involvements), her popular support began to decline and she was criticized for her political failures, particularly her inability to control the potentially explosive situations in Sind and Punjab. Defeated in the 1990 elections, she was subsequently charged with corruption, but fought her way back to win reelection as prime minister in 1993.

Bhutto, Zulfikar Ali (1928–79) Pakistani prime minister and president. Born into a rich and powerful family, Bhutto was educated at the Universities of California and Oxford. A lawyer, he held a number of cabinet posts before becoming foreign minister (1963–6), but resigned in protest from President Ayub Khan's government when it concluded peace with India in the war over Kashmir (1965–6). In 1967 he founded the Pakistani People's Party (PPP) in opposition to Ayub Khan, who was later deposed in a military coup by General Yahya Khan. In the elections of 1970 the PPP was the leading party in West Pakistan, but the Awami League, campaigning for provincial autonomy for East Pakistan, won an overall majority in the National Assembly. Bhutto refused to form a coalition, and succeeded as president of Pakistan in 1971 after East Pakistan, assisted by India, broke away to become the independent state of Bangladesh. Bhutto nationalized major industries and taxed landed families. In 1973 he became prime minister under a new constitution that gave increased powers to this post. He maintained martial law and strengthened Pakistan as an Islamic state. In the 1977 election his party won a large majority, but was accused of electoral fraud. Shortly afterwards, General Zia u-Haq, the head of the army, seized power and arrested Bhutto for allegedly conspiring to murder a political opponent in 1974. He was found guilty, and executed in 1979, despite appeals for clemency from many heads of state.

Biko, Steve (1946–77) South African political leader. As a medical student at Natal university (1966–72) and influenced by the ideas of the US Black Power movement and other Black writers, Biko became a leading figure in the Black Consciousness movement. Advocating militant self-reliance for South Africa's Black peoples, he founded the all-Black South African Students' Organization (1969) and was a cofounder of the Black People's Convention (1972). He worked in community development and set up a trust fund to help political prisoners. Frequently the subject of banning orders, he nevertheless succeeded in getting his ideas heard through his writings. Arrested for subversion, he died in police custody. The South African government originally claimed that his death was accidental, but was later forced to retract its statement.

Binet, Alfred (1857–1911) French psychologist and developer of IQ tests. Binet was the first person to attempt a precise measurement of intelligence,

Léon Blum, who was elected France's first Socialist prime minister in 1936.

and the first to include in such tests questions demanding cognition. A student of law, he took up psychology in 1878, initially concentrating on hypnotism. In 1891 he began work in a research laboratory at the Sorbonne in Paris, becoming its director in 1895. He specialized in child study, working first with his own daughters as subjects; his collaborator was the educational psychologist Théodore Simon. They conducted their first series of intelligence tests in 1905, followed by a second series in 1908. In 1911 they devised the concept of "mental age", thereby creating a measurement for assessing the "intelligence quotient" (or IQ)of individuals.

Birdseye, Clarence (1886–1956) US businessman and inventor. While working as a fur trader in Labrador Birdseye observed the Eskimos' practice of freezing food for consumption during the winter months. On his return to the US he began his own experiments into ways of quick-freezing food and in 1924 formed the General Seafoods Company to sell quick-frozen foods, including fish, fruit and vegetables. Birdseye was not the first producer of frozen foods but his method, using two refrigerated metal plates to freeze packaged food, was efficient, quick, and preserved the original flavor. In 1929 the company was sold for $20 million to become the General Foods Corporation, with Birdseye continuing as a consultant. He was president of Birdseye Frosted Foods (1930–34) and of Birdseye Electric Company (1935–38). He continued to invent and was in possession of 300 patents when he died, including a superfast dehydrating technique for foodstuffs.

Black, Conrad (1944–) Canadian financier and newspaper magnate. Black started his career in the Argus corporation (of which his father had been a major shareholder). Following in the tradition of two other Canadian newspaper magnates, Lords Thomson and Beaverbrook, he set about creating a press empire. He acquired his first two newspapers in Quebec in 1967 and by 1972 owned 21 Canadian local papers. Over the next two decades he built up his newspaper holdings still further, and by 1994 owned more than 250 newspapers around the world, including Australia, Israel, the US and the UK. His major international acquisitions included the London *Daily Telegraph* (1985) and the Chicago *Sun-Times* (1994).

Blum, Léon (1872–1950) French prime minister. Elected to parliament as a Socialist in 1919, Blum rebuilt the party after its 1920 split with the Communists. In 1936 he was elected France's first Socialist prime minister at the head of the Popular Front coalition and introduced a series of radical measures to improve working conditions, including a 40-hour week, paid holidays and collective bargaining. He nationalized the Bank of France and the defense industries. A policy of non-intervention in the Spanish Civil War alienated Communist coalition members and Blum resigned in 1937 after he had been refused emergency powers to deal with France's economic problems, serving again for a brief period in 1938. Following the fall of France in 1940, Blum was arrested and put on trial (1942) by the Vichy government on charges of neglecting France's interests, but defended himself so effectively that the trial was abandoned. A Jew, Blum was held in a concentration camp in Germany from 1943–45. He returned to politics after the war and in December 1946 was appointed premier of a six-week caretaker government, and was vice-premier for a short time in 1948. He later served as France's chief representative to UNESCO.

Boeing, William (1881–1956) US aircraft designer. Boeing took up flying as a hobby and turned it into a business, setting up the Pacific Aero Products Company in 1916 to manufacture aircraft. Renamed the Boeing Airplane Company in 1917, and later still Boeing Aircraft, the company produced a variety of military aircraft and Boeing helped design the first seaplane for the US Navy. From very early on he realized the potential of airplanes for carrying freight and passengers and his company played a leading role in the development of cargo planes. During World War II Boeing produced a number of military planes such as the B-17 Flying Fortress, returning in the 1950s to the production of commercial aircraft. The Boeing 707, the first US jet airplane, was developed shortly after Boeing's death.

Björn Borg, the Swedish player who dominated men's tennis in the 1970s.

Bogart, Humphrey (1899–1957) US actor. A slight, tight-lipped man with a lisp and a sardonic smile, Bogart was unlikely star material but found his niche playing self-reliant, cynical anti-heroes. His major break occurred in the Broadway hit *The Petrified Forest* (1935), in which he played a gangster. A year later he successfully recreated the role in a movie version, and this led to five years of gangster parts. Success came in 1941 with two hit movies: *High Sierra* and *The Maltese Falcon* (in which, for a change, he played the part of a detective). *Casablanca* (1942), probably his most popular movie, followed soon after, and he continued his stream of screen successes with *The Big Sleep* (1946), in which he teamed up with his fourth wife the actress Lauren Bacall, *The Treasure of the Sierra Madre* (1947), and *The African Queen* (1951), for which he won an Academy Award.

Bond, Alan (1938–) British-born Australian business executive. Bond settled in Australia in 1951 and built up a vast corporation, with holdings in insurance and property, gas and oil, the electronic media, minerals and airships. He further expanded the Bond Corporation's activities into Australian newspapers and TV but by 1987, with the economic boom beginning to wane, began to suffer losses. In 1992 he was declared bankrupt. He was imprisoned for dishonest business dealings, and acquitted after three months in prison, only to face further charges of fraud in 1994. In 1983, his syndicate sponsored the yacht *Australia II*, which became the first challenger to win the coveted America's Cup Challenge.

Bonhoeffer, Dietrich (1906–45) German Protestant theologian. Bonhoeffer, who was appointed to a lectureship at the University of Berlin in 1931, became a leading Protestant critic of the Nazi regime. In particular, he attacked its antisemitism and worked against it in the underground resistance movement. He was an active member of the conspiracy against Hitler in 1944, and on its collapse was arrested, imprisoned and hanged. After his death Bonhoeffer's life and work became widely known to an international audience through his writings. Admired for his willingness to confront controversial issues, he influenced both churchmen and academic theologians. His best-known collection of writings, *Letters and Papers From Prison* (published in German in 1951, English translation 1955) called for a "religionless" Christianity aimed at the mature modern man. His views, rejecting the traditional religious positions and advocating a Christianity directed at man not in weakness but when he is strong, have been subjected to much debate and criticism.

Borg, Björn (1956–) Swedish tennis player. The first man to win the Wimbledon singles title five times in succession (1976–80) since the 1900s, Borg began playing at a very young age and turned professional in 1972. He won the Italian Open at 17, the French Open at 18, and by 1975 had broken the record for consecutive cup singles wins. His most effective shots were his powerful serve and his two-handed backhand. He won the French Open six times (1974–75, 1978–81) and the World Championship three times (1978–80). He retired in 1983, and staged an unsuccessful comeback in early 1991.

Borges, Jorge Luis (1899–1986) Argentinian writer. A lover of English language and literature from childhood, Borges traveled in Europe from 1914–21. He came under the influence of the Spanish Grupo Ultra, who believed in "pure" poetry independent of context. He later judged his first three collection of poems too Ultraist, but they contain the metaphysical games that characterize his mature work. On his return to Buenos Aires, Borges wrote articles for a Sunday newspaper and magazine stories as well as essays and poems. Collections of his concise yet intricate stories, acclaimed for their jewel-like clarity and vision, were published in *Fictions* (1944) and *The Aleph* (1949). In the 1960s Borges won international recognition as his work began to find publication in English. He was Director of the National Library of Argentina (1959–73) and wrote much literary criticism. He gradually became blind and later works such as *The Book of Sand* (1975) were dictated.

Marlon Brando as the original motorbike rebel in The Wild One (1953).

Botha, P.W. (1916–) South African prime minister. He entered parliament in 1948 as a member of the National Party, serving in several ministerial posts before becoming prime minister in 1978. Botha strengthened the armed forces to carry out raids into the neighboring countries of southern Africa that supported ANC activity, and funded antigovernment groups within those countries, destabilizing their governments. At home, he abolished some minor apartheid laws, granted nominal independence to the Black homelands and reformed the constitution to allow limited political rights to Asians and coloreds, though not to Black South Africans. As a result of this, the right wing of the party broke away in 1982 to form the Conservative party. Following a cabinet revolt and the onset of ill-health Botha was forced to resign in 1989.

Boutros-Ghali, Boutros (1922–) Secretary-general of the United Nations. Boutros-Ghali was born into an eminent Egyptian family with a strong political background, and studied international law in Paris before becoming a professor at Cairo University. He served both Presidents Sadat and Mubarak as minister for foreign affairs (1977–92), and earned international recognition for his negotiation of the 1979 peace treaty between Egypt and Israel and his activities as intermediary during the Gulf War (1991). As an African and an Arab, his appointment as secretary-general of the UN in 1992 was seen as an important political move, and he came to the post with a personal mission to champion Third World causes. However, he presided over a turbulent period in the history of the organization, beset by financial problems and dominated by the seemingly intractable problems of the civil wars in Somalia and Bosnia, but earned wide respect for his patient and persistent skills in negotiation.

Bradman, Don (1908–) Australian cricketer. Bradman's Test record of a total of 6,996 runs, with an average scored of 99.94 runs per innings, has never been equaled since. Widely regarded as the greatest batsman in the history of cricket, his perfect eye and timing were acquired early in his batting career. He made 334 runs in a Test innings in 1930, during his first tour of England, a record no Australian has equaled, and he scored 19 centuries against England in a Test career that stretched from 1928–48. He was knighted on his retirement from professional cricket in 1949. In later years he became chairman of the Australian Cricket Board and wrote his memoirs *Farewell to Cricket* (1950).

Brando, Marlon (1924–) US actor. A Method actor schooled at the Actors' Studio in New York, Brando's first stage success was on Broadway in 1947, in Tennessee Williams' *A Streetcar Named Desire.* His naturalistic screen performances in *The Men* (1950), and *On the Waterfront* (1954), for which he gained an Academy Award, won him admirers and detractors. No one could deny his charisma, and young audiences in the 1950s saw him as an icon of their generation. His controversial image and growing age made it difficult to acquire parts in the 1960s and he disappeared for a time, coming back to achieve memorable performances in *The Godfather* and *Last Tango in Paris* (both 1972). During the 1980s he became something of a recluse, making only occasional film appearances in cameo roles. In 1990 his family was struck by tragedy and scandal when his son Christian shot dead his daughter's boyfriend.

Brandt, Willy (1913–92) West German chancellor. Growing up in Berlin, Brandt became involved in Socialist politics and fled Nazi Germany in 1933 to escape arrest. He spent the war in Sweden where he supported the anti-Nazi underground movement. Returning to Germany in 1945, he served in the federal parliament (1949–57) as a Social Democrat. Elected mayor of West Berlin in 1957, his term of office coincided with the building of the Berlin wall (1961), and he gained an international reputation. He became leader of the Social Democratic party in 1964, and in 1966 was made vice-chancellor and foreign minister in a coalition government with the Christian Democrats. In 1969 Brandt was elected chancellor, at his fourth attempt, to head a new Social Democrat–Free Democrat coalition. His chancellorship was notable for his attempts to improve relations with

Leonid Brezhnev, who was leader of the Soviet Union from 1964 to 1982.

Eastern Europe. In 1970 he joined with the Soviet Union in calling for the rejection of military force and for the recognition of current European boundaries. He signed a nonaggression pact with Poland the same year, and in 1971 was a party to the "big four" treaty to determine the status of Berlin. For these and other initiatives he was awarded the Noble peace prize (1971). A campaigner for a united Europe, Brandt supported the expansion of the European Economic Community (EEC). He resigned in 1974 over a spy scandal in his administration and later served as a member of the European parliament (1979–83). Appointed to head the Independent Commission on International Development Issues (often known as the Brandt Commission) he issued two reports (1979 and 1983) that, among their other recommendations, advocated increased aid to developing countries.

Branson, Richard (1950–) British business tycoon. Branson was only 21 when he opened his first record shop. Within two years he had gone on to establish the highly successful Virgin record company. In 1984 Branson set up Virgin Atlantic Airlines; his incursion into the air business provoked a savage price-cutting war with the major airlines. When the Virgin Music group was quoted on the stock exchange in 1986, Branson's rapid rise to success seemed very much a reflection of the economic boom of the 1980s and he was often characterized as the self-made whizz kid with unbridled ambition. By the 1990s his business empire included publishing, local radio, construction, mail order, insurance, leisure concerns and soft drinks manufacture. A keen sportsman, Branson actively sought to break new barriers of physical achievement. He captained the powerboat that made the fastest crossing of the Atlantic to win the coveted Blue Riband (1986), and made the first Pacific crossing by hot air balloon (1991).

Braun, Wernher von (1912–77) German–US pioneer of rocket propulsion. After studying engineering in Zurich and Berlin, Braun began rocket research for the German army in 1932, initially with solid fuel propellant but within two years using liquid fuel. In 1938 he was appointed technical director of the German rocket research establishment at Peenemünde on the Baltic, and there he developed the highly destructive V-2 rockets that were launched against London during World War II. In 1945 he and his team surrendered to the US forces and continued their space research program in the US, developing the rocket expertise that ultimately succeeded in landing men on the Moon in 1969. He resigned from NASA in 1972.

Brecht, Bertolt (1898–1956) German playwright and poet. Brecht, considered by many to have been Germany's greatest dramatist, was a controversial writer who conceived the form of "epic theater". He won the Kleist prize for drama for his first two plays, *Drums in the Night* and *Baal* (1922), but his reputation was established with the production of his great musical drama, *The Threepenny Opera* (1928), the first of several collaborations with the composer Kurt Weill. A Marxist, Brecht believed in the power of theater to change society. On Hitler's rise to power he left Germany, seeking refuge in several European countries in turn before settling in Hollywood in 1941. *Galileo* (1938), written in exile in Scandinavia, reflects his growing disaffection from the Communist party organization. Brecht wrote three of his finest plays, *Mother Courage* (1941), *The Good Person of Setzuan* (1943) and *The Caucasian Chalk Circle* (1948), in the US. In 1946 he denied membership of the Communist party before a Senate subcommittee hearing on un-American activities but in 1948 accepted an invitation from the East German government to found a theater company in East Berlin to produce his own plays. Though he was the recipient of the Stalin peace prize (1954) Brecht's views often proved unpalatable to his hosts, and his opera *Lucullus* (1932–51) was withdrawn by order after its first performance.

Brezhnev, Leonid (1906–82) President of the Soviet Union. A Ukrainian, Brezhnev served as a political commissar during World War II and in 1950 was sent as party leader to the newly-ceded republic of Moldavia. Here he attracted the attention of Joseph Stalin, and in 1952 he was appointed to a post on the CPSU

The Jewish philosopher Martin Buber was a highly influential writer and teacher.

(Soviet Communist party) central committee and on the Politburo (1952). Demoted on Stalin's death, he owed his return to prominence in the party hierarchy to his friendship with his fellow Ukrainian Nikita Khrushchev. From 1957–60 Brezhnev served once again on the Politburo. Assuming the ceremonial position of state president in 1960, he began to disassociate himself from Khrushchev as criticism of his policies mounted. He became party leader in 1964, after the fall of Khrushchev, briefly sharing power with Alexei Kosygin. Brezhnev delegated much responsibility and concentrated his attention on foreign affairs and the suppression of internal dissent. Though opposed to liberalization at home, he encouraged the emigration of Soviet Jews. Abroad, he pursued a policy of détente while amassing conventional forces and using Warsaw Pact forces to uphold Communism in neighboring Soviet bloc countries, for example sending tanks into Czechoslovakia to bring the leadership into line in 1968. As his health failed throughout the 1970s, his government was increasingly marked by caution and inaction, leading to economic stagnation.

Britten, Benjamin (1913–76)
British composer. Britten studied under the British composer Frank Bridge, winning a scholarship to London's Royal College of Music in 1930. During the 1930s he wrote music for plays and documentary films and enjoyed a fruitful collaboration with the poet W. H. Auden on several song-cycles including the sociopolitical piece, *Ballad of Heroes* (1939). On the outbreak of war Britten followed Auden to the US with the tenor Peter Pears, his lifelong companion who inspired his finest vocal works. They returned to Britain in 1942 and Britten's first opera, *Peter Grimes* (1945), was performed at Sadler's Wells to resounding success. In 1947 he helped establish the first musical festival in Aldeburgh, the small fishing town on the East

Anglian coast where Britten and Pears had made their home; they remained closely associated with the festival for the remainder of their lives, building it into one of the premier music events in Europe. More operas followed – *Billy Budd* (1951), *Gloriana* (1953, commissioned for the coronation of Queen Elizabeth), and *The Turn of the Screw* (1954). Britten was much interested in composing music for children, including *The Young Person's Guide to the Orchestra* (1946) and a number of "children's operas" such as *Let's Make an Opera!* (1949) and *Noye's Fludde* (1958), based on a medieval mystery play. His later major works include the *War Requiem* (1962) and the opera *Death in Venice* (1973). They confirm Britten's status as one of the major composers of the 20th century, but it is perhaps for his numerous songs, written for Peter Pears and with himself as piano accompanist, that he will be best remembered. He was given a life peerage in 1976.

Buber, Martin (1878–1965) German-Jewish theologian and philosopher. At university Buber was influenced by the work of Nietzsche. He became attracted to the idea of spiritual renewal and to Zionism (the movement for a Jewish homeland) and in 1916 founded the influential monthly *Der Jude* as a forum for Jewish intellectuals. By the mid-1930s, Buber had become director of a Jewish adult education program in Germany, but the rise of Nazism forced him to emigrate in 1938 to Palestine, where he took up a professorship in social philosophy at the Hebrew University in Jerusalem. After the creation of the state of Israel, Buber became head of the Teachers Training College for Adult Education in Jerusalem (1949), whilst continuing to publish his theories on social and ethical problems. He explored the problems of Arab-Jewish relations and worked for the emergence of an Israeli state in which the two peoples could live together in peace. His philosophy and poetry are best demonstrated in *I and Thou* (1923), in which he underlines man's basic duty to his fellow human beings.

Bugatti, Ettore (1881–1947) Italian automobile manufacturer. A designer for several small automobile companies before setting up a factory at Molsheim, Alsace, in 1909, Bugatti's first production model, the Type 13, was raced successfully in 1911. Two of his other racers, the Brescia and the Type 35, were outstanding, the latter being the only car sold at a price within the reach of amateurs that was capable of winning grands prix.

Nikolai Bukhárin, a notable victim of Stalin's staged show trials.

A passionately meticulous man, Bugatti's great folly was the Type 41 (La Royale), designed to be the ultimate supercar: only six were built and three sold. He used the redundant engines in high-speed railcars.

Bukhárin, Nikolai Ivanovich (1888–1938) Communist leader, economist and Marxist theoretician. Bukhárin studied economics at Moscow University but did not graduate. In 1906 he joined the Bolshevik party and was made a member of its Moscow committee in 1908. He was imprisoned and then deported in 1911. Returning to Russia after the 1917 Revolution, Bukhárin was editor of *Pravda* (1917–29). A member of the Politburo from 1924 and a supporter of Lenin, he backed Stalin after Lenin's death, despite distrusting him, but when Stalin abandoned Lenin's New Economic Policy in 1928 Bukhárin tried in vain to move party opinion against him. He opposed Stalin's industrialization policy and argued against his brutal collectivization program. Bukhárin was expelled from the Politburo in 1929, and, although briefly (1934) editor of *Izvestia* and one of the authors of the 1936 Soviet Constitution, his political career had ended. In 1938, after a show trial, he was executed for high treason.

Bush, George (1924–) US president. Bush graduated from Yale University in 1948, after wartime naval service. He made a fortune in the Texan oil industry before entering politics to sit in the house of representatives (1966–70). He was ambassador to the UN (1970–74) and head of the US liaison office in China (1977–76) before appointment to the directorship of the CIA. Bush unsuccessfully contested the Republican presidential nomination with Ronald Reagan in 1980, and became vice-president. He acted behind the scenes as one of Reagan's closest advisers, undertaking many international missions on his behalf. Elected president in 1988, Bush did not possess his predecessor's strong public image, but once in office he acted decisively. On his orders troops were sent into Panama in 1989 to arrest President Noriega and bring him to trial in the US on drugs charges, and he led the international action against the Iraqi invasion of Kuwait, committing large numbers of US troops to the UN-backed Allied force that fought the Gulf War (1991). However, he failed to win reelection to a second term in 1992.

Cage, John (1912–92) US composer. After college, Cage studied classical music in Europe and composition in the USA with Arnold Schoenberg and others. In 1938 he developed his "prepared piano", a piano made percussive by the placing of various objects between the strings, and after teaching in Chicago, settled in New York in 1942, where he became musical director for Merce Cunningham's dance group. Cage was influenced by Eastern philosophers, and in the 1950s, working with the I Ching, began to introduce chance elements into composition, as in *Music of Changes* (1951). In 1952 he organized an event at Black Mountain College which prefigured the 1960s' "happenings". He taught experimental music and continued to push back the musical boundaries. In *Musicircus* (1962), the audience was invited to perform. *Roaratorio* (1979) was the realization of a means of translating James Joyce's *Finnegan's Wake* into music. Cage's influence was immediate but shortlasting. His overriding and controversial aim was to persuade audiences to pay attention to all sound events, since it was his belief that "everything we do is music".

Callas (Kalogeropoulos), Maria (1923–77) Greek–US soprano. After studying at Athens conservatory, Callas played Tosca in Athens (1941) but her international début came in 1947 at La Scala, Milan, when she played the role of La Gioconda in Ponchielli's opera of that name. She joined the La Scala company in 1950 and won especial renown in the title roles of Tosca, Norma, and Lucia di Lammermoor, appearing internationally in these parts. Her repertoire stretched from Italian bel canto (by Bellini, Donizetti, and Rossini), which she revived, to Wagner. Known for the brilliancy of her dramatic interpretations and for her perfectionism, she was an opera singer of genius. In the early 1960s, her relationship with the Greek shipping tycoon Aristotle Onassis attracted much popular attention. She retired, as her voice was losing its clarity, in 1965, and gave master classes at New York's

Albert Camus, the French writer who won the Nobel prize for literature in 1957.

Juilliard School (1971–72). She emerged from retirement to give a final world concert tour in 1972–3, which sadly confirmed the wisdom of her earlier decision.

Calmette, Albert (1863–1933) French bacteriologist. Calmette qualified in medicine in Paris before serving in the French navy (1883–90) in order to study the incidence of malaria and sleeping sickness in Gabon, west Africa. In 1889 he investigated an outbreak of bubonic plague in Oporto, Portugal, before moving to Saigon in Indochina where he established a Pasteur Institute (1891) to develop vaccines against plague and snakebite. In 1895 Calmette returned to France to found another Pasteur Institute in Lille. In 1917 he was appointed administrative head of the Pasteur Institute in Paris, where he spent the rest of his working life. His most important work was done during the years 1906–24 when, with Camille Guérin (1872–1961), he developed the BCG vaccine against tuberculosis.

Calvin, Melvin (1911–) US biochemist. A chemistry graduate, Calvin worked as a research fellow in the UK at Manchester University (1935–37) before returning to the University of California, Berkeley. Here he spent the rest of his working life (except for wartime work on the atomic bomb), latterly as professor of chemistry. He was also director of the Laboratory of Chemical Biodynamics (1960–80) and associate director of the Lawrence Radiation Laboratory (1963–80). Most of Calvin's research concerned photosynthesis, the process by which plants utilize carbon dioxide from the air and convert it, through chlorophyll as an intermediary, into starch and oxygen. He developed the technique of using radioisotopes to follow chemical reactions, and identified a cycle of reactions, now known as the Calvin Cycle. He was awarded the Nobel Prize for chemistry in 1961. In 1969 he was asked by NASA to carry out research on the samples of lunar rock that were brought back to Earth by the Apollo XI and XII space missions.

Camus, Albert (1913–60) French writer. Born in Algeria, Camus' philosophy studies at the university of Algiers were interrupted by TB, and he later found work as an actor, schoolteacher and journalist there and in Paris. He joined the French Resistance in 1942 and became coeditor with the writer and philosopher Jean-Paul Sartre of the leftwing journal *Combat*. His novels *The Outsider* and *The Myth of Sisyphus* (both 1942), brought him instant fame as a writer, and he followed their success with *The Plague* (1947), which discussed the moral problems posed by the German occupation through the analogy of a plague-ridden town. A leading figure in post-war Parisian intellectual life, Camus quarreled with Sartre after denouncing Communism in *The Rebel* (1951). He also rejected Christianity, and his last novel, *The Fall* (1956), is a work of great pessimism and painful self-doubt. Camus wrote of the absurdity of the human condition and the futility of life in view of death; he himself died prematurely, in a car crash three years after winning the Nobel prize for literature in 1957.

Capone, Al (1899–1947) US gangster. Son of an Italian barber in Brooklyn, Capone abandoned school for the street gang and petty crime. An associate, Johnny Torrio, summoned him to run a brothel network in Chicago, and after the introduction of Prohibition in 1920 the two of them turned to the easy profits to be made from bootlegging, Torrio was injured in a street fight, and Capone (now nicknamed "Scarface") inherited his empire. With unprecedented violence, he seized control of Chicago's underworld: the most notorious of his outrages was the St Valentine's Day massacre of 1929. His annual take in 1927 was estimated at around $1,000,000, and he wielded enormous political influence. In 1931 he was given an 11-year jail sentence for tax evasion, but he was released in 1939, paralysed from advanced syphilis. He died, a recluse, in Florida.

Carnegie, Dale(1888–1955) US author and teacher of public speaking. An active member of debating clubs at school and college, Carnegie worked as a salesman and an actor before teaching public speaking at the YMCA. A successful response and large attendances led to the publication of pamphlets, eventually collected in book form in *Public Speaking: A Practical*

Jimmy Carter, 39th US president, speaking in Washington in 1977.

Course for Business Men (1926). The publication of *Little Known Facts About Well Known People* (1934) led to a radio series of the same name, but his most successful and influential book was *How to Win Friends and Influence People* (1936). In this Carnegie offered common-sense advice for overcoming handicaps in order to become successful, emphasizing the importance of a positive attitude.

Carothers, Wallace (1896–1937) US industrial chemist. In 1928 Carothers became head of the organic chemistry department of the giant chemicals company Du Pont. Charged with investigating substances of high molecular weight, he produced neoprene (1932), one of the first satisfactory synthetic rubbers. He then went on to study the fiber-forming properties of polymers, a line of research that led to the discovery of nylon, first marketed commercially in 1939, two years after Carothers' suicide due to depression.

Carrel, Alexis (1873–1944) French-born US surgeon. Carrel joined the Rockefeller Institute for Medical Research, New York, in 1906, where he studied the problems of organ transplantation in animals. A major task was to reconnect the severed blood vessels of the transplanted organs. Using new microtechniques for suturing, he successfully removed organs and replaced them in the same animal. He was, however, unable to overcome the problem of rejection when transplanting an organ from one animal to another. His suturing techniques found further application in vascular surgery, and he is also remembered for his pioneer research on tissue culture. He was awarded the Nobel prize for physiology or medicine in 1912.

Carson, Johnny (1925–) US broadcaster and personality. Starting out as a magician, Carson turned to writing comedy routines and began to work in local radio in the 1950s. His humorous monologs on *The Johnny Carson Show* led NBC to give him a spot on *The Tonight Show* (1962). His naughty boy image and "desk and sofa" interview technique made it the most popular show on US television, and Carson became the highest-paid entertainer. until his retirement in 1992.

Carter, James Earl ("Jimmy") (1924–) US president. Carter served in the US Navy (1946–53) before joining the family peanut farming business in Plains, Georgia. He was Democratic governor of Georgia (1970–74) and came from behind to win the Democrat presidential nomination in 1976, going on to defeat Gerald Ford in the presidential election. His program of social reform was blocked by Congress. Carter won an international reputation as a mediator and peace-maker. He signed the Panama Canal treaty, hosted the Camp David peace talks between Egypt and Israel (1978), opened full diplomatic relations with China and signed the SALT II treaty to limit strategic nuclear arms. The failure of a military operation to free hostages held in the US embassy in Iran in 1980 severely dented Carter's image at home. Meanwhile, he applied economic sanctions against the Soviet Union in response to its invasion of Afghanistan (1979) and called for a boycott of the 1980 Moscow Olympics. Rising inflation and high unemployment added to Carter's unpopularity, and he failed to win reelection in 1980, losing to Ronald Reagan.

Cartier-Bresson, Henri (1908–) French photographer. Cartier-Bresson took up photography in Africa in about 1930, after studying painting and literature in Paris and Cambridge. His first exhibitions were held in Madrid and New York (1933). He worked as assistant to the French film director Jean Renoir (1936–39), and made two documentary films, *Return to Life* (1937), about the Spanish Civil War, and *Le Retour* (1945), on the postwar experiences of French prisoners-of-war. In 1947 he was involved in the setting up, with Robert Capa and others, of Magnum Photos, a pioneering cooperative photographic agency. He traveled in India, China, Indonesia, Egypt and the Soviet Union taking photographs that appeared in *The Decisive Moment* (1952) and *People of Moscow* (1955). Always concerned with the experience and response to "great events" of ordinary people, Cartier-Bresson was out on the streets of Paris with his Leica during the riots of 1968. A major retrospective exhibition of his photographs was held at the New York Museum of Modern Art in 1988.

The Marxist leader Fidel Castro whose rule in Cuba outlasted Soviet communism.

Caruso, Enrico (1873–1921)
Italian opera singer. Born into a poor family in Naples, Caruso began singing in church and at street festivals. From these inauspicious beginnings he went on to become the best-loved operatic tenor of his day, and perhaps of all time. He sang at Milan's La Scala and London's Covent Garden but was particularly associated with the New York Metropolitan where he made his debut in *Rigoletto* (1903). Famous for his roles in *La Boheme, I Pagliacci* and *Tosca*, Caruso was among the first to take the gramophone seriously, and it was through his many records of operatic arias and Neapolitan folksongs that he reached a worldwide audience. He died at the early age of 48.

Castro (Ruz), Fidel (1926–)
Cuban revolutionary leader. A lawyer, Castro staged an unsuccessful rising against President Batista in 1953. He was imprisoned, but released in an amnesty two years later and fled to the US and Mexico. Returning to Cuba in 1956 with a small band of insurgents, he waged a guerrilla war against Batista's regime, amid growing support. Batista was overthrown in 1958 and Castro appointed prime minister. He proclaimed a Marxist–Leninist program of reform adapted to Cuban requirements in industry, agriculture and education. US-owned companies were nationalized, a free welfare system established, ownership centralized and the media government controlled. After the defeat of the US-backed invasion at the Bay of Pigs in 1961, Cuba became increasingly dependent on Soviet aid, leading to the Cuban missile crisis of 1962. A committed revolutionary, Castro gave assistance to Marxist, pro-Soviet forces in Angola and Ethiopia, and by the 1980s had 40,000 troops stationed in some 25 countries. He was a strong critic of Gorbachev's reforming policies in the late 1980s. The subsequent collapse of the Soviet Union saw a deepening of his political isolation, while the removal of Soviet aid plunged Cuba into economic crisis.

Ceausescu, Nicolae (1918–89) Romanian political leader. Ceausescu joined the then illegal Rumanian Communist party in 1933. He owed his appointment as deputy minister of agriculture (1948–50) and deputy minister for the army (1950–4) in the postwar Communist government to the patronage of Gheorghe-Dej, the party leader, and rose rapidly through the central committee and Politburo to become secretary general (1965), head of state (1967), and president (1974). An orthodox Marxist-Leninist, he accelerated industrialization and imposed strict party controls, at the same time fostering a personality cult around himself. His pursuit of economic and politic independence from the Soviet Union endeared his regime to Western leaders in the 1970s, but his personal rule, which he shared with his equally narrow-minded and self-obsessed wife Elena, became increasingly harsh and irrational. The country's once stable economy was destroyed by policies which included the exportation of most of the food and fuel needed for domestic consumption and the destruction of rural society through the demolition of villages and the forcible removal of the rural population to the cities. Legislation was passed to compel every Romanian woman of child-bearing age to have six children. In 1989 the military joined a popular rising against the regime. Ceausescu and his wife tried unsuccessfully to flee but were captured, tried and executed.

Chagall, Marc (1889–1985) Russian–Jewish-born French painter. Chagall studied art at St Petersburg and Paris, where he was introduced to Cubism and Fauvism. These strongly influenced his paintings of Jewish rural life in works like *I and the Village* (1911). Returning to his hometown of Vitebsk, he married Bella Rosenfeld, the subject of many of his paintings. He was made commissar of fine arts in Vitebsk after the Russian Revolution but left Russia for Paris in 1923. The dealer Ambroise Vollard commissioned many illustrations from him, notably a series of etchings for Gogol's *Dead Souls*. The years 1941–47 were spent in the US. Chagall's sorrow at his wife's death in 1944 is reflected in paintings like *Around Her* (1945). He is best remembered for his dreamlike paintings peopled by animals, objects and people from his Russian–Jewish past and from his own poetic imagination. In the 1950s he took up sculpture, stained-glass and ceramics. His public commissions include the ceiling of the Paris Opera (1964) and two large murals for the New York Metropolitan Opera (1966).

Charlie Chaplin as the immortal Little Tramp, seen here in City Lights (1931).

Chamberlain, Neville (1869–1940) British prime minister. Elected to parliament as a Conservative in 1918 at the age of 50, Chamberlain became chancellor of the exchequer (1923–24, 1931–37), and prime minister (1937–40). Coming to the premiership at a time of mounting crisis in Europe, he pursued a policy of nonintervention in the Spanish Civil War, and one of appeasement toward Mussolini's Italy and Nazi Germany. He dropped the sanctions that had been introduced against Italy after its occupation of Ethiopia in 1936, and in 1938 signed the Munich Pact with Hitler which recognized the German occupation of western Czechoslovakia. Meanwhile, the pace of British rearmament increased. When, in 1939, Hitler occupied all of Czechoslovakia in defiance of the Munich Pact, war became a certainty. Chamberlain introduced conscription, and promised armed assistance to Poland, Romania and Greece. He declared war on Germany in September 1939 following Hitler's invasion of Poland. Criticized for early military setbacks and in ill health, he resigned the war leadership to Winston Churchill in 1940.

Chanel, Coco (1883–1971) French couturier. Starting from a tiny hat shop which she opened in 1913, Chanel rose swiftly to dominate the Parisian fashion scene, persuading generations of women to choose casual, understated elegance. She introduced several classics, notably the little black dress, as well as costume jewelry and bobbed hair. Her empire grew to include a textile business, jewelry workshop and perfume laboratory: the perfume Chanel No. 5 was introduced in 1922. She retired in 1938 but made a comeback in 1954, introducing another classic, the cardigan suit.

Chaplin, Charlie (1889–1977) British actor and movie director. A child music-hall performer from a poor background in London's East

End, Chaplin created one of the world's greatest screen clowns. With his pantomimic performances of balletic delicacy he transformed the Little Tramp, created for a 1914 Hollywood movie – pathetic, heroic, naively full of impossible aspirations and yet finally triumphant – into one of the great icons of early cinema. His masterpieces of the silent screen include *The Tramp* (1915), *The Kid* (1921), *The Gold Rush* (1925). He made some concessions to the coming of sound in *City Lights* (1931) and *Modern Times* (1936), but his full sound movies, *The Great Dictator* (1940), a caricature of the rise of Adolf Hitler, and *Limelight* (1952), an affectionate portrait of his music-hall days, were less successful and his later Hollywood years were dogged by scandal and controversy. An unabashed supporter of radical causes, Chaplin was refused reentry into the US in 1952, at the height of the anticommunist fervor of the McCarthy era. He settled in Switzerland and did not return to the US until 1972 when he received an emotional Hollywood tribute. He was knighted in 1975.

Chomsky, Noam (1928–) US linguistic theorist and political activist. Chomsky studied mathematics and philosophy at Pennsylvania University, and became interested in linguistics. It was while he was a research fellow at Harvard and the Massachusetts Institute of Technology that he developed his theories of generative grammar. These led to the creation of a new school of linguistics and profoundly influenced philosophy and psychology. Chomsky was involved with New Left politics and opposed US foreign intervention in Vietnam during the 1960s and 1970s and in the Gulf War (1990–91). His views on socio-political matters can be found in *American Power and The New Mandarins* (1969) and *At War with Asia* (1970).

Chrétien, Jean (1934–) Canadian prime minister. Chrétien studied law in Quebec and entered legal practice in 1958. Elected to the House of Commons in 1963, he represented the Quebec riding of Saint Maurice for the next 23 years. During this period he held nine successive cabinet posts and acquired a reputation as an astute politician and able administrator. In 1980, as minister of justice and attorney general of Canada, he took on the delicate negotiations with the provincial and British governments over the repatriation of the Canadian constitution. In 1986 Chrétien left politics to return to the law, but four years reentered the fray as leader of the Liberal Party, becoming prime minister when

Winston Churchill, Britain's wartime leader, with his famous V-for-Victory sign.

the Liberals were returned to power in November 1993. A supporter of a united Canada, Chrétien presided over the referendum that narrowly decided against independence for Quebec and faced strong opposition from the Bloc Québecois in parliament.

Christie, Agatha (1890–1976) British detective novelist. Christie turned to writing in the 1920s and during a long career produced more than 76 novels. Her enormous international popularity was based on ingenious plotting and the brilliant use of suspense. Among her best-known novels were her first major success, *The Murder of Roger Ackroyd* (1926), *Murder on the Orient Express* (1934) and *Death on the Nile* (1937). Several have been made into successful movies and TV series. Christie was also the author of several plays, including *The Mousetrap* (1952), the longest-running play in London's West End.

Christo (1935–) Bulgarian sculptor. Born Christo Javacheff, he studied in Sofia and Vienna (1955–57), then went to Paris, where he joined the Nouveaux Réalistes, a movement deeply critical of consumerist culture and materialist values. He began wrapping objects in 1958, at first bottles and cans, and then (after moving to New York in 1964) larger and larger things such as trees, cars and buildings. In 1969 he wrapped a 1.5-mile long bay on the Australian coast and in 1971 created *Valley Curtain*, a long fence made of sheet plastic, in Colorado. The Pont Neuf bridge in Paris was draped in plastic in 1985 and the Reichstag building in Berlin in 1995. Christo also produced, from 1961, assemblages made out of oilcans.

Churchill, Winston (1874–1965) British prime minister. Born into an aristocratic family, Churchill was a soldier and war correspondent before entering parliament as a Conservative in 1900. He broke with his party in

1904 over tariff reform to join the Liberals, and on their election to power was appointed colonial undersecretary (1906). He went on to hold a number of other ministerial posts before resigning from the government as first lord of the Admiralty during World War I after the failure of the Dardanelles expedition (1915). He was colonial secretary (1921–22) in Lloyd George's postwar government but rejoined the Conservative party as chancellor of the exchequer (1924–29). Regarded as a man of undoubted ability but unreliable judgement, he became politically isolated during the 1930s but, as a relentless opponent of Nazi appeasement, was the natural choice as successor to Neville Chamberlain in 1940. Churchill was an outstanding wartime prime minister. His leadership qualities, oratorical skills and determination rallied and inspired the British people, and he forged close ties with Britain's US and Soviet allies. Overwhelmingly defeated in the 1945 postwar election, he used his time in opposition to warn against the expansion of Soviet power and wrote a history, *The Second World War* (1948–53). He was reelected prime minister in 1951 at the age of 77, and resigned in 1955. An historical writer of considerable literary skill, Churchill was awarded the Nobel prize for literature in 1953.

Citroën, André-Gustave
(1878–1935) French engineer and industrialist. During World War I Citroën applied mass-production techniques to the French munitions industry. Converting his munitions plant to an automobile factory after the war, he began mass production of a small model, the Citroën, in 1919 and went on to build one of the largest automobile manufacturing companies in France. He introduced the front-wheel-drive Citroën Seven in 1934 during the Depression but it was not enough to stave off bankruptcy and Citroën lost control of the company. In the 1920s he sponsored a number of scientific and geological expeditions and provided the lighting for the Arc de Triomphe and the Place de la Concorde as gifts to the city of Paris.

Clemenceau, Georges
(1841–1929) French premier. A politician of strong radical views, Clemenceau was involved in the Paris Commune (1871). From 1876 he served in the National Assembly as leader of the far left and used his radical paper *La Justice* to denounce France's colonialist policies. His opposition brought down two premiers, and it was during this period that he acquired a reputation as a powerful antagonist who would not take office

Bill Clinton's presidency was troubled by rumors of scandal and corruption.

himself. His unpopularity grew and he was defeated in the elections of 1893. An outstanding political writer, he campaigned vigorously in his newspapers on behalf of Dreyfus, the Jewish army officer who became the victim of injustice and antisemitism. In 1902 Clemenceau was reelected to the Assembly and as interior minister (1906) broke with the left when he ordered out troops against striking miners. He served two terms as prime minister (1906–09, 1917–20). Known as "the Tiger", he inspired popular resistance to Germany and presided at the Paris Peace Conference (1919), energetically defending French interests and pressing demands for German disarmament. Nevertheless the Treaty of Versailles was attacked for having conceded too much to Germany, and Clemenceau failed in his attempt to win the presidency in 1920.

Clinton, Bill (William) (1946–) US president. A Democrat, Clinton set his sights on a political career after meeting his hero, President John F. Kennedy, in the early 1960s. He studied at Oxford and Yale Law School and in 1977 was elected state attorney general for Arkansas. In 1978 he became the state's youngest governor, at 32, holding the office for five terms (1979–81, 1983–92). His campaign for the US presidency in 1991–92 was overshadowed by charges of marital infidelity and draft dodging, but he survived to win election with 43 per cent of the popular vote. Seen by many of his supporters as an energetic figure in the Kennedy mold, Clinton's domestic policies soon ran into problems as his economic and welfare measures were consistently blocked by Congress. His popularity declined as rumors circulated in Washington concerning his and his wife Hillary's involvement in alleged property fraud in the 1970s. However, his diplomatic efforts in working for peace in Ireland, Israel and Bosnia contributed to increase his political stature abroad.

Cockcroft, John Douglas (1897–1967) British physicist. A mathematician, Cockcroft joined Ernest Rutherford's team of atomic physicists working at the Cavendish Laboratory, Cambridge in 1924 and, in partnership with E.T.S.Walton, succeeded in splitting atoms of lithium and boron by bombardment with protons (1932), for which they shared the Nobel prize for physics in 1951. During World War II Cockcroft was associated with the development of radar and other aspects of air defense while serving as Jacksonian Professor of Natural Philosophy at Cambridge (1939–46). He was director of the Canadian Atomic Energy Commission (1944–46), director of the UK Atomic Energy Research Establishment, Harwell (1946–58), and master of Churchill College, Cambridge (1959–67).

Cocteau, Jean (1889–1963) French writer, film-maker, and artist. It was in Paris during World War I, in which he had served as an ambulance driver, that Cocteau met the avant-garde group of composers known as Les Six: his first ballet, *Parade* (1917), was a collaboration with Erik Satie, one of their number, and Picasso. Such glittering cooperation and virtuosity was to be the keynote of Cocteau's career. Though known primarily as a writer and film-maker, his artistic endeavors ranged widely: he worked in glass and ceramics, illustrated books, decorated buildings, wrote libretti, designed ballets and composed music, frequently in association with many famous artists and writers. His best-known works are the novel *Les Enfants Terribles* (1929), which he later filmed, and the play *La Machine Infernale* (1934). His films include *The Blood of a Poet* (1932), *Beauty and the Beast* (1945) and *Orpheus* (1950). In 1955 he became the first person to be elected to the Académie Française without paying court to its members.

Colette, (Sidonie Gabrielle) (1873–1954)) French writer. Born in Burgundy, Colette married and moved to Paris when she was 20. Her first four semiautobiographical "Claudine" novels were published under her husband's pseudonym of Willy. They were divorced in 1906, and she married twice more. Her best-known novels include *Chéri* (1920), *The Cat* (1933) and *Gigi* (1944), later made into a film musical. She also published numerous short stories and memoirs of her country childhood. Her writing, largely concerned with the pleasure and pain of love, is remarkable for its rich sensory qualities, combined with acute observation of the physical world.

Noel Coward with leading lady Gertrude Lawrence in Private Lives (1930).

Connolly, Maureen (1934–69) US tennis player. Popularly known as "Little Mo", she won three consecutive US singles titles (1951–53) and Wimbledon singles titles (1952–54) and was the first woman to win tennis's Grand Slam, the Wimbledon, US, Australian and French championships in one year (1953). A tiny, tough player, her competitive career was tragically ended after a horseriding accident in 1954, but she continued to coach until her early death from cancer.

Conrad (Korzeniowski), Joseph (1857–1924) Polish-born English writer. Son of a revolutionary Polish poet who died when he was young, Conrad spent 20 years at sea. During this time he studied English and in 1884 became a British subject. His first novel, *Almayer's Folly* (1895) was written when he was nearly 40. He settled in Kent and devoted himself to writing. His novels drew heavily on his experiences as a sailor. *Lord Jim* (1900) and *Nostromo* (1904) are often regarded as his masterpieces: they demonstrate the power and beauty of his style, and the depth and complexity of plot and character that distinguish his work. Conrad's novels are psychological studies of men put to the utmost test; the settings are often menacing – the sea, the jungle, even the world of political espionage – but the real threat comes from the "heart of darkness" (the title of one of his stories) that lies within.

Conran, Terence (1931–) British designer and retailer. In the 1960s Conran's Habitat stores had great success in making available a coordinated collection of inexpensive, well-designed furniture and articles for the home. Using natural materials such as wood, terracotta and cotton, they were in marked contrast to the plastic and nylon goods of the 1950s. Conran's entrepreneurial skills later took him into popular retailing and into the restaurant business. His strong interest in design led him to become involved in the Boilerhouse Project, a design exhibition at London's Tate Gallery, and he also played a major part in setting up London's Museum of Design. He was knighted in 1983.

Coolidge, Calvin (1872–1933) US president. Coolidge first came to national attention in 1919 when, as Republican governor of Massachusetts, he called out the state guard to restore order during a police strike. Appointed vice-president by President Harding in 1921, Coolidge succeeded to the presidency on Harding's death in 1923 and went on to win the presidential election in 1924. He reduced government intervention in the economy (though high, protectionist tariffs remained), cut taxes and paid off a large proportion of the national debt. Coolidge successfully opposed farm relief, but his opposition to bonuses for World War I veterans was defeated by Congress. He did not seek reelection in 1928.

Cooper, Gary (1901–61) US film actor. One of Hollywood's most popular stars, Cooper's laconic style and lanky looks appealed to men and women alike: he was the strong, silent man of adventure and romance. Raised on a Montana ranch, he drifted into the movie business in the early 1920s, finding work as an extra and stunt-rider in Westerns. His break came quickly, as replacement second lead in *The Winning of Barbara Worth* (1926). Lead roles followed in *Wings* (1927) and *The Virginian* (1929) and, encouraged by the directors Capra and Hawks, he went on to extend his range into comedy. Credits include *A Farewell to Arms* (1932), *Mr Deeds Goes to Town* (1936), *For Whom the Bell Tolls* (1943) and *High Noon* (1952). In 1961 he received a special Academy Award for his contribution to the movie industry.

Coward, Noël (1899–1973) British actor, director, and playwright. Born into a musical family, Coward started as a child actor. In the 1920s and 1930s he found fame as the writer of sophisticated and technically brilliant comedies that frequently defied moral convention. He was an excellent actor, taking the lead in many of his plays, memorably *The Vortex* (1924) and *Private Lives* (1930). *Hay Fever* (1925) and *Blithe Spirit* (1941) are among his most accomplished works. In 1942 he wrote, produced, coordinated-directed and starred in the wartime sea drama *In Which We Serve*. He later became a noted nightclub and cabaret performer and appeared in numerous film cameo roles.

Marie Curie, Polish-born French scientist and discoverer of radium.

Crawford, Joan (1904–77) US film actress. One of the most tenaciously durable Hollywood stars, Crawford was not particularly pretty or sexy but she had glamor and she worked hard, achieving success mostly through her ambition and adaptability. A flapper to rival Clara Bow in the 1920s, she played working-girl parts in the 1930s, melodramas a decade later, the mature *femme fatale* in the 1950s and horror film roles in the 1960s. Credits include *Our Dancing Daughters* (1928), *The Women* (1939), *Mildred Pierce* (1945) and *Johnny Guitar* (1954). Her last great role, opposite her arch-rival Bette Davis, was in *Whatever Happened to Baby Jane?* (1962).

Crick, Francis (1916–) British molecular biologist. A physics graduate, after postgraduate research in Cambridge Crick spent the war years as a scientist with the Admiralty (1940–47), before returning to Cambridge as part of a Medical Research Council unit investigating the structure of large biological molecules by means of X-ray crystallography. In 1951, the unit was joined by J.D. Watson, an American biologist with a particular interest in genetics. The two men complemented each other, both personally and professionally, and they joined forces to search for a way of describing the chemical structure of deoxyribonucleic acid (DNA). With their own X-ray pictures of DNA, and some others supplied by M.H.F. Wilkins, a New Zealand biophysicist working in London, they eventually constructed a model containing a double helix – connected at intervals by rungs like those of a ladder – which was fully consistent with the observed X-ray patterns. Crick, Watson and Wilkins were awarded a Nobel prize in 1962. In 1977 Crick joined the Salk Institute in San Diego.

Cronkite, Walter (1916–) US newscaster. Cronkite worked as a journalist for the *Houston Post*, covering World War II and the Nuremberg Trials, before joining CBS in 1950. He became a popular figure on the *You Are There* series and from 1962–81 was the anchor-man of his own nightly newscast. His low-key broadcasting style earned him the title of "The Most Trusted Man in America".

Crosby, Bing (1904–77) US vocalist. Band leader Paul Whiteman signed Crosby as one of the Rhythm Boys trio in 1927. It was in 1931, when he was heard over the radio on a nationwide CBS broadcast, that Crosby's unique singing voice first made its impression on the US public: his unique crooning sound was attributed to nodules on the vocal cords. His relaxed, casual style was much imitated. Hollywood signed him to make several musical romances in the 1930s; the famous "Road" movies with Bob Hope and Dorothy Lamour followed in the 1940s, and Crosby later took some dramatic roles. With over 2,600 releases, by 1975 he had sold over 400 million discs. His recording of "White Christmas" from the 1954 film of that title is one of the world's all-time biggest sellers.

Curie, Marie (1867–1934) Polish-born French physicist. Daughter of a Warsaw physics teacher, she worked as a governess before entering the Sorbonne in Paris in 1891 to study physics and mathematics. There she met, and soon married (1895), Pierre Curie, director of laboratory work at the newly founded Municipal School of Physics and Chemistry. Both were intensely interested in the newly discovered phenomena of X-rays and radioactivity (a term Marie Curie invented) and they collaborated in a search for substances with properties similar to those of uranium. Their discovery in 1898 of polonium and radium brought fame to both. Together with Antoine Becquerel they shared the 1903 Nobel prize for physics. In 1904 Pierre was appointed professor of physics in the Sorbonne but, tragically, was killed in a street accident in 1906. Marie succeeded to his chair, and was awarded a Nobel Prize for chemistry in 1911 for her continued work on radium. She died of leukaemia, a condition that was brought on by her exposure to radiation.

Curzon, George Nathaniel, Marquis Curzon of Kedleston (1859–1925) British politician. Academically brilliant and a man of huge conceit, Curzon was elected a Conservative member of parliament in 1886. In 1895, at the age of 36, he was appointed the youngest ever Viceroy of India and made a baron. He set about the task of ruling British India with

Salvador Dalí, the Spanish Surrealist painter, famous for his showmanship.

great energy, though there was personal rivalry and intrigue between him and his military commander, Lord Kitchener, and in 1905 Curzon tendered his resignation. In 1915 he became Lord Privy Seal in Asquith's coalition government. He went on to become a member of Lloyd George's war cabinet in 1916, and served as foreign secretary (1919–24) but never gained the premiership himself despite believing he had earned it. In 1919, he proposed the "Curzon Line" across Poland, which formed the basis of the Polish–Soviet border after World War II. He was instrumental in helping rebuild Anglo–German relations after World War I.

Dalí, Salvador (1904–89) Spanish painter. Imprisoned for subversion during his studies at Madrid Fine Art School, Dalí was expelled in 1926 and went to Paris, where he met his fellow Spanish painters Pablo Picasso and Joan Miró and studied the work of Sigmund Freud. In 1928 he joined the movement of Surrealist painters and collaborated with the Spanish film director Luis Buñuel on two Surrealist films, *Un Chien Andalou* (1928) and *L'Age d'or* (1930). His painting, *The Persistence of Memory* (1931), popularly known as *The Limp Watches*, which combined quasi-hallucinatory images with a brilliantly realistic style of execution, made him the most popular of the Surrealists. In the 1930s he flirted with Fascism, which led to a rift with his fellow Surrealists, though he continued to exhibit with them. From 1940–55 he lived in the US. His work drew more and more on Catholic themes, as in *The Crucifixion of St John of the Cross* (1951) and *The Last Supper* (1955). He returned to Spain and devoted his time to decorating the museum of his works in the Catalan town of Figueras, his birthplace.

Dean, James (1931–55) US film actor. After studying at the University of California, Dean briefly attended the Actors' Studio in New York. His film career was short – a few bit parts (1951–53) and three starring roles in *East of Eden* and *Rebel Without a Cause* (both 1955) and *Giant* (1956). His brooding good looks, sulky drawl and nonconformist attitudes catapulted him to fame and he became the symbol of teenage rebellion in the mid 1950s. His death in a car crash aroused displays of mass grief only paralleled by Rudolf Valentino's death in 1926.

de Beauvoir, Simone (1908–86) French novelist and feminist. Privately educated, de Beauvoir attended the Sorbonne (1926–9) where her lifelong relationship with the philosopher Jean-Paul Sartre began. Her most famous work is *The Second Sex* (1949) in which she argued for the rejection of the myth of women's feminity. This work was to be enormously influential in the feminist movement of the 1960s and 1970s. De Beauvoir's novels such as *She Came to Stay* (1943), *All Men are Mortal* (1946) and *The Mandarins* (1954), for which she won the Prix Goncourt, were discussions of existentialism and feminism. She wrote her autobiography in four volumes (1958–72). Rejecting marriage and motherhood for herself, de Beauvoir was active in the women's movement, especially in the campaign for the legalization of abortion in France.

Debussy, Claude (1862–1918) French composer. In 1872 Debussy entered the Paris Conservatoire to study piano. He won the prestigious Prix de Rome in 1884, but did not take it up, choosing to complete his studies in Paris. His first major work, *La Damoiselle élue* (1888), shows the influence of Wagner. However, more lasting influences were to be the gamelan music of Southeast Asia, the Russian composer Modest Moussorgsky, and his French contemporary, Erik Satie. *Prélude à l'après-midi d'un faune* (1894) brought Debussy to public attention, earning him the epithet "Impressionist", though he repudiated this attribution. Debussy's subtlety of touch did not lend itself readily to opera: *Pelléas et Mélisande* (1902), his only successful opera, aroused considerable controversy on its first performance. Both poetry (particularly that of Prosper Mallarmé and Maurice Maeterlinck) and painting inspired his work, as in *La Mer* (1905). *Les Préludes* (1910–13) contain some of his best-known pieces. Debussy retained the discipline of the classical tradition, but introduced unusual harmonic procedures into his compositions. He employed orchestral color in a way that has been highly influential in the development of music throughout the 20th century.

Deng Xiaoping, who headed China's drive to modernization in the 1980s.

de Gaulle, Charles (1890–1970) French general and president. De Gaulle was mentioned in dispatches three times during World War I. He was an instructor in military strategy after the war, though his efforts to modernize the French army met with little success. On the fall of France in 1940, he fled to England where he formed and led the Free French Army and in 1943 was elected president of the French Committee of National Liberation. He entered Paris at the head of the liberation forces in August 1944 and headed the provisional French government, but resigned in 1946. A consistent campaigner in parliament against the government of the Fourth Republic, he was asked in 1958 to form a temporary administration to avoid the impending chaos caused by nationalist unrest against French colonial rule in Algeria. He reformed the constitution, and in 1958 was elected president and established the Fifth Republic. As president, he strengthened the French economy, gave independence to 12 African colonies, withdrew France from NATO and acquired an independent nuclear deterrent. Regarded as a difficult man to deal with abroad and as an autocrat at home, de Gaulle received a boost for his waning popularity after the student–worker riots of 1968, but this success was short-lived. After losing a national referendum, he resigned in 1969. His published writings include memoirs and lectures on leadership.

de Klerk, F.W. (1936–) South African president. De Klerk worked as a lawyer before entering parliament for the National Party in 1972. He served in a number of ministerial positions (1976–82) and as minister of internal affairs in P. W. Botha's hardline government stood out for promoting a policy of racial power-sharing as the only route to peace and stability. He was made leader of the ruling National Party (1982), becoming South African president in 1989. Embarking on the process of dismantling apartheid, in

1990 he lifted the ban from the African National Congress (ANC) and released Nelson Mandela from prison. The last major apartheid laws were removed the following year, thus allowing international sanctions against South Africa to be lifted. Working in close cooperation with the ANC, he led the way toward South Africa's first multiracial elections in 1994, when he lost the presidency to Nelson Mandela. The two men were joint recipients of the Nobel prize for peace in 1993.

Delors, Jacques (1925–) French Socialist politician, president of the European Community (EC). Delors worked in banking and as a university lecturer before entering the European parliament (1979), becoming chairman of its economic and monetary committee. As French finance minister (1981–84) he demanded a slowing-down of social reform, devalued the franc and froze prices and wages, and was criticized for his excessive austerity. He was president of the EC (1985–94), in which role he was an enthusiastic advocate of European economic unity.

de Mille, Cecil B. (1881–1959) US film director, producer and screenwriter. A cofounder of the Lasky company, later to become Paramount Pictures, de Mille pioneered the switch to feature-length films, developed his own regular company of actors and concentrated on improving production values. His early romantic comedies and later epic Biblical spectaculars such as *The Ten Commandments* (two versions: 1923 and 1956) and *Samson and Delilah* (1949) demonstrate the same successful formula: explicit visual detail combined with clearly stated Christian values. De Mille was also an entrepreneur in commercial aviation.

Deng Xiaoping (1904–) Chinese Communist leader. Born into a landowning family, Deng studied in France (1920–25), joined the Communist party and spent six months in Moscow before returning to China. A supporter of Mao Zedong, he took part in the Long March (1934), and fought against the Japanese (1935–36) and in the civil war against the Nationalists (1945–49). By the mid 1950s Deng had become secretary general of the Chinese Communist party (CCP) and a Politburo member, but was attacked during the Cultural Revolution (1966–69) and dismissed from his posts. Reinstated in 1973, in 1975 he was appointed vice-chairman of the CCP Central Committee, a member of its Politburo, and chief of staff. His push to modernize China alienated

Walt Disney, creator of the world's best-loved cartoon characters.

Mao Zedong, and he again fell from favor. After Mao's death (1976) Deng led the campaign against the ultra-left Gang of Four, which included Mao's widow. By 1979 he had gained effective control of the government and launched a far-reaching program of economic reform. Bureaucratic restrictions were swept away to increase agricultural and industrial efficiency, and his "open door" policy permitted the introduction of foreign technology and capital to facilitate modernization. In 1989, Deng's credibility as a reformer was severely damaged after pro-democracy demonstrations in Peking's Tiananmen Square were crushed with savage force, leaving thousands dead.

Derrida, Jacques (1930–)
Algerian-born French philosopher. Derrida studied in Paris and taught at the Sorbonne (1960–4) and Ecole Normale Supérieure (1965–84). His most important works include *Of Grammatology* (1967), *Writing and Difference* (1967) and *Dissemination* (1972). In them he developed a deconstructionist style of criticism, which became a major influence in Marxist literary criticism. Critical deconstruction, as argued by Derrida, aimed to show that any and every text inevitably undermines its own claims to a determinate meaning, and he challenged traditional schools of criticism by emphasizing the role of the reader in the production of meaning.

de Valera, Eamon (1882–1975)
Irish prime minister and president. A commander of the Irish Volunteers in the unsuccessful Easter Rising in Dublin (1916), de Valera was imprisoned until 1917, when he was elected president of the separatist party Sinn Fein ("We ourselves"). He was voted into the British parliament in 1918 when Sinn Fein won three-quarters of the Irish seats, but was imprisoned again and escaped to the US in 1919. Returning to Ireland in 1921, he unsuccessfully opposed the partition of the island. In the ensuing civil war

(1922–23), de Valera backed the Republicans against the victorious Free Staters, who imprisoned him. Released in 1924, he broke away from Sinn Fein, abandoning its extremist positions, and in 1926 founded the alternative Republican party Fianna Fail ("Warriors of destiny"). Elected to the Irish parliament, the Dail, he became prime minister in 1932. In 1937 the sovereign state of Eire was created, claiming sovereignty over all Ireland. In 1939, de Valera outlawed the Irish Republican Army (IRA) but maintained Eire as a neutral state during World War II. He was defeated in the 1948 elections, but served two further terms as prime minister (1951–54, 1957–59) before becoming president (1959–73).

Dietrich, Marlene (1901–92) German-born actress and singer. Dietrich studied with the great theater director Max Reinhardt. Successful as a stage and screen actress, a starring role in Joseph von Sternberg's *The Blue Angel* (1930), Germany's first sound movie, brought her wider fame. She traveled to Hollywood where, under contract to Paramount, she made six of her first seven films with Sternberg. Most notable were *Shanghai Express* (1932) and *The Scarlet Empress* (1934), both of them indulgent pieces that featured her as a sexual icon, alluring in fur and feathers or drag. In 1935 the partnership with Sternberg ended, and her later movies never achieved the same success. During World War II Dietrich entertained Allied troops and made anti-Nazi broadcasts. She afterwards became a highly successful international cabaret artist, performing well into the 1970s.

Dior, Christian (1905–57) French couturier. After working for Parisian designers Robert Piguet and Lucien Lelong in the 1930s, Dior opened his own salon in 1947 with the backing of textile manufacturer Marcel Broussac. His highly popular "New Look", with long swirling skirts that turned their back on the austerity clothes of the war years, reestablished Paris's place at the top of the fashion world. He later launched the "Sack Look" in the 1950s and was quick to discover talent in the next generation of designers such as Yves Saint-Laurent.

Disney, Walt (1901–66) US film animator, producer and executive. A pioneer of animated cartoons, Disney taught himself art by correspondence course. His most famous cartoon character, Mickey Mouse, first appeared in *Steamboat Willie* (1928) and was followed by a stream of anthropomorphic

The Spanish tenor Placido Domingo in concert performance.

cartoon animals – Minnie Mouse, Donald Duck, Goofy and Pluto. A leader in the technical field, Disney's animated movies matched action to prerecorded sound. He was using Technicolor by the mid 1930s, developed a multiplane camera that improved perspective and action shots, and produced the first feature-length cartoon, *Snow White and the Seven Dwarfs* (1937), followed by *Fantasia* (1940) and *Bambi* (1942). He later turned to making live-action adventure movies, the first of which was *Treasure Island* (1950), and full-length nature documentaries, as well as moving into television. In 1955 he opened the first Disneyland amusement park in California, still one of the world's leading tourist attractions.

Domingo, Placido (1941–) Spanish tenor. Domingo's parents were famous zarzuela singers (a popular Spanish form of operetta). He was brought up in Mexico and studied piano at the National Conservatory. After trying his hand at a number of jobs, including bullfighting, he made his operatic debut in Mexico City in 1961. He joined the Hebrew National Opera in Tel Aviv as leading tenor (1962–65) and in 1965 made his opera début in New York with the City Opera. He sang for the first time with the New York Metropolitan Opera in 1968 and with La Scala, Milan, a year later. Thousands of concerts and recordings followed. A man of striking looks, strong stage presence, and a fine actor and musician, Domingo's powerful, yet lyrical, voice put him in the very first rank of singers. In the late 1980s and 1990s, starring as one of the "three tenors" (with Luciano Pavarotti and José Carreras), he achieved enormous worldwide exposure and popularity in a series of broadcast concerts.

Dorsey, Tommy (1905–56) US jazz bandleader and trombonist. With his brother Jimmy (1904–57), a cornetist, saxophonist and clarinetist, he played with a number of leading dance bands before forming the shortlived Dorsey Brothers Orchestra (1933–35). Musical and personality differences led to a split and both went on to form their own bands. An ambitious perfectionist, Tommy created a versatile, disciplined swing orchestra by securing the best talent. During the 1930s and 1940s he built up a huge radio following and made a series of hits, including "I'm Getting Sentimental Over You" and "The Sunny Side of the Street".

Dubcek, Alexander (1921–92) Czechoslovakian politician. Elected Communist party leader in January 1968, Dubcek adopted the slogan "Socialism with a human face". During the so-called "Prague Spring" he increased freedom of speech, removed Stalinists from high office and published a program of reform, "Czechoslovakia's Road to Socialism". The pace of change alarmed the leadership of the Soviet Union, who feared it would lead to a breakup of the Eastern bloc. Dubcek refused to make any but the most minor concessions, and after several weeks of confusion and uncertainty a Warsaw Pact army invaded Czechoslovakia in August 1968. Dispatched for talks to Moscow , Dubcek was forced to abandon his policies. He served as ambassador to Turkey (1969–70) but was expelled from the party and faded into obscurity, working as a forestry administrator. After the collapse of Communism (1989) he came out of retirement and was appointed chairman of the new Czechoslovak parliament.

Dulles, John Foster (1888–1959) US secretary of state. Dulles was appointed US legal advisor at the 1919 Paris Peace Conference and served on the War Reparations Commission. He was a senior advisor at the San Francisco United Nations Conference (1945), and a UN delegate (1946, 1947, 1950). As advisor to the secretary of state, he negotiated the Japanese peace treaty (1951). Appointed President Eisenhower's secretary of state (1953–59), he was prominent in the setting up of SEATO (Southeast Asia Treaty Organization). Firmly opposed to Communism, he introduced the concept of "brinkmanship" and active intervention into the Cold War, threatening "massive nuclear retaliation" against any Soviet aggression.

Duncan, Isadora (1878–1927) US dancer. Rejecting the constraints of ballet, Duncan evolved her own distinctive style in which she aimed to bring expressive life to her improvised dances. Her movements came from the solar plexus and she worked with gravity, not (as in classical ballet) against it. Her ideas would later influence

Albert Einstein, whose theory of relativity reshaped understanding of the universe.

modern choreography, but her daringly flowing draped costumes and unconventional movements shocked American audiences and in 1899 she moved to Europe, where she built a successful career. In 1921 she was invited to Moscow to found a school of dance. Here she met and married the Soviet poet, Sergei Yesenin, but the marriage was short-lived and he killed himself in 1925. Isadora moved to the south of France until her own tragic death in a car accident.

Dylan (Zimmerman), Bob (1941–) US folk/rock composer, singer and guitarist. The leading exponent of US folk/protest music and a musical legend, Dylan was a passionate lyricist of politically slanted songs with a unique rasping voice and staccato delivery. Influenced by the folksinger of an earlier generation, Woody Guthrie, Dylan enthralled New York audiences in the early 1960s with songs such as "A Hard Rain's A Gonna Fall" and "Blowin' in the Wind" (both 1963). His two great landmark albums were *Highway 61 Revisited* (1965) and *Blonde and Blonde* (1966). His rambling movie *Renaldo and Clara* (1978) flopped and the religious trend in later albums such as *Slow Train Coming* (1979), *Saved* (1980) and *Shot of Love* (1981) was not popular with his fans, though his occasional concert tours continued to attract large (and aging) audiences.

Eastwood, Clint (1930–) film actor, director and producer. Eastwood first came to public notice in the 1960 TV series *Rawhide* before winning international fame in Sergio Leone's spaghetti Westerns (which were shot in Almeira, Spain) such as *The Good, The Bad and the Ugly* (1966). His image as the laconic hero under pressure brought worldwide popularity. In 1986 he was elected mayor of his Californian hometown, Carmel. His later movies (many of which he directed and produced himself) include

Dirty Harry (1971), *Play Misty for Me* (1971), *Escape from Alcatraz* (1978) and *The Unforgiven* (1992), for which he won the Academy Award for best director.

Eden, Anthony (1897–1977) British prime minister. Elected to parliament as a Conservative in 1923, Eden served as foreign secretary from 1935–38, resigning in protest over the appeasement of Germany and Italy. Returning to government as dominions secretary after the declaration of war in 1939, he served as war secretary (1940) and foreign secretary (1940–45), a post he resumed on the Conservatives' return to power in 1951, together with that of deputy prime minister. When Churchill finally stood down in 1955, Eden took over as prime minister, despite being in poor health. He was criticized for his indecisive handling of the Suez Crisis (1956) and resigned the following year. In 1961 he was given an earldom.

Edward VIII (1894–1972) King of Great Britain and Northern Ireland. The eldest son of King George V and Queen Mary, Edward was thoroughly trained for the job of king, serving in the army, touring the Empire and making token visits to depressed industrial areas. But his playboy image was never far beneath the surface, and after a series of affairs he formed a liaison with an American divorcee, Wallis Simpson. Determined to marry her as well as ascend the throne, Edward precipitated a constitutional crisis after acceeding to the throne on his father's death in 1936, and was forced to abdicate. He married Wallis Simpson and was created Duke of Windsor. After serving as governor of the Bahamas during World War II, he and his wife withdrew from public life to live as lonely exiles in France.

Einstein, Albert (1879–1955) German–Swiss–US mathematical physicist. Born in Bavaria, Einstein completed his studies in Zurich and acquired Swiss citizenship. The first of his three seminal papers on the theory of relativity was published in 1905, and Einstein held senior academic posts in Prague and Zurich before going as director to the Kaiser Wilhelm Institute of Physics, Berlin, in 1914. His most important work, *The Foundations of the General Theory of Relativity*, was published in 1916 and he was awarded a Nobel prize in 1921. He was in the US when Hitler came to power and never returned to Germany, taking up a position at the Institute of Advanced Study at Princeton. In 1952 Einstein, now a revered figure, was offered, and declined, the presidency of Israel.

Crowned in 1953, Queen Elizabeth II is the world's most enduring head of state.

Eisenhower, Dwight D. ("Ike") (1890–1969) World War II commander and US president. A career soldier, Eisenhower took command of US forces in Europe (1942), and led the successful invasions of North Africa and Italy in 1942–43. Appointed commander of the Allied forces in 1943, he was in overall charge of the D-Day landings when 1 million men and supplies were transported across the English Channel to Normandy on 6 June 1944. After the German surrender (7 May1945), Eisenhower was appointed chief of staff and oversaw the process of demobilization, later becoming NATO supreme commander (1950–52). His wartime popularity swept him into power as Republican president, and he served two terms in office (1953–61). As president, he tended to delegate responsibility. His administration at home put through a number of tax reforms, deregulated prices, rents and wages and saw a reduction in federal powers. The Civil Rights Act was passed in 1957, and minimum wage and social security payments were increased. Overseas, Eisenhower helped end the Korean War in 1953, and the following year presided over the formation of SEATO. The Eisenhower doctrines, by which military assistance was offered to Middle Eastern countries perceived to be under threat from Communism, were introduced in the wake of the Suez Crisis of 1956 and the International Atomic Energy Agency was set up in 1957, at Eisenhower's instigation, to share nuclear materials and information.

Eliot, T. S. (1888–1965) US-born British poet, playwright and critic. Eliot read philosophy at Harvard, then studied under Henri Bergson and Alain-Fournier at the Sorbonne in Paris, where he absorbed the Symbolist poetry of Jules Laforgue and became interested in Indian philosophy. "The Love Song of J. Alfred Prufrock" (published 1915) revolutionized poetic diction, imagery, and tone. In 1914 he moved to London where Ezra Pound encouraged him and edited the text of his pessimistic early masterpiece *The Waste Land* (1922). In 1922 Eliot founded *The Criterion*, a literary journal, and in 1925 left his job in a bank to join a publishing firm. He became a British citizen in 1927, and an Anglo-Catholic. The *Four Quartets* (1935–41), a long meditation on time and history, both personal (it contains elements of autobiography) and collective, contributed to his receiving the Nobel prize for literature (1947). He wrote a number of verse dramas, including *Murder in the Cathedral* (1935). As a critic Eliot helped bring about a revival of interest in Elizabethan and Jacobean drama and the Metaphysical poets. But it is the directness and clarity of his poetry, unsurpassed in modern literature, for which he is best remembered.

Elizabeth II (1926–) Queen of Great Britain and Northern Ireland. The elder daughter of King George VI, Elizabeth was on tour in Kenya with her husband Philip when, at the age of 27, she inherited the throne. The great state occasion of her coronation in 1953 was one of the first ceremonial events to be seen on television around the world. She became one of the most public and hard-working of modern monarchs, making frequent visits to the Commonwealth and other parts of the world, dedicated to carrying out the demanding duties of her role. Towards the end of the century she appeared at times a remote and embattled figure as she faced growing controversy about the role of the monarchy in present-day society, both in Britain and in many parts of the Commonwealth. She had to ride out a succession of crises within her own family, in particular over the issue of Prince Charles' and Princess Diana's divorce, but her own personal popularity was never in doubt.

Elgar, Sir Edward (1857–1934) British composer. The son of a church organist, Elgar was largely self-taught. After his marriage in 1889 he settled in Malvern in the west of England and devoted himself to composition, particularly for local choral societies, winning gradual wider acceptance. His reputation was established with the *Enigma Variations* (1899) and the oratorio *The Dream of Gerontius* (1900), which won particular acclaim in Germany. Other compositions include *Pomp and Circumstance* (1901) and the Violin Concerto in B Minor (1910). Noted for its deep emotional intensity and rich orchestration, his music has remained consistently popular throughout the 20th century.

Georges Escoffier, the world's best-known chef, celebrates his 80th birthday.

Escoffier, Georges (1846–1935) French chef of international renown. Escoffier, a blacksmith's son, began to cook aged 13 in his uncle's restaurant, and was apprenticed in 1865 to a famous Parisian chef. An army cook in the Franco–Prussian war (1870–71), he worked from 1883 as head chef at the Grand Hotel, Monte Carlo for César Ritz. Using teamwork to enhance efficiency, Escoffier refined and simplified contemporary French cuisine. He also ran the Ritz kitchen at the Savoy Hotel in London. Regarded as the supreme chef of all time, he cooked for kings, emperors and the great. Among his famous creations were peach Melba and Melba toast, both inspired by the opera singer Nellie Melba. From 1899 to 1919, still in partnership with Ritz, he was in charge of the Carlton Hotel kitchen in London. He was awarded the Légion d'Honneur in 1920 in recognition of his services to French cooking. In his retirement, he helped run L'Hermitage restaurant in Monte Carlo. Escoffier wrote several cook books.

Fairbanks (Ulman), Douglas, Sr (1883–1939) US actor. Fairbanks overcame an uncertain early start to his career to find stardom on Broadway in 1910. Moving to Hollywood in 1915, he won instant success. Cheerful, athletic and courageous, he epitomized the American male ideal during the 1920s playing tongue-in-cheek swashbuckling roles such as *Robin Hood* (1922) and *The Thief of Baghdad* (1924). He was a leading mover in the formation of United Artists (1919) and the first president of the Academy of Motion Picture Arts and Sciences. He was married to Mary Pickford, Hollywood's sweetheart, from 1920 to 1935. His appeal survived the coming of sound but not of age, and he retired in 1936.

Fangio, Juan (1911–95) Argentinian racing driver. Considered by many to have been the greatest racing driver in the history of the sport, Fangio found employment as a mechanic before building his own racing car which he drove in South American events. In 1949 he joined the European circuit, and won his first world championship in 1951, going on to take the title four more times between 1954 and 1957. He drove for Alfa Romeo, Mercedes-Benz, Ferrari and Maserati, and after his retirement from racing was president of Mercedes Benz, Argentina. A popular figure who was without enemies, he died in the house in which he had been born, in the town of Balcarce.

Faulkner, William (1897–1962) US novelist. Born in Mississippi, Faulkner served with the Royal Canadian flying corps in World War I and traveled in Europe before returning to the south. After publishing a book of poetry, *The Marble Faun* (1924), he met the influential writer Sherwood Anderson, and turned to fiction. *Soldier's Pay* (1926) was followed by a stream of novels set in the country of his southern upbringing and charged with a passionate moral concern: *The Sound and the Fury* (1929), *As I Lay Dying* (1930), *Sanctuary* (1931), *Light in August* (1932), *Absalom, Absalom* (1936) and *Go Down, Moses* (1942). Their complex structure and shifting chronology are often baffling, and their outspoken content matter brought both praise and blame. He worked for a time for Hollywood and scripted *The Big Sleep* (1946). In 1950 he received the Nobel prize for literature. Since his death his reputation has grown, and he is recognized as a brilliant innovator in American fiction.

Fellini, Federico (1920–93) Italian film director. Fellini worked in a variety of jobs before collaborating with documentary movie maker Roberto Rossellini (1945–48). His début as a solo director came with *Luci dei Varieta* (1950). His later films, which brought him international fame, have a kaleidoscopic quality, part fantasy, part autobiography. His major credits include *I Vitelloni* (1953), *La Strada* (1954), *La notte di Cabiria* (1956), *La dolce vita* (1960), *8 1/2* (1963), *Giulietta degli Spiriti* (1965), *Roma* (1972) and *Amarcord* (1973).

Ferrari, Enzo (1898–1988) Italian automobile manufacturer. Ferrari joined Alfa Romeo as a race driver in 1920. He formed his own agency – Scuderia Ferrari – in 1929, though in reality this operated for some of the time as Alfa's works team. In 1939 he set up a company to manufacture racing cars, but the outbreak of war halted production. His first postwar cars (1946) were racers, and one of these

Ella Fitzgerald, one of the greatest interpreters of popular song this century.

developed into his earliest road car, the 166 Inter (1947). The successful 250 Europă series (1954) suggested a commitment to manufacturing road cars, but Ferrari's heart was in racing and that shaped the company's subsequent technical and commercial development. Ferrari cars have won nearly one quarter of the races they have competed in since 1951.

Fitzgerald, Ella (1918–96) US jazz vocalist. Probably America's greatest interpreter of popular song, Fitzgerald was discovered singing at an amateur show in Harlem at the age of 16. She sang with Chick Webb's band in the late 1930s, leading for two years before going solo in 1941. Her international reputation grew as she honed her performance, developing an individual cabaret-style: she possessed superb technical virtuosity and a remarkable flexible range. She worked with all the jazz greats such as Louis Armstrong, Count Basie and Duke Ellington and is best known for her songbook recordings of the great American composers: George Gershwin, Johnny Mercer, Jerome Kern, Cole Porter, Irving Berlin and Duke Ellington. Her high-speed scat improvisations on numbers like "Lady Be Good" and "Flying Home" were equally brilliant.

Fitzgerald, F. Scott (1896–1940) US writer. Fitzgerald was an advertising copywriter when he wrote *This Side of Paradise* (1920). Based on his experiences at Princeton, it fitted the brittle mood of the times and was an immediate popular success, making him rich enough to marry Zelda Sayre, an unstable beauty who inspired many of his heroines. The couple became part of the French Riviera's glamorous "jet set", living dangerously beyond their means. Despite this, Fitzgerald produced a succession of glittering, well-crafted short stories and novels, including *The Great Gatsby* (1925), to continued acclaim. In 1930 Zelda suffered a schizophrenic breakdown. She was hospitalized in 1935, the year after *Tender is the Night* was published. Perhaps Fitzgerald's finest novel, this dealt with the subject of his troubled married life. In 1937 Fitzgerald, by now ill with heart problems and incipient TB, tried his hand as a Hollywood writer, but the experiment was not a happy one. He died of a heart attack at the age of 44. His last great novel *The Last Tycoon*, published posthumously in 1941 and based on his Hollywood experiences, proved that heavy drinking had done little to diminish his undoubted literary powers.

Fleming, Alexander (1881–1955)
British bacteriologist. Fleming qualified in medicine at St Mary's Hospital London and, apart from military service during World War I, spent the rest of his working life as a bacteriologist there. During these years he made two major discoveries. The first (1922) was lysozyme, an enzyme present in nasal and other bodily secretions that is able to digest certain types of bacteria. This demonstrated the existence of substances that could destroy bacteria while remaining harmless to human tissues. In 1928 Fleming observed the similar action of a mold that had accidentally contaminated a staphylococcal culture. He rightly attributed this to the production of an antibacterial substance, to which he gave the name penicillin. However, he failed to recognize the uniquely powerful chemotherapeutic characteristics of penicillin, and by 1934 had given up all work on it. It was left to the biochemists H.W. Florey and E.B. Chain, working at Oxford University in the early 1940s, to establish the importance of penicillin as an antibiotic drug and to develop its use in clinical medicine. All three men shared the Nobel prize for physiology or medicine in 1945.

Forbes, Malcolm (1919–90)
American publisher and businessman. Forbes studied at Princeton and served with distinction in World War II before taking over control, in 1957, of the family-owned business magazine, *Forbes*. He quickly revived the magazine's ailing fortunes, increasing its circulation from 100,000 to 720,000 and laying the foundations of his own wealth – it is reckoned that in his lifetime he amassed a personal fortune of $400 million.Thus enabled to indulge in a life of conspicuous consumption, his extravagance and taste in attractive women guaranteed that he was rarely out of the gossip columns. He was well known as an art collector, accumulating one of the world's greatest collections of Fabergé eggs.

Henry Ford poses in the driver's seat of his latest model in the early 1900s.

Ford, Harrison (1942–) US movie actor. Ford took up acting at college and on leaving was soon signed up by Columbia Pictures. Cast in a succession of bit parts, he became disillusioned with life in the world of movies and began work as a carpenter. He had a part in the very popular *American Graffiti* (1973), but it was *Star Wars* (1977), the blockbusting science-fiction space epic, in which he played a leading heroic role, that made his name. He appeared in its equally popular sequels, *The Empire Strikes Back* (1980) and *Return of the Jedi* (1983). Other good, if small, parts followed; and then came the enormous success of *Raiders of the Lost Ark* (1981) and its successors, in which he played an adventure-seeking archaeologist in the 1930s. Later movies included the serious and moving *Witness* (1985); *Working Girl* (1988); *Presumed Innocent* (1990) and a remake of the 1970s TV hit *The Fugitive* (1993).

Ford, Henry (1863–1947) US automobile manufacturer. Ford constructed his first automobile in 1896, and set up the Ford Motor Company (1903). Production of the Model T Ford, the world's first inexpensive standardized car, began in 1908. When it ceased in 1927 more than 5 million models had been sold – half the world's total auto output at that time. It was the high demand for his product that led Ford to introduce mass-production methods into his plant, with the first assembly-line in 1913, thereby bringing about the rapid worldwide expansion of the automobile industry. Ford also introduced a $5 minimum wage for an eight-hour day and profit-sharing schemes for his employees. The Ford Company produced motor vehicles for the US government during World War I though Ford himself opposed US intervention and dispatched a "Peace Ship" to Scandinavia in 1915 to seek mediation. The company survived the post-war crisis of 1920–21 but Ford failed to take account of the changing needs of consumers who now demanded style and speed as well as economy. The company lost its dominance of the automobile market in the face of increased competition, especially from General Motors. In the 1930s Ford took a strong stand against organized labor, and his mounting political aspirations led him to run for the Senate as a Republican. Most of his personal estate was placed in the hands of the Ford Foundation (a philanthropic institution) before his death.

Ford, John (1895–1973) US film director. Ford began directing in 1917. Two of his silent movies won him particular acclaim: *The Iron Horse* (1924), a film that inspired a new wave of popular Westerns, and *Four Sons* (1928). An instinctive artist, Ford's cinematic work has a folk quality, and the Westerns in particular demonstrate a nostalgia for America's past that is transmitted through evocative musical scoring and powerful images of men within the landscape. The list of his work is impressive, including such all-time greats as *Stagecoach* (1939), *The Grapes of Wrath* (1940), *How Green Was My Valley* (1941), *They Were Expendable* (1945), *My Darling Clementine* (1946), *She Wore a Yellow Ribbon* (1949), *The Quiet Man* (1952), *The Searchers* (1956) and *The Man Who Shot Liberty Valance* (1962). A director without artistic pretensions, Ford once remarked that the key to his art was to "photograph the people's eyes."

Forster, Edward Morgan (1879–1970) British novelist and critic. After a boarding-school education he hated, Forster relished the freedom of thought he found at university in Cambridge. On leaving, he traveled in Greece and Italy. His first writing endeavors were short stories, then followed *Where Angels Fear to Tread* (1905), a novel set partly in Italy, and *Howard's End* (1910), claimed by many as the best of his works. *Maurice* (1912), a novel portraying an "ideal" homosexual relationship, was published posthumously in 1971. His best-known novel, the last he wrote, is probably *A Passage to India* (1924), which followed a trip to the subcontinent. A collection of lectures, published as *Aspects of the Novel* (1927), confirmed Forster's reputation as a literary critic of note. As a social commentator, he spoke for the virtues of honesty and kindness, whose demise he feared among the shibboleths of materialism, and he was the first president of the National Council for Civil Liberties. He was made an honorary fellow of his Cambridge college, King's, in 1946.

Sigmund Freud, whose theories profoundly influenced 20th-century thought.

Fox, William (Wilhelm Fried) (1879–1952) Hungarian-born film executive. A pioneer of the movie business, Fox bought his first nickelodeon in 1904 . This led him to start up an independent movie distribution company, and in 1915 he merged it with a production company and motion-picture theater chain to found the Fox Film Corporation. The business grew, building much of its success on Fox's introduction of the cinema organ and comfortable seats in his theaters. He launched the Movietone News in 1927 and created a number of stars, including Theda Bara. By the end of the 1920s the company, with an estimated value of $200 million, was making about 50 films each year. However, the Depression hit Fox hard. The cost of converting his cinemas to sound added to his problems, forcing him into eventual bankruptcy.

Franco, Francisco (1892–1975) Spanish dictator. An army officer, Franco served in the Balearic Islands and Morocco in the 1920s and 1930s, achieving the rank of general. He was made the army's chief of staff (1935) but after the left-wing Popular Front won power in 1936, was demoted and posted to the Canary Islands. One of the leaders of the army revolt against the government, he launched an attack on Spain from Morocco in July 1935, thereby beginning the Civil War (1936–39). Proclaimed commander-in-chief and head of state (1936), he obtained military aid from the Fascist governments of Italy and Germany and led the Nationalist forces to victory in 1939. Emerging as Spain's undisputed leader, he presided over the creation of a single-party state, using the army to suppress political dissidence. Spain remained neutral in World War II, though Franco was openly sympathetic to the Axis nations. The Spanish state was reaffirmed as a monarchy in 1947, with Franco named as effective regent and head of state for life. As the Cold War took hold in the postwar period,

Western attitudes to Franco's regime began to soften. In 1953, he permitted the establishment of US bases on Spanish soil in return for economic aid, and in 1955 Spain was accepted as a member of the United Nations. As economic conditions improved, largely as a result of Spain's tourist prosperity, the gap between Franco's reactionary regime and the society over which it ruled was made increasingly apparent and opposition became more overt. In 1969 Franco named Prince Juan Carlos as his successor. He resigned as premier in 1975, retaining the positions of party leader, head of state and commander-in-chief until his death, which was not long delayed.

Fraser, Dawn (1937–) Australian swimmer. Born in Sydney, Fraser first represented Australia at the Olympic Games of 1956, where she won the gold medal for the 100 meters freestyle. She repeated this win in 1960 and 1964, becoming the first woman swimmer to win three consecutive Olympic gold medals, and went on to take six Commonwealth Games gold medals. She held 27 world records, and in 1962 became the first woman to break one minute for the 100 meters. Fraser attributed her success to a grueling training programme, estimating that she had covered 10,000 miles in her ten-year swimming career. Voted Australia's greatest female athlete in 1988, she subsequently entered politics, serving in the New South Wales Legislative Assembly (1988–91).

Fraser, Malcolm (1930–) Australian prime minister (1975–83).The youngest person to be elected to the Australian House of Representatives, at the age of 25, Fraser held several ministerial posts in Liberal governments before succeeding to his party's leadership in 1975 and becoming head of the Liberal–National coalition government. He introduced measures to curb inflation, such as cutting government spending and discouraging union demands for large wage increases, and supported greater initiative for state governments. Defeated in the 1983 national elections, he gave up his seat in parliament to become a farmer in Western Victoria, but maintained an involvement in politics through his work for the Commonwealth Group of Eminent Persons, which lobbied to remove the system of apartheid in South Africa.

Freud, Sigmund (1856–1939) Austrian pioneer of psychoanalysis. Freud graduated in medicine in Vienna in 1881 and specialized for a time in neurology before going to work in

Yuri Gagarin, the Soviet cosmonaut on his epoch-making mission in 1961.

Paris (1883–85) with the eminent French neurologist J.M. Charcot. On his return to Vienna, Freud set up in practice as a consultant on nervous disorders. Disillusioned with existing forms of treatment, notably hypnotism and electrotherapy, he developed a technique of "free association" to penetrate the patient's subconscious. This revolutionary approach laid the foundations of what is now known as psychoanalysis and his theories soon attracted a group of supporters, including Alfred Adler and Carl Jung. In 1908 they came together to call themselves The Vienna Psychoanalytic Society., but Freud later broke with Adler and Jung who went their separate ways to develop their own theories of human behavior and personality. Freud developed other treatment modes, including the interpretation of dreams, and formulated the concept of the "id" (the subconscious drive) and the "ego" (the executive force). He published his theories in seminal works such as *The Interpretation of Dreams* (1900), *Totem and Taboo* (1913), *Beyond the Pleasure Principle* (1920) and *The Ego and the Id* (1923). His ideas have had enormous influence on 20th-century thought, art and literature. A Jew, Freud was forced to leave Vienna after the Nazi takeover of Austria in 1938, and he died in London.

Friedan, Betty (1921–) US feminist. Regarded by many as the founder of the modern US women's movement, Friedan campaigned on a wide range of women's issues and advocated an individualist and liberal form of feminism which was later rejected by more radical feminists. *The Feminine Mystique* (1963) is one of the earliest and most influential books on the women's movement. Describing the discrepancy between the ideals to which women try to conform and the frustrated reality of their lives, it called for women to reject the "mystique" wherein their highest achievement is fulfillment through domesticity and motherhood and to develop fully as individuals through education and work. Friedan herself had given up a career in psychology for marriage and a family. In *The Second Stage* (1981) she warned of the dangers of competing with men rather than insisting on the right to be different from them while still cooperating with them. She founded the powerful National Organization for Women (1966).

Friedman, Milton (1912–) US economist. Friedman was professor of economics at Chicago University (1945–76). In his book *Studies in the Quantity Theory of Money* (1956) and subsequent paper, *A Theory of the Consumption Function* (1957) he challenged the then widely accepted theories of the British economist John Maynard Keynes, who called for high levels of government spending to prevent economic stagnation, advocating instead the control of the money supply as the key to a strong economy. A believer in a laissez faire capitalist economy with minimal government intervention, Friedman's ideas radically altered the perspective of economics and marked the start of the now familiar dichotomy between the Keynesian and monetarist approaches to economic management. He received the Nobel prize for economics in 1976.

Gable, Clark (1901–60) US film actor. Signed by MGM in 1931, Gable seemed destined to play mostly gangsters in movies such as *Possessed* (1932) and *Red Dust* (1932) until his starring role in *It Happened One Night* (1934), a romantic comedy, softened his image. *Gone With the Wind* (1939) was his most important and popular film, but he continued to attract audiences with his portrayal of tough, unsentimental heroes who appealed to men and women alike. Many consider his best performance was his last, in *The Misfits* (1961).

Gagarin, Yuri (1934–68) Soviet cosmonaut. Born on a collective farm, Gagarin entered the Soviet cosmonaut program in 1959. On 12 April 1961 he orbited the Earth for 1 hour 48 minutes at a maximum speed of nearly 18,000 miles an hour in the spacecraft *Vostok I*, thus completing the first manned space flight in history.

Galbraith, John Kenneth (1908–) US economist. Galbraith was professor of economics at Harvard University (1949–75) and served as US ambassador to India (1961–63). In his numerous writings he challenged many of the traditional assumptions of economic theory, advocating, for example, the use of price control and

Indira Gandhi, India's first woman prime minister who was assassinated in 1984.

rationing in peace as well as war. In *The Affluent Society* (1958), his most popular book, he argued that demand for luxury goods is artificially created by the producer, resulting in a society with private wealth but public poverty. *The New Industrial State* (1967) protested the domination of "big business". He wrote prolifically on other subjects as well as economics, including a novel in 1990.

Gandhi, Indira (1917–84) Indian prime minister. The daughter of Jawaharlal Nehru, Indira Gandhi became president of the Congress party in 1959 and prime minister in 1966. The party split in 1969 over her policy to nationalize the major banks, and she lost her overall majority. She regained it in 1971, but in 1975 the Indian High Court ruled that she had breached election laws by misappropriating funds. Declaring a state of emergency, she centralized power in herself, curtailing civil liberties and arresting political opponents. After defeat in the 1977 elections she founded the new Congress (I) party the following year. This was returned to power in the 1980 federal elections and she became prime minister once again. Abroad, Indira Gandhi worked to build up India's role among the developing nations and remained on good terms with the Soviet Union, though she opposed the occupation of Afghanistan (1979). She introduced social and economic reform at home, but faced with increasing opposition from Sikh separatists, in 1984 she ordered an army assault on the Golden Temple of Amritsar, the Sikhs' holiest site, resulting in 450 deaths. Five months later Mrs Gandhi was assassinated by her own Sikh bodyguards in revenge for this attack.

Gandhi, Mohandas (1869–1948) Indian nationalist leader. Born in the state of Gujarat, Gandhi studied law in England before going to work as a lawyer in South Africa. Here he became actively involved in protests against the discrimination suffered by his fellow Indians, in the course of which he developed the concept of nonviolent resistance. Returning to India in 1914, Gandhi identified himself with the plight of the poor. Increasingly disillusioned with British rule after World War I, in 1919 he launched a campaign of nonviolent noncooperation through protest marches and strikes, but called for its abandonment after the massacre of unarmed demonstrators at Amritsar by British soldiers. The following year he called for Indians to boycott British goods, but again was forced to end the campaign after it erupted into violence. As president of the Congress party from 1924–34, he helped turn it into a nationwide movement and worked to promote unity between Hindus and Muslims. He campaigned for the rights of untouchables and women, and was an ardent advocate of self-sufficient cottage industries. In 1930 he led a march more than 300 kilometers to the sea where he illegally distilled salt as a protest against the salt tax. Despite several periods of imprisonment, Gandhi never abandoned his program of protest fasts and civil disobedience. In 1942, during World War II, he launched a nationwide campaign calling on the British to quit India. He was again imprisoned and released in 1944. He played a major role in the negotiations that preceded Indian independence in 1947. A fierce opponent of the partition of the subcontinent, after it had taken place he fasted to appeal for an end to rioting. He was assassinated by a Hindu nationalist on 30 January 1948.

Gandhi, Rajiv (1944–91) Indian prime minister. The elder son of Indira Gandhi, Rajiv Gandhi studied engineering. Choosing to remain outside politics, he followed a career as a commercial pilot until his brother Sanjay's premature death in 1980 forced him onto the political arena. As a member of India's ruling political dynasty, great hopes were placed in him, and his honesty and dignified manner won him much popular support. By 1983 he had become leader of the Congress (I) Party and automatically assumed the role of prime minister after his mother's assassination (1984), becoming the third member of his family to serve in that position. But despite his liberalizing influence on Indian society, his leadership ultimately proved ineffectual and he was unable to take control of the growing conflict with Sri Lanka. He was killed in 1991 at a political rally in south India, whilst campaigning for re-election, the victim of a Tamil terrorist bomb attack.

Computer billionaire Bill Gates presents his "Windows" software system in 1995.

Garbo, Greta (1905–90) Swedish film actress. A successful actress at home, Garbo made the move from Sweden to Hollywood in 1925, where the first film she made, *The Torrent* (1926), took the public by storm. Famous for her brooding looks and unattainable allure, she specialized in ill-fated heroines: her greatest roles were in *Queen Christina (*1933) and *Camille* (1936). She retired in 1941, at the height of her fame, to live as a recluse in a New York apartment.

Garvey, Marcus (1887–1940) US Black nationalist leader. Born in Jamaica, Garvey founded the Universal Negro Improvement Association (UNIA) in 1914. Unable to attract support, he moved its headquarters to New York in 1916 and founded branches in the main Black communities of the northern US. At the first UNIA convention in 1920, attended by delegates from 25 countries, Garvey broke new ground in speaking on Black rights, achievements and culture. An advocate of economic independence for Blacks, he began various enterprises to forward this aim. However, his belief in racial purity and separation (which led him to endorse the Ku Klux Klan) and his dubious business practices brought him enemies. His influence declined and he was convicted of fraud (1923) but following commution of his sentence by President Coolidge he was deported to Jamaica. Unable to revive the dwindling support for his movement, Garvey died several years later in obscurity in London.

Gates, Bill (1955–) US computer pioneer and business tycoon. Gates' rise to billionaire status was meteoric. A mathematical genius, he devised his first computer program at the age of 13 and six years later cowrote his first BASIC software program with his friend Paul Gardner Allen. By now convinced that personal computers were the coming thing, he dropped out of his studies at Harvard in 1975 to concentrate on developing his basic system, DOS. Two years later he founded the Microsoft Corporation in Seattle. In 1981 IBM adopted Gates' DOS system for its personal computers, giving Microsoft an unassailable marketing advantage. Within a few years MS-DOS had been licensed to vendors all around the world and Microsoft had become the biggest computer software corporation of the late 20th century. Gates went on to introduce his Windows operating system in 1995, and by the age of 31 was the world's youngest self-made billionaire. His book *The Road Ahead* (1995) outlined his vision of the information highway of the future and spelled out his view of how technology would transform people's everyday lives in the 21st century.

Geiger, Hans Wilhelm (1882–1945) German pioneer of atomic physics. After graduating in physics in Germany in 1906 Geiger conducted postdoctoral research on the discharge of electricity through gases before moving to England to work with the physicist Ernest Rutherford in Manchester. Together they devised a method for counting alpha-particles which eventually led to Rutherford's initial concept of the nuclear atom (1912). Geiger returned to Germany and in 1925 became professor of physics at Kiel University. There, with Walther Müller, he perfected his famous particle counter, which resulted in the Geiger counter for use in the detection of radioactivity (1928).

George VI (1895–1952) King of Great Britain and Northern Ireland. The second son of King George V and Queen Mary, George grew up in the shadow of his elder brother David, later King Edward VIII. Never expecting to be king himself, he became a naval officer and married Lady Elizabeth Bowes-Lyon in 1923. They had two daughters, Elizabeth (1926), the future Queen Elizabeth II, and Margaret (1930). Handicapped by shyness and a stammer, it was the love and support of his family that helped him adjust to his demanding new role when he succeeded to the throne after the abdication of Edward VIII in 1936. Throughout World War II he and the Queen worked hard to raise public morale, particularly during the bombing raids on London.

Gershwin, George (1898–1937) US composer. Gershwin wrote his early musicals in partnership with his brother, Ira (1896–83), who provided the lyrics. They collaborated on *Lady, Be Good* (1924), *Funny Face* (1927) and *Of Thee I Sing* (1931), which was the

John Paul Getty, who used his oil millions to found an unrivaled art collection.

first musical comedy to win a Pulitzer prize. Gershwin's more serious compositions include *Rhapsody in Blue* (1924) and *An American in Paris* (1928), both of which now belong to the popular classical repertoire. His folk opera *Porgy and Bess* (1935) also combined classical and jazz elements.

Getty, John Paul (1892–1976) US oil multimillionaire. The son of a wealthy oil man, Getty graduated in economics from Oxford University in 1913. Returning to the US, he entered the oil business on his own account and had made his first million dollars by 1916. He inherited $15 million on his father's death in 1930 and merged his father's interests with his own, going on to acquire over 100 oil companies. Building a huge financial empire, he reportedly kept most policy decision-making in his own hands, despite the size of his operations. A noted eccentric, he was married and divorced five times. He accumulated a very valuable art collection, which he housed in the J. P. Getty Museum, opened in Malibu in 1954, to which he bequeathed most of his estate.

Gide, André (1869–1951) French writer. Gide was a delicate child from a wealthy family. The beginning of his writing career in the 1890s coincided with his realization of his homosexuality, and his early works such as *Fruits of the Earth* (1897) and *The Immoralist* (1902), as indeed almost the whole of his writing, are concerned with his lifelong struggle between puritanism and hedonism. His most ambitious and famous novel (the book he later described as his only fiction), *The Counterfeiters* (1926), deals with sexual ambivalence in teenage boys. Gide published more than 50 works, including his autobiography *If it die...* (1926), plays such as *Oedipus* (1931), libretti, essays, and his *Journal* (1939–50), widely regarded as his finest literary work. He battled with religious ideas, finally settling for agnosticism. His travels in Africa led him to write on colonialism, and he briefly espoused Communism until put off by a visit to Russia in 1936. He won the Nobel prize for literature in 1947.

Giscard d'Estaing, Valéry (1926–) French president. Born into a prominent French family, Giscard served with the Free French army in North Africa and Germany during World War II and later trained at the Ecole Nationale d'Administration for a career in the civil service, which he entered in 1952. He was elected to the national assembly as a Gaullist deputy in 1956 and in 1959 became secretary of state for finance under President de Gaulle, later serving in the same capacity (1969–74) under President Pompidou. After Pompidou's death from cancer, Giscard was elected to the presidency, as the youngest French head of state since 1848, but his term of office was tainted by political scandals, including his alleged acceptance of gifts of diamonds from the discredited Emperor Bokassa of the Central African Republic. These played a part in his defeat by François Mitterrand in the presidential elections of 1981. Thereafter, Giscard concentrated his political efforts on strengthening the European Community (EC) as a member of the European Parliament.

Glenn, John (1921–) US astronaut and politician. Glenn served as a fighter pilot with the marines in World War II and the Korean War, and became a test pilot in the 1950s. He made the first nonstop transcontinental supersonic flight in 1957 and two years later was picked as one of the original team of astronauts as the US entered the space race against the Soviet Union. On 20 February 1962 Glenn made the first orbital space flight for the US, and immediately assumed the status of national hero. He later entered politics as a Democratic senator from 1975, and made an unsuccessful bid for the US presidency (1984).

Goebbels, Joseph (1897–1945) German Nazi political leader. Goebbels joined the Nazi party in 1924, becoming head of the Berlin branch in 1926. Given responsibility for party propaganda in 1929 and elected to the Reichstag in 1930, Goebbels was heavily involved in the Nazis' rise to power, and in 1933 was made government minister of enlightenment and propaganda. A skilled and manipulative orator, he orchestrated the huge Nuremberg rallies of 1933–38 and used his control of the media to justify policies like the persecution of the Jews. Retaining his post throughout World War II, he constantly fanned the public

Mikhail Gorbachev, whose reforming policies led to the breakup of the Soviet Union.

appetite for continuing conflict, and in 1944 was given the title of Reich Plenipotentiary for Total War. He killed himself, together with his wife and six children, shortly after Hitler's suicide in April 1945.

Goering, Hermann (1893–1946) German Nazi political leader. Soon after meeting him in 1922, Hitler appointed Goering to command the storm troopers. He fled Germany after the unsuccessful Munich putsch in 1923, and did not return until 1927. Elected to the Reichstag a year later, he became its president in 1932. The following year Goering was made interior minister for Prussia, in which capacity he organized the local Gestapo and established the first concentration camps. By 1935 he was commander of the German airforce, the Luftwaffe, and was the most important man in Germany after Hitler. Appointed minister of economic affairs in 1936, he was given the task of putting the German economy on a war footing. He amassed a large personal fortune through his control of the state-owned giant mining and industrial enterprise created by Hitler and added to it by plundering Jewish communities and acquiring many priceless works of art from occupied Europe. His fall from favor began after the Luftwaffe's defeat in the Battle of Britain (1940), and ended in his expulsion from the Nazi party in 1945. Found guilty of war crimes at the Nuremberg trials, he poisoned himself rather than face execution.

Gorbachev, Mikhail Sergeyevich (1931–) Soviet statesman. A member of the Communist party central committee from 1971, Gorbachev was made a member of the Politburo (1980) and general secretary of the Communist party (1985). He immediately undertook a campaign against corruption and economic mismanagement in the party bureaucracy, launching the drive for *glasnost* (openness). In 1987, Gorbachev announced proposals for economic *perestroika* (reconstruction) with the aim of decreasing the authority of central government and promoting democracy. The industrial sector was modernized and encouraged to become self-financing. Gorbachev withdrew the Soviet army from Afghanistan in 1988–89, initiated the ending of the Cold War and signed the INF treaty with the United States in 1988 to dismantle nuclear arms in Europe. These moves raised his status with Western leaders, but at home he was not so fortunate. He was elected to the newly created post of president of the Soviet Union in 1990, but the failure of his agricultural policies, the continuing weakness of the Soviet economy and the desperate shortage of consumer goods rendered him increasingly unpopular, and he was further criticised for using military force to suppress unrest in Lithuania (1991). As secessionist fervor spread through the Soviet Union, Gorbachev found himself having to tread an uneasy path between the Communist old guard and progressives like Boris Yeltsin, who demanded an acceleration of the pace of reform. Gorbachev's response was to accumulate formal power in his own hands, precipitating an attempted Communist takeover in August 1991. He was outwitted by Yeltsin in the coup's political aftermath and resigned shortly afterward on the dissolution of the Soviet Union.

Graham, Billy (William Franklin) (1921–) US evangelist. Converted to fundamendalist Christianity at the age of 16, Graham was ordained a Southern Baptist minister in 1939. Ten years later he began a series of preaching tours across the US, and soon came to be regarded as the most powerful promulgator of the fundamentalist message. His large-scale, highly organized revivalist campaigns during the 1950s led to the conversion of thousands and the re-energizing of the Christian movement. Widening his support to include all the major denominations, he went on to preach his form of evangelistic Christianity throughout the world, organizing tours in Europe (1954–55), Africa and the Holy Land (1960), and Korea (1973). Though his preaching style remained simple, direct, energetic and popular, Graham proved adept in the use of modern communication methods to reach vast audiences. By the 1990s he controlled one of the largest electronic churches in the US, and he also used modern business methods to establish the Billy Graham Evangelistic Association Inc. to communicate with his followers. He produced religious films, published books and developed friendships with several world leaders and US presidents, including Presidents Truman, Eisenhower and Nixon.

Guerrilla leader Che Guevara became a student icon of revolt in the 1960s.

Graham, Martha (1894–1991) US choreographer and founder of "modern dance". Graham explored ethnic and primitive dance at the Denishawn dance school (1916–23), before joining the Greenwich Village Follies revue (1923). From 1924 she taught dance and began to choreograph, making her first appearance as an independent artist in 1926. As a performer, Graham was intense, graceful and dramatic, and her social and feminist conscience showed in her work, such as *Revolt* (1927). In 1929 she founded her own school, The Martha Graham School of Contemporary Dance, an all-women company. She went on to create a dance technique that is disciplined yet radically different from classical ballet, and is now widely taught. Graham explored myth, ethnic and ancient dance with vigor and certainty, as in *Appalachian Spring* (1944), *Cave of the Heart* (1946), and *Clytemnestra* (1958). Fusion of dance and design, and three-dimensional sets, were central to her work, and she also used Japanese mime and Absurdist themes.

Grass, Günter (1927–) German writer. Grass was a member of the Hitler Youth and was later taken prisoner of war. After the war he had various jobs before studying art in Düsseldorf and Berlin, and in 1956 he moved to Paris. His first novel *The Tin Drum* (1959), the first of a trilogy exposing Hitler's grip on ordinary people, aroused controversy and affronted many with its obscenity, but despite its intractable style, won international acclaim. As a playwright, Grass was influenced by the theater of the Absurd and the playwright Bertholt Brecht. A supporter of the Social Democratic party in the late 1960s, he wrote speeches for Willy Brandt. Widely seen as "the nation's conscience" because of his commitment to numerous political and social crusades, Grass preferred to call himself "the court jester". His novel *The Flounder* (1977) is regarded by many as his literary masterpiece.

Greer, Germaine (1939–) Australian writer and feminist. Greer studied at Melbourne and Sydney Universities before moving to Britain, where she worked for her doctorate at the University of Cambridge (1964–67) and lectured at the University of Warwick (1968–73). She shot to fame with the publication of her first book, *The Female Eunuch* (1970), which discussed the prevalence of misogyny in society and culture, portraying marriage as a legalized form of slavery for women. Always ready to give forthright, articulate, and sometimes arrogant, expression to her views on a wide range of subjects, she became a well-known media figure. Never afraid of controversy, in *Sex and Destiny* (1984) she diverged from current feminist theories by advocating the return to large extended families and claiming that women have been harmed by modern permissiveness. *The Change* (1991), a discussion of the female menopause, continued her reputation for stating the unacceptable.

Gromyko, Andrei (1909–89) Soviet statesman. A Communist party member from 1931, Gromyko joined the Soviet foreign service in 1939. After a spell as counselor at the Soviet embassy in Washington he was appointed Soviet ambassador to the US in 1943 and attended the Allied wartime conferences at Tehran, Yalta and Potsdam. In 1946 he sat on the UN Security Council, where he used his veto 25 times. Promoted to deputy foreign minister (1946), he became chief Soviet representative in the UN General Assembly (1949), and ambassador to the UK (1952–53). A full member of the Communist party central committee from 1956, he served an unprecedentedly long period as foreign minister from 1957–85. During this time he took part in talks with President Kennedy to resolve the Cuban crisis (1962) and paved the way for the nuclear nonproliferation treaty (1967). Though a champion of détente, he remained in Western eyes a grim-faced and somewhat humorless figure, nicknamed "Mr Nyet" (Mr No) by the popular press. As Soviet president (1985–88), he is widely regarded as having been the principal engineer of Gorbachev's subsequent rise to power.

Guevara, Che (Ernesto) (1928–67) Argentinian-born revolutionary. Guevara combined his medical studies in Buenos Aires with revolutionary politics. He joined Fidel Castro's Cuban revolutionary movement in Mexico, and played a leading role in the guerrilla war against the Batista regime (1956–59). (He was

The Ethiopian emperor, Haile Selassie, who was later executed in a Marxist-led coup.

later, in 1960, to write an influential manual on guerrilla warfare.) On gaining power, Castro conferred Cuban citizenship on Guevara and gave him a series of important posts, including directorship of the National Bank. As minister of industry (1961–65), he was charged with implementing mass nationalization but abandoned politics in 1965 to return to the revolutionary struggle. After spending time in the Congo, he returned to South America and attempted to establish a guerrilla base in the jungles of Bolivia, but he was captured and executed by a Bolivian army unit. Guevara's life and writings inspired many student radicals during the 1960s.

Haile Selassie (Tafari Makonnen) (1892–1975) Ethiopian emperor. A member of the imperial family, he instrumented a palace revolution in 1916, securing for himself the title of regent and heir apparent. He became king in 1928 and emperor in 1930, taking the name of Haile Selassie ("Might of the Trinity"). He introduced a new constitution (1931), which concentrated power in himself and made parliament redundant, strengthened the police and abolished feudal taxation. After Italy's invasion of Ethiopia (1935) Haile Selassie went into exile, appealing for help to the League of Nations conference the following year, and was reinstated on Ethiopia's liberation by British forces (1941). He attempted to modernize the country and improve education, but power remained in the hands of a wealthy elite. Accused of economic mismanagement following a severe famine, he was deposed by a Marxist-led military coup (1974) and executed.

Hammarskjöld, Dag (1905–61) Swedish diplomat. A former academic and career civil servant, Hammarskjöld was Swedish foreign minister (1951–53) and secretary general to the UN (1953–61), the second man to hold the post. He helped resolve the Suez Crisis (1956) by establishing the first UN Emergency Force in Sinai and Gaza. He was killed in an aircrash in Zambia while on a mission to negotiate an end to the civil war in the Congo (now Zaire). His independent peace-making initiatives were censured by the Soviet Union and others, but he was awarded the Nobel peace prize posthumously in 1961.

Hammerstein, Oscar
(1895–1960) US lyricist, writer and producer. Hammerstein wrote or part-wrote about 45 musicals for theater, film and TV from 1920–59. He worked with a number of composers including Vincent Youmans, Rudolf Friml, Sigmund Romberg and Jerome Kern on musicals such as *Rose Marie* (1924), *The Desert Song* (1925), and *Show Boat* (1927), before entering the exclusive partnership with Rodgers (1943) for which he is best known. Their collaboration on *Oklahoma!* (1945), *Carousel* (1945), *South Pacific* (1949), *The King and I* (1951) and *The Sound of Music* (1959), all later made into successful films, won them both honors and acclaim.

Hart, Lorenz (1895–1943) US song lyricist. During his 25-year collaboration with Richard Rodgers, they produced about 1,000 songs, among them such great standards as "My Heart Stood Still" (1927), "With a Song in My Heart" (1929), "Lover" (1933), "Blue Moon" (1934), "My Funny Valentine" (1937), "Falling in Love with Love" (1938) and "Bewitched, Bothered and Bewildered" (1940). In contrast to Rodgers, Lorenz's attitude toward work remained that of the determined non-professional. Though his writing was impaired by a growing addiction to alcohol, his lyrics were as well crafted as serious poetry.

Havel, Vaclav (1936–) Czech playwright and statesman. Havel put himself through night school and later worked as a stagehand in a Prague theater while establishing himself as a playwright. *The Garden Party* (1963) and *The Memorandum* (1965) satirized the position of intellectuals in a Communist state and won him acclaim at home and abroad. He was out of the country for the US première of *The Memorandum* when Soviet forces invaded Czechoslovakia in 1968. Seizing the opportunity to address himself to "Western intellectuals" he broadcast a demand for human rights at home and abroad and was promptly interrogated on his return and barred from writing. Compelled to do menial work, his plays were circulated secretly and could only be staged abroad. A founder member and signatory of the

The British physicist Stephen Hawking, who popularized the "big bang" theory.

Charter 77 manifesto demanding human rights, Havel was arrested a number of times and was imprisoned for four years in 1979. As the Communist hold weakened in Czechoslovakia in 1989, he campaigned vigorously for democratic reform as leader of Civic Forum, gaining the presidency in the country's first free elections. A much respected figure, in 1993 he became president of the new Czech Republic.

Hawking, Stephen (1942–) British theoretical physicist. After studying physics at Oxford, Hawking became a research fellow at Cambridge, and in 1979 was appointed to the Lucasian professorship of mathematics. Despite a degenerative disease which robbed him of speech and movement and would eventually make him dependent on a specially-devised computerized voice, he devoted himself to elucidating the structure of black holes, showing (1971) that these can issue not only from the collapse of stars but also, as mini-black holes, from the time of the original "big bang". Hawking popularized his "big bang" theory of the origin of the universe in his best-selling book, *A Brief History of Time* (1988). Its unprecedented success transformed Hawking into a scientific guru with a huge following worldwide.

Hawke, Bob (1929–) Australian prime minister. Hawke built up a position of great influence in the Australian trade union movement during 20 years with the Australian council of trade unions. His ten-year term as the council's president (1970–80) and his leadership of the Australian Labor party (1973–8) put him in a strong position when he entered parliament in 1980. Becoming prime minister after the Labor party's electoral victory in 1983, his flamboyant personality made him a popular leader., though he was criticized for taking the Labor party away from its traditional values through his deregulation of banking and removal of state ownership from key industries. In 1990 he became the Labor party's longest-serving prime minister, but was replaced the following year after press allegations about his extra-marital affairs.

Hawks, Howard (1896–1977)
US film director, screenwriter and producer. A professional craftsman and realistic storyteller involved in every aspect of his films, Hawks made some of Hollywood's best films in genres ranging from action-films to detective thrillers and comedies. His credits include *Scarface* (1932), *Bringing Up Baby* (1938), *Only Angels Have Wings* (1939), *Ball of Fire* (1942), *The Big Sleep* (1946), *Red River* (1948), *Gentlemen Prefer Blondes* (1953) and *Rio Bravo* (1959).

Hewlett, William (1913–) and **Packard, David** (1912–) US electronics pioneers. Hewlett and Packard studied electrical engineering together at Stanford University before setting up their first business in a garage in Palo Alto, California in 1938, with a capital of only $538. It was here, in what was to become known as Silicon Valley, that the world's largest electronics empire had its modest beginnings, as the two men began production of a range of electronic measuring equipment. In 1971 Hewlett and Packard brought out the HP-35, a hand-held calculator, the success of which could be said to mark the beginning of the age of the personal computer. By the 1980s the company was producing desk-sized computers with the same capacity as the early postwar mainframe computers that had occupied whole rooms.

Hearst, William Randolph
(1863–1951) US newspaper publisher. Hearst took control of his father's San Francisco *Examiner*, turning it to profit (1887–89) and then bought the ailing New York *Morning Journal* (later *Journal-American*) in 1895. He reshaped the paper, using copious illustration, bold headlines and a sensation-seeking approach. Famed for his ruthless methods, by 1925 he owned newspapers and magazines all over the US, but his empire was depleted by the Depression and his own extravagances. He was forced to sell off some of his priceless art collection which he kept in his vast mansion, San Simeon, in California. His meteoric career was immortalized in Orson Welles' film *Citizen Kane* (1941).

Hefner, Hugh (1926–) US publisher. Raised a strict Methodist in the American Midwest, Hefner graduated from Illinois University in 1949 and started work in the subscriptions

Jimi Hendrix, who came to represent the psychodelic music of the 1960s.

department of *Esquire* magazine. Four years later he founded *Playboy* magazine. With its combination of nude photography, glossy advertising and feature articles, the magazine was aimed at young, affluent, urban males. Hefner was himself a practitioner of the hedonistic lifestyle that his magazine advocated. In 1968 he grossed $100 million, but in the 1970s his daughter took over to rescue the ailing business, which by now had expanded into real estate and nightclubs.

Helpmann, Robert (1909–86)
Australian ballet dancer, choreographer and actor. Born in Victoria, Helpmann began dancing professionally at the age of 14. After seeing the legendary Anna Pavlova perform in Australia, he joined her touring company and moved to Britain, where he was to become the principal male dancer at the Vic-Wells (later Sadler's Wells) Ballet (1933–50), frequently partnering Margot Fonteyn. In 1937 he played the first of many Shakespearean roles, as Oberon in *A Midsummer Night's Dream*, at the Old Vic and Stratford-upon-Avon, and in the 1940s began working in films. He gave one of his most memorable dance performances in the film classic *The Red Shoes* (1948). He was artistic director of the Australian Ballet (1965–76) and was knighted in 1968 .

Hemingway, Ernest (1899–1961)
US writer. Hemingway saw service in World War I as an ambulance driver, but was invalided out aged 18 and became a reporter. Appointed foreign correspondent for the *Toronto Star*, he settled in Paris, where his novels *The Sun Also Rises* (1926) and *A Farewell to Arms* (1929), describing his wartime experiences, were written. Critically well received, they secured him instant fame. He reported on the Spanish Civil War (1936–39), afterwards writing *For Whom the Bell Tolls* (1940). His novel about a fisherman's lone battle against the elements, *The*

Old Man and the Sea (1952) won him a Pulitzer prize, and in 1954 he was awarded the Nobel prize for literature. Despite evident literary flaws – cardboard characterization, a self-conscious and sentimental machismo that barely conceals an anguished sensitivity – Hemingway retains his reputation as one of the mid-century's great writers, remembered for his stark, resonant style and outstandingly beautiful descriptive passages. He married four times and never overcame his struggle with recurring bouts of depression, committing suicide in 1961.

Hendrix, Jimi (1947–70) US rock guitarist and composer. Born in Seattle, Hendrix put together his group, the Jimi Hendrix Experience, in Britain. Successful appearances on TV and at the Olympia in Paris created its first hit single, "Hey Joe" (1966). Hendrix's impact was phenomenal: the power of his blues playing seemed to re-create the electric guitar, and it was the heaviest rock sound around. In 1969 he disbanded the group and formed Band of Gypsies. His most highly rated album, *Are You Experienced* (1967), become a classic of the psychedelic music of the 1960s. Hendrix's premature, drugs-related death mirrored many of his rock contemporaries, and cut short an outstanding musical talent.

Heston, Charlton (1923–) US actor. His splendid physique and presence ensured epic Hollywood roles and though criticized for a certain woodenness of style, this did not prevent him achieving international status in some of the finest movies of the postwar era. Credits include *The Ten Commandments* (1956), *Ben-Hur* (1959), *El Cid* (1961), *The Greatest Story Ever Told* and *The Agony and the Ecstasy* (both 1965) and *Antony and Cleopatra* (1972), which he adapted and also directed.

Himmler, Heinrich (1900–45) German Nazi political leader. Himmler joined the Nazi party in 1923 and was appointed head of Hitler's bodyguard, the SS (*Schutzstaffel*) corps, in 1929, which he turned into a powerful force. In 1933 he was made head of the Gestapo (secret police) in Bavaria and soon took control of the national organization. The infamous Night of the Long Knives (1934), when a list of Hitler's opponents in the SA (storm troopers) were murdered by the SS, was carried out at his instigation. Using the SS and the Gestapo, Himmler set up a network of 17 concentration and extermination camps. In 1943 he became minister of the interior, and in 1944 head of the German home forces and effective second in command. Toward

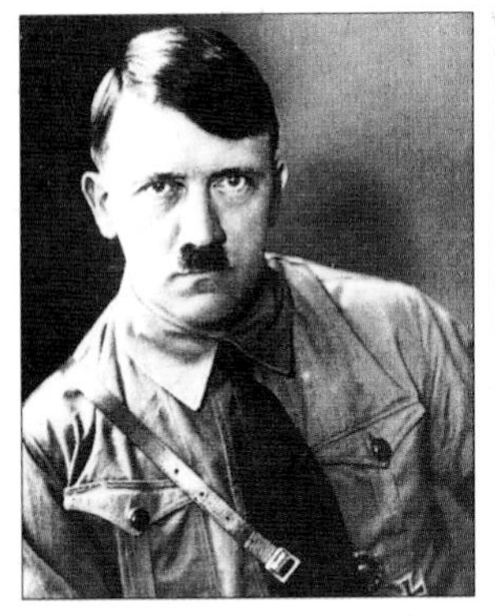

Adolf Hitler, the German dictator and proponent of racial supremacy.

the end of the war, realizing that all was lost, Himmler secretly proposed surrender to the Allies in the hope of saving his own neck. Captured by British troops, he committed suicide to avoid identification as a war criminal.

Hirohito (1901–89) Japanese emperor. Hirohito succeeded his father Taisho to become the 124th Japanese emperor in 1926. An expert on marine biology, he is frequently portrayed as an unworldly pacifist who ineffectually urged restraint on Japan's military leaders in the 1930s and 1940s, but it is now clear that he was more than just a figurehead. Though he did not actively promote the army's plans for expansion, he did little to discourage them and took an intense interest in the conduct of the war. His power within the state system was revealed when he advised capitulation in 1945. His subsequent surrender broadcast on 15 August 1945 caused all but a few diehards to lay down their arms. The following year he ended centuries of tradition by repudiating the legendary divinity of Japan's emperors. Continuing as ceremonial ruler only, he reigned for a record 63 years.

Hitchcock, Alfred (1899–1980) British-born film director. A meticulous planner with a superb visual sense, Hitchcock specialized in making well-crafted psychological thriller-dramas. His years in Britain produced many of his most famous suspense classics: *Blackmail* (1929), the first successful British talkie, *The Man Who Knew Too Much* (1934), *The Thirty-Nine Steps* (1935) and *The Lady Vanishes* (1938). Moving to Hollywood in 1939, he achieved an instant success with *Rebecca* (1940), one of cinema's all-time greats The period 1954–60 was a particularly creative one for Hitchcock, producing a string of successful films such as *Rear Window* (1945), *North by Northwest* (1959), *Psycho* (1960) and *The Birds* (1963). He produced two series for American TV between

1955 and 1965 which were famous for their spine-chilling introductions by Hitchcock himself. He was also noted for appearing fleetingly in his own films, as a face in a crowd or an anonymous passenger on a train.

Hitler, Adolf (1889–1945) Austrian-born German dictator. Hitler studied art unsuccessfully in Vienna before seeing service in World War I. He sought refuge for his bitterness against the politicians who had led Germany to defeat in the nationalistic politics of the tiny German Workers' party, which he renamed the National Socialist German Workers' (Nazi) party and came to dominate, inspiring their unsuccessful *putsch* (coup) in Munich in 1923. Imprisoned for nine months, he wrote *Mein Kampf (My Struggle)*, in which he outlined his doctrine of German racial supremacy and identified Marxism and the international Jewish conspiracy as Germany's enemies. A magnetic orator and manipulator of public opinion, his movement gathered growing support among the public who wanted scapegoats to blame for Germany's economic plight. He was narrowly defeated in the presidential elections of 1932, but was made chancellor the next year and soon afterwards assumed dictatorial powers with the help of the Gestapo (secret state police). Concentration camps were established for political opponents and Jews, who were systematically persecuted, and a program of nazification set in motion through an all-powerful propaganda machine. Rebuilding the armed forces, Hitler restored national pride by occupying the demilitarized Rhineland zone (1936). In 1938 he began his program of territorial expansion by annexing Austria and the German-populated areas of Czechoslovakia. After signing a nonaggression pact with Stalin, he invaded Poland in 1939, precipitating a European war. As a war leader, Hitler's greatest gift was his energy and his eagerness to take risks, but his hypnotic hold over his subordinates ultimately worked against him. He lived in a world of dreams, losing all touch with reality. As the war turned against him and Germany's bombed cities lay in ruins, he refused to sanction any retreats, finally withdrawing to Berlin where he committed suicide on 30 April 1945.

Ho Chi Minh (Nguyen That Thanh) (1890–1969) Vietnamese revolutionary and president. Ho fled a background of poverty to become a seaman. Settling in France, in 1917 he joined the newly-formed French Communist party (PCF)and later went to Moscow (1923), where he addressed

David Hockney, the British painter, in California with one of his dogs.

the 1924 Communist International on the importance of the peasantry in revolution. He visited China as a representative of Comintern (1924–27) and returned to Vietnam, where he helped to found the League of Oppressed Peoples, the Vietnamese Revolutionary Youth League, and, in 1930, the Indochinese Communist party. In 1940 he organized a resistance force, the Vietminh, to oppose the occupying Japanese army. Following Japan's defeat in 1945, he established the Democratic Republic of Vietnam in Hanoi with himself as president. For the next eight years he conducted a war against the French who had taken repossession of their colonial territories in southern Vietnam. Humiliatingly defeated at Dien Bien Phu (1954), the French withdrew and Vietnam was partitioned. Ho's Marxist government in the North was supported by China and the Soviet Union. In 1959 he gave his backing to the Vietcong guerrillas seeking to overthrow the US-sponsored government in the South and unify Vietnam. He remained a leading force in the Vietnam war throughout the 1960s.

Hockney, David (1937–) British painter, designer and photographer. Hockney began to attract notice while a student at London's Royal College of Art, where he won several prizes including the Gold Medal (1961). A leading exponent of Pop Art, his early paintings showed an originality and wit that remained characteristic of his work. A series of etchings, *The Rake's Progress* (1965), was based on his first visit to New York, and he later went to California, which became his home in 1978 and where, inspired by the light and his fascination with water, he painted many pictures of swimming pools. He designed several stage-settings, including *The Magic Flute* at Glyndebourne (1978), and produced a book of photomontages, *Camerawork* (1984). A brilliant draftsman, his later work embraced realism and Cubism, and included many portraits.

Holiday, Billie (1915–59) US jazz vocalist and composer. Known as "Lady Day" and the "first lady of the blues", Holiday was indisputably the greatest singer of jazz from the 1930s to the 1950s, with a small but incomparable bell-like voice. Her career started in Harlem's nightclubs and she made her first record, with Benny Goodman, in 1933. She worked with several bands in the 1930s, including Goodman's, Artie Shaw's and Count Basie's, before going solo in 1940. By the end of the decade her addiction to heroin (which was eventually to kill her) was beginning to damage her voice, though public interest in her turbulent private life kept her career alive till 1957.

Holly, Buddy (Charles Hardin) (1936–59) US singer, guitarist and songwriter. Born in Lubbock, Texas, Holly's career lasted only two years before he was killed in an aircrash. It was only after his death that his enormous contribution to the development of rock-and-roll came to be recognized, though he only issued three albums during his lifetime. The first to add rhythm-and-blues beat to a basic country style, Holly was also influenced by Mexican music. His most popular singles, made with The Crickets, include "Peggy Sue","That'll Be the Day" and "It Doesn't Matter Anymore".

Honda, Soichiro (1906–91) Japanese businessman. In 1934 Honda established a factory producing piston rings which he sold to Toyota after the war. Using army surplus parts, he began manufacturing motorcycles, forming the Honda Motor Company (1948) and becoming its president (1948–73) and director (1973–83). Honda made major technical innovations and his machines had won all the most prestigious international motorcycle racing prizes by 1959. He then established the American Honda Motor Company to break into the US and European markets and become the world's largest manufacturer of motorcycles. In 1967 Honda began producing small economy cars, having great success with the Honda Civic (1973).

Hoover, Herbert (1874–1964) US president. Hoover amassed great wealth as a mining engineer while still a young man. In 1914 he was appointed to head war relief in Europe. Serving as secretary of commerce under Presidents Harding and Coolidge (1921–28), he oversaw the construction of the Hoover Dam on the Colorado River and the St Lawrence Seaway. In 1928 he was elected Republican president. Entering the White House at a time of great prosperity, he soon had to face the problems of the Great Depression

Harry Houdini mesmerized audiences with his daring escapes.

but failed to cope with this crisis, believing that the slump would last only a short time and adhering rigidly to accepted economic strategy. As the Depression spread to Europe Hoover postponed international debt repayments in 1931 and established the Reconstruction Finance Corporation. His failure to undertake a major program of social relief destroyed the humanitarian reputation he had earned during World War I and later, and his popularity quickly declined. The presidential election of 1932 brought a decisive victory for Franklin D. Roosevelt. During and after World War II, Hoover again involved himself in famine-relief work in Europe.

Hoover, William (1849–1932) US industrialist. Hoover started out in business in Ohio where he ran a tannery and manufactured horse harnesses. When the motor car threatened to destroy his business, he bought the rights to a crude prototype upright vacuum cleaner which had been developed by J. Murray Spangler, a department store janitor. Hoover produced a commercial version of Spangler's design which he advertised for sale in 1908 at a price of $70. Selling the product through a trial purchase scheme, Hoover built up a network of dealers and formed the Electric Suction Sweeper Company. Later renamed the Hoover Company, it was soon selling vacuum cleaners around the world, and by the 1920s Hoover had become the generic name for one of the great labor-saving devices of the century.

Hope, Bob (1903–) British-born US film actor and entertainer. Hope began his career in vaudeville on Broadway, and later became a radio star. His film break came in *The Big Broadcast* (1938). The following year he had a hit with *The Cat and the Canary* and the hugely popular "Road" series of movies, in which he starred with Bing Crosby and Dorothy Lamour, began in 1940. Of his other films, *The Paleface* (1948) probably rates highest, but

Hope also built his reputation on live stage appearances around the world, enlivening his act with a rapid-fire stream of fast gags and topical wise-cracks. He entertained US troops during World War II and the Korean and Vietnam Wars, and in later years was an indefatigable golfer. He was one of the richest entertainers ever.

Houdini, Harry (1874–1926) Hungarian-born US escapologist. The son of a rabbi, Houdini came to the US as a child and found work as a trapeze artist performing in circuses and vaudeville. By the early 1900s his amazing ability to extricate himself from shackles, ropes, handcuffs, strait-jackets and locked containers, sometimes while weighted and submerged in water or suspended head down high above the ground, had brought him world fame. Also a successful conventional illusionist, Houdini denounced mind readers and mediums as charlatans, arguing his case in two books published in the 1920s.

Hubble, Edwin (1889–1953) US astronomer. Hubble studied law at the Universities of Chicago and Oxford, but an amateur interest in astronomy led to his making this his life's work. In 1924 he announced the findings of two years' research, carried out at the Mount Wilson Observatory, California, which showed that the nebulous outer part of the Andromeda galaxy consisted of a myriad of individual stars. Hubble then went on to measure the speed of recession from the Earth of 18 other galaxies, and demonstrated that this speed is proportional to their distance. This proposition became known as Hubble's Law and gave the first positive proof of the concept of an expanding Universe, which had been advanced some years previously. Hubble estimated the boundary of the Universe at a distance of 18 billion light years and its age as two billion years, but more recent research suggests that this was a tenfold underestimate.

Hughes, Howard (1905–76) US millionaire, film producer and aviator. Hughes inherited his father's tool company at the age of 18 and two years later moved to Hollywood, investing in such movies as *Hell's Angels* (1930) and *Scarface* (1932). In 1932 he suddenly began work as a pilot under an assumed name and then formed the Hughes Aircraft Company to design, build and fly aircraft. Between 1935 and 1938 he broke most of the world's air speed records. Returning abruptly to Hollywood, he produced his best-known film, *The Outlaw* (1943) as a vehicle for Jane Russell. He continued

The singer Michael Jackson today heads a multibillion dollar business empire.

to build a large business empire, including RKO Pictures Corporation, and maintained his involvement in aviation, designing for and controlling Trans World Airlines. Long known as an eccentric, in 1950 he became a recluse and ran his vast business interests from secluded hotel rooms.

Hussein (1935–) King of Jordan. Hussein became king in 1953, when his father was forced to abdicate because of mental illness. Steering a middle way through the Middle East's turbulent politics, he exercised a strong personal rule during four decades, lending his support to Western policies while at the same time pacifying Arab nationalism: Jordan is home to more than a million Palestinian refugees. His earliest achievement was the strengthening of Jordan's economy, doubling output between 1956 and 1963. He took his country into the Arab war against Israel in 1967 and later helped draft the UN resolution 242 calling for the return of the Israeli-occupied West Bank. He had to face assassination threats after expelling the Palestinian Liberation Organization (PLO) from Jordan in 1970. He denounced the Israel–Egypt Camp David peace accords (1978) as unfair to the Arab states, in particular Palestine and Jordan, and resisted huge pressure from the US government to help implement them. In later years Hussein came to be seen as a moderating force in Middle Eastern affairs. In 1988 he surrendered Jordan's claim over the West Bank in favor of the PLO, and during the Gulf War (1990) put himself forward as a mediator between Iraq and the US-led Allied force, at no little risk of damaging his reputation with both sides.

Iacocca, Lee (1924–) US businessman. The son of Italian immigrants, Iacocca joined the Ford Motor Company in 1946. Quickly gaining a reputation as a marketing genius, he gradually worked his way up through the corporation to become president (1970–78). Disagreements with Henry Ford II led him to leave the company, and he joined Ford's competitor, Chrysler, as president and later chairman. Chrysler was then in trouble, but in a short time Iacocca had turned the company's fortunes around through a program of production cutbacks and layoffs, helped by tax concessions and a loan guarantee, bringing it into profit by 1984. His autobiography *Iacocca* (1984), which extolled the work ethic and family values, had instant success, selling more copies than almost any other book this century.

Ibarruri, Dolores (1895–1989) Spanish political leader. The daughter of a Basque miner, Ibarurri worked as a journalist in the workers' press under the pseudonym of "La Pasionaria" ("the passion flower"). In 1920 she helped found the Spanish Communist party. A member of parliament, she acquired international notoriety during the Spanish civil war (1936–39) for her vehement broadcasts in which she famously exclaimed of the fascists, "They shall not pass!". She left Spain on Franco's acquiring power, to spend the next 34 years in exile in the Soviet Union. Returning to Spain after the restoration of democracy in 1977, she was again elected to parliament.

Jackson, Michael (1958–) US popular singer and dancer. Jackson began his career singing with his brothers as the Jackson Five in 1969, making an early impression with his energetic dancing. He went solo in the early 1970s, recording a steady stream of hit singles. His album *Off The Wall* (1979) launched him into the big time, followed by *Thriller* (1982), *Bad* (1987)and a quasi-autobiographical film *Moonwalk* (1988). A double album *History* came out in 1995. His releases were backed by skillfully packaged videos exploiting his brilliant dancing and choreography. Jackson's international fame was enormous, and he accumulated a vast fortune through clever business deals. As he became more and more reclusive in his private Californian estate, he excited endless press comment, first of all concerning his use of plastic surgery to alter his facial appearance and later over accusations of child abuse which led to his paying a huge out of court settlement. He was briefly married to Lisa Marie Presley, the daughter of Elvis Presley.

Jagger, Mick (1943–) British rock singer. Jagger was the charismatic lead vocalist and spokesperson for the Rolling Stones, the British rock group formed in 1962. Their blues-inspired, aggressively sexual music and their

Pope John Paul II, who has addressed vast audiences on his many worldwide tours.

uninhibited lifestyles epitomized the rebelliousness of the 1960s. Remembered for such hits as "Satisfaction" (1965), "Jumpin' Jack Flash" (1968) and "Honky Tonk Women" (1969), their live performances drew vast audiences. Their greatest albums include *The Rolling Stones* (1964) and *Beggars' Banquet* (1968). Jagger's looks and energetic stage act were exceptional. Though his behavior was frequently criticized – he was twice convicted of drugs possession, and his private life was the subject of gossip – his musical status was never in doubt. He later gained press respect through his status as a rock survivor and was still performing in his fifties.

Janácek, Leos (1854–1928)
Czech composer. A teacher of organ who founded and taught at the Brno Organ School (1881–1919), Janácek's music incorporated themes and sounds from nature, myths and Czech folk tales, as in his opera *Jenufa* (1903). He formulated a musical theory based on speech-rhythms and composed principally choral and operatic works, for which he usually wrote his own libretti. His period of greatest flowering was 1916–28 when he produced the superb operas *Katya Kabanova* (1921), *The Cunning Little Vixen* (1923), and the powerfully religious *Glagolitic Mass* (1926). Janácek was a Czech nationalist and he intended his orchestral work *Sinfonietta* (1926) "to cleave to the simple Czech soul".

Jinnah, Mohammad Ali
(1876–1948) Pakistani statesman. Born into a mercantile Muslim family in Karachi, Jinnah studied law in Britain (1892–65) and later practised in Bombay, where he had a brilliant career at the bar in the early years of the century. A great liberal and constitutionalist, he supported the early Indian National Congress and joined the All-India Muslim League in 1913, becoming its president. Increasingly opposed to Gandhi's program of civil disobedience, which he believed would

be harmful to Muslim interests, he came into his own as a political leader in the late 1930s when his concern for the adequate protection of the Muslim minority led him to head the movement for an independent Muslim state of Pakistan. He displayed consummate political skill in the negotiations (1946–47) that resulted in the partition of the subcontinent, and earned for himself the title "Qaid-i-Azam" (Founder of the Nation), becoming the first Governor-General of the independent state of Pakistan in 1947.

John XXIII (Angelo Roncalli) (1881–1963) Italian pope. Ordained priest in 1904, Roncalli was an army chaplain in World War I and afterward a Vatican diplomat (1925–52). He was appointed patriarch of Venice in 1953. Elected pope in 1958, he was viewed by many as a "caretaker" holder of the office but confounded his critics when, in 1959, he announced the summoning of an ecumenical council, the first for almost a century, in order to reinvigorate Catholic Christianity and promote Christian unity. Pope John took an informal approach to the papacy and emphasized his pastoral role. His encyclicals *Mater et Magistra* (1961) and *Pacem in Terris* (1963) contained reminders not to confuse error with the erring person; for example, Marxism with the governments that espoused it. The former was to be rejected, the latter understood. A humble and compassionate man, he won the respect and affection of millions, Catholic and non-Catholic alike, with his openness to change within the church.

John Paul II (Karol Wojtyla) (1920–) Polish-born pope. Wojtyla become a priest just after World War II and rose quickly through the Polish Catholic hierarchy to become auxiliary bishop (1958), archbishop of Cracow (1964) and cardinal (1967). The first non-Italian pope in 456 years and the first Pole ever to hold the office, his election in 1978 was seen as a surprising and imaginative one. He immediately began a global tour to redefine the tenets of Catholicism and clarify their relation to the modern world. An assassination attempt in 1981 left him seriously wounded. John Paul II was a conservative who underlined the orthodox Catholic position on such issues as abortion, divorce and contraception, addressing the public directly and avoiding the complexities of theological dogma. During the 1990s he had to contend with increased criticism of his uncompromising stance on doctrinal issues and, despite failing health, maintained his punishing schedule of overseas visits.

Amy Johnson, the record-breaking aviator who later disappeared on a wartime flight.

Johnson, Amy (1903–41) British aviator. Johnson caught the public imagination when, with no long-distance experience, she made an unsuccessful attempt to break the record for a light-airplane solo flight to Australia (May 1930): her time to Karachi (6 days) was a record. She went on to establish other flight records, including Siberia to Tokyo (1931); London to Cape Town (1932); and London to the Cape return (1936). She disappeared on a wartime flying mission in 1941.

Johnson, Lyndon B. (1908–73) US president. A Texan, Johnson entered the House of Representatives in 1937 as a Democrat and strong supporter of President Franklin D. Roosevelt. He was elected to the Senate (1948), where he was majority whip (1951–53) and party leader (1955–61). In 1960, after unsuccessfully challenging John F. Kennedy for the Democratic presidential nomination, he became Kennedy's running mate and was elected vice-president (1961–63). Assuming the office of president after Kennedy's assassination in November 1963, Johnson ensured continuity, seeing through the passage of Kennedy's civil rights and voting rights bills. Reelected by a big majority in 1964, he undertook an extensive program of social reform, aimed at creating what he termed the "Great Society". This had to be largely abandoned to fund US military commitments in South Vietnam and his popularity waned when involvement in the Vietnam war escalated. Wearied by the war, and by the increasingly powerful antiwar movement, he stepped down in 1969.

Jolson, Al (Asa Yoelson) (1886–1950) Russian-born US singer and actor. Jolson is best remembered as the star of Hollywood's first sound feature, *The Jazz Singer* (1927), but he had first performed his famous act as a blacked-up singer down on one knee on Broadway in 1911. The son of a rabbi, he began his career singing on the streets and in circus, café and vaudeville spots. He first performed the Gershwin number "Swanee" that became his trade mark in *Sinbad* (1918). He made several other movies after *The Jazz Singer* and dubbed Larry Parks' singing in the movie of his life, *The Jolson Story* (1946).

Joplin, Scott (1868–1917) US ragtime pianist and composer. The son of a former slave, Joplin was self-taught and began his career as a saloon-bar player in St Louis. He later moved to Sedalia, Missouri, before enrolling at the George R. Smith College for Negroes (1896) to study music. It was here that he began to write down the popular rags he heard. In 1899 his "Maple Leaf Rag" was published, selling 75,000 copies in the first year. Other successes included "Easy Winners", "Elite Syncopations" and "The Entertainer". He turned ragtime into an art form, but his later compositions, including an opera, failed to win recognition and he died in a mental institution in New York.

Joyce, James (1882–1941) Irish novelist. In 1905 Joyce escaped from what he felt were the constraining influences of Irish society to Trieste, Italy, where he wrote his series of stories, *Dubliners*. The autobiographical *Portrait of the Artist as a Young Man*, published in serial form, followed in 1914–15. He moved to Zurich (1915) and then to Paris (1920), where he wrote his great stream-of-consciousness novel *Ulysses*. Initially appearing chapter by chapter in a magazine, on its first publication in book form in 1922 it was banned in many countries for obscenity, and copies were seized and destroyed. *Finnegan's Wake*, a vast iconoclastic, inaccessible, poetic dream-piece, devastated the literary establishment on its appearance in 1939. In this work James drew heavily on myth, using Wagnerian themes. His radical treatment of form and linguistic innovations revolutionized language and changed the face of literature in the 20th century.

Juan Carlos (1938–) King of Spain. The grandson of Alfonso XIII, he was groomed for the monarchy by General Franco, who nominated him as his successor in 1969. After Franco's death in 1975, Juan Carlos adopted the role of a constitutional monarch and played an important role in guiding Spain's progress toward democracy. In 1981, Francoist soldiers occupied parliament and held its members hostage. Juan Carlos's prompt and courageous denunciation of this action saved the new democratic constitution.

Franz Kafka, whose novels of alienation greatly influenced 20th-century writing.

Jung, Carl (1875–1961) Swiss psychiatrist and psychologist. After studying medicine at Basel, Jung became a pupil of Sigmund Freud in Vienna (1907). They soon began to have fundamental differences in their interpretation of the human unconscious, in particular over the sexual basis for neurosis. In 1912 Jung published his independent researches in *The Psychology of the Unconscious*, precipitating a break with Freud (1913). The cornerstone of Jung's school of "analytical psychology" was the defining of different personality types, as part of which he coined the terms "introvert" and "extrovert", describing them in his major published work, *Psychological Types* (1921). He developed his theories further by describing and exploring the "Collective Unconscious" made up of man's memories, dreams and his artistic and anthropological heritage, seeing this pattern of shared ideas and experience as the wellspring of man's creativity. As a professor at Zurich (1933–41) and Basel (1941–61) universities, Jung made a major study of schizophrenia and developed methods of psychotherapy which have been highly influential in the development of psychiatry in this century.

Kafka, Franz (1883–1924) Austrian–Jewish writer. Kafka was born into the German-speaking Jewish community of Prague, then part of the Austro-Hungarian empire. A law graduate, he worked in an insurance company (1908–22), writing short stories and novels at night. Closely attached to his father, Kafka was sensitive and introspective, painfully aware of his apartness from society: the only one of his novels to be published in his lifetime, *Metamorphosis* (1916), deals with the impossibility of communication. In 1917, after TB was diagnosed, Kafka told his friend and amanuensis, Max Brod, to burn his unpublished work. Brod disobeyed and preserved two great unfinished novels, *The Trial* (1914–15) and *The Castle* (1922), which were published in 1925. Kafka's writings portray the hopeless struggle of individuals against anonymous forces, and have been highly influential in the development of 20th century, particularly German, literature.

Kaunda, Kenneth (1924–) Zambian president. Born in Northern Rhodesia, Kaunda was involved in nationalist politics for many years before becoming leader of the United National Independence party (UNIP). He played an important role in the negotiations leading up to Northern Rhodesia's independence as Zambia, becoming its first president (1964). He was reelected in 1968, and in 1972 proclaimed Zambia a single-party state. From 1965 he provided bases for the anticolonial forces of Southern Rhodesia (Zimbabwe) and Namibia. His disastrous economic policies resulted in Zambia's having the world's highest per capita foreign debt. After an attempted coup in 1990 he restored multiparty politics in 1991 but was defeated in the subsequent elections.

Keating, Paul (1944–) Australian prime minister. A lawyer, Keating entered politics in 1969 and served in two Labor governments before succeeding to leadership of the Labor party and the Australian premiership in 1991. He injected new life into the party and confounded his critics when he was reelected in 1993. In 1996 Keating fought a general election in which he sought a mandate to declare Australia a republic and replace the British monarch as head of state with an Australian president by the year 2001. But after six elections in 13 years the Australian electorate showed distinct signs of ballot fatigue and he was defeated.

Keaton, Buster (1895–1966) US comedy actor and director. An accomplished child acrobat, Keaton worked in vaudeville and in 1917 turned to making comedy film shorts. *One Week* (1920), *The Goat* (1921) and *Cops* (1922) established his famous "deadpan" style of humor, and he later starred in and directed full-length silent classics such as *Our Hospitality* (1923), *The Navigator* (1924) and *The General* (1927). He continued making films into the 1960s but his silent films remain his finest work.

Kelly, Gene (1912–96) US dancer, actor, choreographer and director. Kelly first appeared in a Broadway chorus line in 1938. He starred in *Pal Joey* (1941) and made his screen debut in *For Me and My Gal* (1942). His spontaneous, athletic style made him the

President John F. Kennedy, whose election promised a new era in US politics.

natural successor to Fred Astaire as Hollywood's leading dancer, and his choreography, first seen in *Cover Girl* (1944), revitalized film dance. Among his other movies are *Anchors Aweigh* (1945), *On the Town* (1949), *An American in Paris* (1951) and *"Singin' in the Rain"* (1952).

Kelly, Grace (1928–82) US film actress. Born into a wealthy Philadelphia family, Kelly starred in a number of Hollywood films in the mid-1950s. Her popular image as a superficially cool yet latently passionate woman was established in three movies directed by Alfred Hitchcock: *Dial M for Murder* (1954), *Rear Window* (1954), and *To Catch a Thief* (1955). Shortly after making *High Society* in 1956, she married Prince Rainier of Monaco and retired from Hollywood. She died tragically in a car crash.

Kennedy, John F. (1917–63) US president. Kennedy was the second son of millionaire and Democratic power-broker Joseph P. Kennedy. He graduated from Harvard in 1940 and saw service with the marines in World War II.
In 1947 he entered the House of Representatives as a Democrat, and in 1952 was elected to the Senate. His father's wealth helped secure his selection as the Democratic presidential candidate (1960) and he won the election to become the youngest and first ever Roman Catholic US president. Handsome and intelligent, he and his glamorous wife Jackie seemed to signal a fresh start in politics, but his "new frontier" program of radical social reform was stalled by Congress. Other initiatives included the establishment of the Alliance for Progress between the US and several Latin American countries, and of the Peace Corps, through which volunteers supplied Third World countries with skilled labor. In 1961 he authorized the US-backed Bay of Pigs invasion of Cuba, planned during the previous administration, accepting responsibility when it went disastrously

wrong. The following year Kennedy demanded the removal of Soviet nuclear bases from Cuba and ordered a US naval blockade. For 13 days the world seemed close to nuclear war until the Soviet Union agreed to remove the weapons in return for a US assurance that Cuban territorial integrity would be respected. Relations between the two superpowers improved, and in 1963 the US, Soviet Union and Britain signed a limited nuclear test ban treaty. On 22 November 1963 Kennedy was assassinated while campaigning in Dallas, Texas.

Kennedy, Robert F. (1925–68) US politician. Kennedy graduated from Harvard (1948) and from the University of Virginia law school (1951). He became an attorney, and in 1960 managed the successful presidential campaign for his brother John, who appointed him attorney-general and his chief advisor on all matters, domestic and foreign. A supporter of the civil rights movement, Robert Kennedy won respect from disadvantaged Americans and others for his championship of the poor and the oppressed, though his onslaught on organized crime outraged the Mafia. Grief-stricken at his brother's assassination in 1963, he resigned as attorney-general in September 1964, to be elected senator for New York a month later. In 1968 he ran for the US presidency, but was shot on 5 June while celebrating his victory in the California primary and died the next day.

Kenyatta, Jomo (c.1889–1978) Kenyan politician. Educated at a mission school, Kenyatta became president of the nationalist Kikuyu Central Association (1928). He lived in London from 1931–46, and on his return to Kenya became president of the Kenya African Union. As leader of the Mau Mau guerrilla organization he was held in detention by the British from 1952–62. On his release he led the Kenya African National Union (KANU) to victory in the pre-independence elections and became Kenya's first president from 1964 until his death. His leadership, which owed much to his powerful personality, provided stability and sustained economic growth, but after the banning of the rival Kenya People's Union (KPU) in 1969, Kenya became effectively a one-party state.

Keynes, John Maynard (1883–1946) British economist. A lecturer in economics and fellow of King's College, Cambridge (1909–41), Keynes became the leading critic of established economic theory and strongly attacked Churchill's moves to

The Ayatollah Khomeini greets his supporters on returning to Iran in 1979.

restore the gold standard (1925). The Depression led him to develop his argument that full employment could be achieved only by adopting a cheap money policy and undertaking a program of public investment. His views on a planned economy influenced Roosevelt's New Deal administration in the 1930s. As chief British delegate at the Bretton Woods Conference (1944), he played an important part in the establishment of the International Monetary Fund.

Khomeini, Ruhollah (1900–89) Iranian religious and political leader. A Shiite Islamic scholar, Khomeini was proclaimed "ayatollah" (religious leader) in the 1950s. For long a fierce opponent of the Shah of Iran's pro-Western policies, he was exiled in 1964 for his denunciation of his land reforms. Living in turn in Turkey, Iraq and France, he campaigned for the Shah's overthrow and returned to Iran to great popular acclaim after the regime's collapse in 1979, to launch the Islamic revolution. A constitution establishing an Islamic state granted Khomeini wide-ranging powers approved by referendum. Western music and alcoholic beverages were banned, women were obliged to wear veils, and the Sharia (Islamic legal code) was reintroduced. Khomeini gave his support to Islamic revolutionaries in other Middle Eastern countries. He issued a *fatwa* (execution order) in 1989 against the British author Salman Rushdie whose book, *The Satanic Verses* (1988), he had declared to be blasphemous.

Khrushchev, Nikita Sergeyevich (1894–1971) Soviet political leader. A Ukrainian, Khrushchev joined the Communist party in 1918 and fought in the civil war, later rising through the party ranks to become a member of the Politburo in 1939. As head of the party organization in Ukraine (1938–47) he organized resistance to the German occupation after 1941 and later presided over Ukraine's postwar reconstruction. Appointed by Stalin to reorganize Soviet agriculture (1949), he emerged from the power struggles following Stalin's death (1953) as first secretary of the Communist party. Three years later at the 20th Party Congress he denounced Stalin's personality cult and overcame all other rivals in the Politburo to become premier in 1958. Khrushchev introduced a degree of liberalization into Soviet society, and allowed the eastern bloc countries more independence, but resorted to military intervention in Hungary after it threatened to withdraw from the Warsaw Pact (1956). Urging peaceful coexistence with the West, he traveled to the US to meet Presidents Eisenhower (1959) and Kennedy (1961). But his conciliatory gestures alternated with threats and stand-offs: in 1961 he ordered the building of the Berlin Wall and his attempt to install nuclear missiles in Cuba (1962) led to a major confrontation with the US. He was a signatory of the nuclear test ban treaty (1963), a year before he was ousted from power by Leonid Brezhnev.

Kim Il Sung (1912–1994) Leader of North Korea. Born Kim Sung Ju, he served his political apprenticeship as a Communist revolutionary in the 1930s, organizing guerrilla activities against the occupying Japanese forces. He received a military training in the Soviet Union and fought with the Soviet forces during World War II. Following Korea's partition along the 38th Parallel (1948), Kim was installed with Soviet backing as the head of the new Democratic People's Republic of North Korea. His refusal to accept the partition led to his invasion of the South and the outbreak of the Korean War (1950–53), a conflict that cost three million lives and ended in stalemate. Kim became deeply entrenched as the godlike head of a repressive regime, isolating himself even from his Communist allies, the Soviet Union and China. A huge and slavish personality cult grew up around him as he restructured North Korea into a collectivized authoritarian state. Though he relaxed his stance toward the South a little toward the end of his life, fears of North Korea's nuclear potential remained. His death sparked a national outpouring of anguish and grief, and he was succeeded by his son Kim Jong Il (1941–), whom he had nominated as his heir in 1972.

King, Billie Jean (1943–) US tennis player. King won her first tournament at the age of 13 and took the first of six Wimbledon singles championship titles

Martin Luther King delivers his "I have a dream" speech in Washington in 1963.

(1966–68, 1972–73, 1975) when she was 17. She won the US singles title four times (1967, 1971–72, 1974), the Australian title in 1968 and the French title in 1972, and was a formidable player in doubles competitions as well. Turning professional in 1968, she was the first woman athlete to win more than $100,000 in a season. In 1973 she defeated former champion Bobby Riggs in a highly publicized battle of the sexes. She helped form a separate tour for women and was co-founder of the Women's Tennis Association in 1974. A shrewd, determined and tactical player, her ceaseless campaigning for women's tennis did much to help raise the status of the game.

King, Martin Luther, Jr
(1929–68) US civil rights leader. An ordained Baptist minister, it was while he was studying for a PhD in theology in the early 1950s that King became influenced by Gandhi's teachings of nonviolent protest. He became a nationally known figure after leading a successful boycott against racial segregation on local buses in Alabama (1955–56). He then went on to found, and became first president of, the Southern Christian Leadership Conference, which oversaw civil rights organizations throughout the south. In the early 1960s King headed the civil rights movement, orchestrating generally successful demonstrations against localized examples of racial discrimination. In 1963, while in jail, he wrote his famous "Letter from Birmingham", spelling out the principles of nonviolent noncooperation, and the same year helped to organize the March on Washington of more than 200,000 people. It was on this occasion that he delivered his powerfully moving "I have a dream" speech. Following the passing of he Civil Rights Act (1964) and the Voting Rights Act (1965), King's campaign moved to the north, where the Black Power movement was attracting support, and had some success in protesting against segregated housing in Chicago. He broad-

ened the civil rights agenda, publicly condemning the Vietnam War and campaigning against poverty in the US, but was assassinated in Memphis, Tennessee, on 4 April 1968. He received the Nobel prize for peace in 1964.

Kinsey, Alfred (1894–1956) US zoologist and sexologist. As professor of zoology at Indiana University, Kinsey's particular area of research was the behavior of wasps until in 1938 he turned his attention to human sexual behavior. He founded an Institute of Sex Research in 1942, and in 1948 published *Sexual Behavior in the Human Male* based on his statistical findings from more than 18,500 personal interviews. This was followed by *Sexual Behavior in the Human Female* (1953). Both books became huge bestsellers, and Kinsey's revelations on the variety of human sexual practice caused widespread controversy, challenging as they did established concepts of "normal" sexual behavior. The Kinsey Report, as the books were collectively called, though criticized for its narrowly biological approach and its unscientific use of personal interviews, prepared the ground for later research into the broader social issues of human sexuality and did much to encourage open discussion of a long-repressed topic.

Kissinger, Henry (1923–) US secretary of state. Born in Germany, Kissinger settled in the US in 1938 and wrote *Nuclear Weapons and Foreign Policy* (1957), which became a key influence in US strategic policy, while he was teaching government at Harvard. He acted as security advisor to Presidents Eisenhower, Kennedy and Johnson and, as President Nixon's assistant for national security (1969–73) and secretary of state (1973–77), dominated US foreign policy for a decade. Famous for his style of shuttle diplomacy, he pursued a policy of détente with the Soviet Union, culminating in the SALT I treaty (1972), and restored relations with China. His advocacy of the bombing and invasion of Cambodia (1971) was criticized as helping to prolong the Vietnam war, but in 1973 he played a part in negotiating a ceasefire (for which he shared the Nobel peace prize with the Vietnamese leader Le Duc Tho) and the same year mediated a ceasefire in the Arab–Israeli "Yom Kippur" war, restoring US relations with Egypt. Kissinger also came under fire for his backing of CIA operations to destabilize Allende's socialist government in Chile and support of anti-Cuban forces in Angola. Following his resignation in 1977 he acted as an international consultant on diplomacy.

Rod Laver, the Australian tennis star, in action at Wimbledon in 1968.

Klee, Paul (1879–1940) Swiss painter. Klee studied art in Munich, where he became associated with the *Blaue Reiter* (Blue Rider) group. He won international acclaim with an exhibition of his work (1919) and taught at the Bauhaus in Weimar and Dessau (1920–31) and in Düsseldorf until dismissed in 1933 by the Nazis who condemned his work as degenerate. Klee's small-scale, mainly abstract, works, often akin to doodling, were highly influential.

Klein, Calvin (1942–) US fashion designer. Klein graduated from New York's Fashion Institute of Technology in 1962 and found work in the city's garment district before setting up his own company in 1968. His designs, noted for their understated sophistication and simplicity, made use of quality materials in neutral colors. His readiness to sell his lines, particularly designer jeans, through sexy, provocative advertisements set a fashion trend in the 1980s. He later diversified into other fashion lines such as accessories, cosmetics and perfumery.

Kohl, Helmut (1930–) German chancellor. A Rhinelander from a Roman Catholic family, Kohl studied at the universities of Frankfurt and Heidelberg. He served as a Christian Democrat in the Rhineland parliament (1959–69) and as minister-president of the state (1969–73) before entering the Bundestag (federal parliament) as leader of the opposition. He ran unsuccessfully for the chancellorship in 1976 and became interim chancellor in 1982, in coalition with the Christian Social Union and the Free Democrats, on the collapse of Helmut Schmidt's Social Democrat government. The coalition won the 1983 elections with Kohl as chancellor. A conservative, he pursued moderate economic policies at home with a strong commitment to NATO and to the European Union. Reelected in 1987, he masterminded German reunification in the wake of the collapse of communism in East Germany. and in 1991 became the first postwar chancellor of a united Germany. But unification brought major economic and social problems and Kohl hung on to the chancellorship by only a narrow margin in the 1994 elections.

Korbut, Olga (1956–) Soviet gymnast. A tiny 17-year-old, Korbut literally leapt to public notice at the 1972 Olympic games in Munich. Her diminutive figure delighted millions of viewers around the world as she performed with consummate ease and grace in the women's gymnastic competition, winning gold medals for the balance beam and floor exercises, a silver medal for the parallel bars, and a third gold medal as a member of the winning Soviet team. The first of a stream of girl gymnasts from the Soviet bloc countries, she almost single-handedly helped to make gymnastics a major spectator sport.

Laver, Rod (1938–) Australian tennis player. Laver dominated men's tennis in the 1960s with his powerful ground strokes and quick thinking, determined game. He was only the second man in history to win the Grand Slam in 1962, and then turned professional in 1963 to win the professional world single's title five times. When the the major tennis tournaments were opened to both amateur and professional players (1968) he won a second Grand Slam (1969). In 1971 he became the first tennis professional to take over $1 million in prize money.

Lawrence, David Herbert (1885–1930) British writer. Lawrence's mother, a teacher, protected her delicate son from her violent coal-miner husband and encouraged him to become a teacher himself, but after the publication of his first novel *The White Peacock* (1911) Lawrence devoted himself to writing. In 1912 he eloped with Frieda von Richthofen, the German wife of a professor at Nottingham University. They traveled in Europe until Frieda obtained her divorce and married in 1914. Lawrence meanwhile had published *Sons and Lovers* (1913), an exorcism of his childhood which shocked the public with its sexual frankness but made his name. *The Rainbow* (1915) was prosecuted for obscenity, and Lawrence left England in protest for Italy where he wrote *Women in Love* (1921), considered by many to be his best novel. The Lawrences' journeys took them to Australia and Mexico and during this time he wrote nearly a thousand poems, as well as essays, short stories,

V. I. Lenin, founder of the Bolshevik party and creator of the Soviet Union.

travel pieces and a huge number of entertaining letters. Lawrence's last novel, *Lady Chatterley's Lover* (1929), a tale of passion across class barriers, was not finally published in an unexpurgated version until 1960. Lawrence was unquestionably a great writer who gave powerful expression to the human "life-force" in his work. He died of TB in the south of France.

Le Corbusier (Charles Jeanneret) (1887–1965) Swiss-born French architect. Perhaps the most significant architect of his day, after studying in Paris, he traveled extensively in Europe from 1908-17, gathering ideas which he later developed into his theory of the interrelation between machines and contemporary architecture (he famously called a house "a machine for living in"). He produced the steel-framed concrete Domino Housing Project (1914) and in 1917 began working with a Parisian building company specializing in the use of reinforced concrete. He adopted the name "Le Corbusier" in 1920 as a pseudonym when writing for *L'Esprit Nouveau*, the magazine he cofounded. His book *Towards a New Architecture* (1923) remains the most influential writing by any 20th-century architect. He later devised the Modulor technique (a system using standardized units based on the proportions of the human figure) and first put it to use in the *unité d'habitation*, a concrete block of flats in Marseilles (1945–50) which prefigured his city design, begun in 1951, for Chandigarh, the new state capital of Punjab. Among his best-known projects is the Cubist chapel of Ronchamp (1950–55). Through the work of the many lesser architects he influenced, he is associated in the public mind with today's ubiquitous concrete cityscapes.

Leigh, Vivien (1913–67) British actress. A woman of extraordinary beauty, her career was largely dominated by her relationship with the actor

Laurence Olivier whom she married in 1940, a year after her first Hollywood role in *Gone With the Wind* (1939), for which she won an Academy Award for best actress. Leigh and Olivier were the leading couple of British theater until her increasing mental instability led to the breakdown of their marriage in 1960. Her finest film role was in *A Streetcar Named Desire* (1951), which revealed previously unseen depths to her acting, and for which she won a second Academy Award.

Lenglen, Suzanne (1899–1938) French tennis player. A volatile player with enormous flair, Lenglen was among the first personality players in tennis. She dominated the women's game from 1919 to 1926, losing only one game during this period and winning the Wimbledon and the French singles championships six times each, before becoming the first player to turn professional in 1926. She is best remembered today for setting new fashions in tennis dress.

Lenin (Ulyanov), Vladimir Ilych (1870–1924) Russian revolutionary leader. Introduced to revolutionary politics as a student at Kazan University, he moved to St Petersburg in 1894 and in 1897 was exiled to Siberia for his subversive views. On his release in 1900 he went to Western Europe, where he became involved with the Russian Social Democratic Labor party. In 1903 he split the party, forming the Bolshevik (majority) wing. On the outbreak of war in 1914 he denounced the conflict as imperialist and from exile in Switzerland called on workers everywhere to transform it into civil war. Returning to Russia after the tsar's overthrow in April 1917, he orchestrated the coup in October that replaced the liberal-controlled Constituent Assembly with the Soviet of Peoples' Commissars, and immediately made peace with Germany. Three years of civil war and anarchy followed (1918–21). Industry was compulsorily nationalized, private trade abolished and strikes declared illegal, but Lenin's "New Economic Policy" (1922) reintroduced limited private enterprise to allow time for recovery before entering the era of giant state planning. He created a secret police, the Cheka, and was intolerant of opposition as well as increasing party and state bureaucratization, both of which assisted the rise of Stalin after his death. A prolific writer, Lenin was Marxism's greatest exponent. Despite the rigor and narrowness of his theoretical approach, he was a charismatic leader. After his death, his embalmed body was placed on display in Moscow's Red Square.

John Lennon, the most outspoken member of the Beatles.

Lennon, John (1940–80) British pop singer, guitarist, composer and lyricist. Lennon formed the Beatles with Paul McCartney, George Harrison and Ringo Starr in Liverpool in 1960, and by the mid 1960s the group had become the most successful in the history of pop music. Lennon and McCartney were brilliant co-writers, producing hit after hit, ranging from early successes such as "Love me Do" to the more complex melodies and rhythms of "Strawberry Fields Forever" and "Penny Lane" (both 1967). Lennon, regarded as the most radical of the group (he returned his MBE, awarded in 1965, in protest against the Vietnam war), brought a degree of social consciousness to their lyrics. Their album *Sergeant Pepper's Lonely Hearts Club Band* (1967) is regarded as marking a new stage in the development of pop music, but Lennon's marriage in 1969 to the Japanese artist Yoko Ono added to the existing strains between the Beatles, and the group broke up, amid painful legal wrangling, in 1970. Lennon wrote and recorded with Yoko Ono in the US, bringing out an innovative album, *Imagine,* in 1971. He was on the point of resuming his recording career after a five-year silence from 1975–80 when he was murdered outside his New York apartment building.

Levi, Primo (1919–87) Italian writer. Of Jewish descent, Levi studied chemistry at Turin University. On Italy's involvement in World War II, he joined a small guerrilla force in the mountains but was betrayed in December 1943 and handed over to the Germans. He survived ten months in Auschwitz concentration camp. His first book, *If This is a Man* (1947), was a graphic and moving account of life in the camp, written with a scientific detachment that adds immeasurably to its power. He subsequently combined his career as a chemist with that of a writer. *The Periodic Table* (1985), which blends autobiography with philosophical reflection, brought him long-delayed international fame. Levi committed suicide in 1987, possibly as a result of his experiences of the Holocaust, which never ceased to haunt him throughout his life.

Lévi-Strauss, Claude (1908–) French social anthropologist. Lévi-Strauss studied philosophy and law at the University of Paris and taught sociology in Brazil (1935–39), where he became interested in anthropology and did field research among Amerindian tribes. He later worked at the New School for Social Research in New York before returning to Paris. His earliest published book *The Elementary Structures of Kinship* (1949) introduced a new analytical method into anthropology. This was followed by *The Savage Mind* (1962) and his extensive and hugely influential four-volume study, *Mythologiques* (1964–72), which included the *The Raw and the Cooked* (1966)and *The Naked Man* (1971). His approach drew on structural linguistic theory to show that it is communication that structures how we perceive the social world.

Lewis, Carl (1961–) US athlete. A runner from the age of eight, Lewis achieved a long jump of over 25 feet in his junior year, becoming the top US high school track athlete. He was a member of the Houston University track team (1979–82) and in 1981 came within .04 sec of the 100 meters world record. An outstanding long-jumper as well, he consistently turned in jumps of over 28 feet. In 1983 he won three gold medals at the world championships in Helsinki and at the 1984 Olympics in Los Angeles won gold in the 100 meters, 200 meters, long jump, and 400 meter relay, emulating Jesse Owens' legendary achievement at the 1936 Berlin Olympics. Two further gold medals at the Barcelona Olympic Games (1992) made him the most successful track and field athlete ever.

Lindbergh, Charles (1902–74) US aviator. Lindbergh shot to public fame in 1927 when he made the first nonstop solo transatlantic flight in the *Spirit of St Louis* in 33 and a half hours, a feat for which he was awarded the Congressional medal. Five years later he became the center of one of the most notorious crimes of the 1930s after the sensational kidnap of his infant son. A handyman, Bruno Richard Hauptmann, was later tried and executed for the child's murder.

Lloyd, Clive (1944–) Guyanese cricketer. Lloyd gained his first West Indies Test cap in 1966. He captained the West Indies team from 1974–88,

Lloyd George, the British prime minister popularly known as "the Welsh wizard".

building into one of the most impressive test teams in the world, winners of the World Cup in 1975 and 1979. During his career, Lloyd took part in 110 test matches, scoring 7,515 runs and 19 centuries. He retired from test cricket in 1985 and first-class cricket in 1986. He was manager of the West Indian tour of Australia in 1988.

Lloyd George, David, Ist Earl Lloyd George of Dwyfor

(1863–1945) British prime minister. Lloyd George grew up in impoverished circumstances in North Wales. He trained as a solicitor and entered parliament as a Liberal in 1890, building a reputation as a fiery orator staunchly opposed to British policy in the Anglo-Boer War (1899–1902). In 1905 he became president of the board of trade, and from 1908–1915 served as chancellor of the exchequer, in which post he was responsible for piloting through parliament a series of social reform measures. In 1909 he incurred the wrath of the propertied classes and the Conservative Party by proposing a supertax and tax on land values to pay for them. The House of Lords rejected his finance bill out of hand, and two general elections followed. Returned to power, the Liberal government passed the Parliament Act (1911) to abolish the House of Lords' power of veto. During World War I Lloyd George was minister of munitions (1915–16). He succeed Asquith as coalition prime minister (1916–22), putting new energy into the conduct of the war, and was one of the three principal negotiators of the Treaty of Versailles. However, support for his policies began to wane after the Anglo-Irish war of 1919–21, which resulted in the partition of Ireland and created a rift with the Conservative members of the coalition. The Liberals were soundly defeated in the elections of 1922, and have never held office since. Lloyd George retained his seat in parliament until 1945, when he was created an earl.

Lloyd Webber, Andrew (1948–) Lloyd Webber's father, a composer, was director of the London College of Music and his mother a piano teacher; he began writing music aged nine. His first full-length theater piece, the "pop oratorio" *Joseph and the Amazing Technicolor Dreamcoat* (1968), brought him and his lyricist Tim Rice instant acclaim, and they went on to collaborate on the hugely successful musicals, *Jesus Christ Superstar* (1971) and *Evita* (1978). After his partnership with Rice ended in 1978, Lloyd Webber had further successes with *Cats* (1981), *The Phantom of the Opera* (1986) and *Sunset Boulevard* (1993). The progenitor of "rock opera", Lloyd Webber's music fused different styles: classical, rock and folk.

Lorca, Federico García (1898–1936) Spanish poet and playwright. Spain's leading 20th-century literary figure, Lorca was born into an affluent family in Granada, where he went to university. Moving to Madrid, he formed a close friendship with the Surrealist painter Salvador Dalí, and flirted himself with Surrealism. A play *Mariana Pineda* (1927) and collection of poetry, *Gypsy Ballads* (1928), both based on the stories and imagery of his native Andalusia, brought instant popularity. Lorca visited New York (1929–30), where his empathy with Black Americans helped radicalize him further. He returned via Cuba to Spain, where a trilogy of plays, *Blood Wedding* (1933), *Yerma* (1934), and *The House of Bernarda Alba* (1936) – elegiac and powerful tragedies dealing with the magnetic, dark forces of Andalusian folk stories – crowned his dramatic achievement. Lorca's use of songs, children's games and Surreal devices in his drama influenced later playwrights such as Arthur Miller and Eugene O'Neill. Of known left-wing sympathies and a leading supporter of the Second Spanish Republic, he was captured by Francoist soldiers after the fall of Granada at the beginning of the Civil War in 1936, and executed. His writings were banned during the early years of the Franco regime.

Louis, Joe (1914–81) US heavy weight boxer. Louis began boxing at the age of 18 and turned professional two years later in 1934. Known as the "Brown Bomber", he became world heavy weight champion in June 1937 and held the title for a record-breaking 12 years until his retirement in March 1949, successfully defending it 25 times and scoring 21 knockout defeats. Louis returned to the ring in 1950 but failed to regain the heavyweight championship, finally retiring in 1951.

The popstar Madonna has adopted many styles to promote her image.

MacArthur, Douglas (1880–1964) US general. MacArthur graduated from West Point Military Academy in 1903, and served with distinction in France during World War I. From 1919–22 he was superintendent of West Point, and from 1922–37 served in the Philippines, first as US commander, then as chief of staff, and finally (from 1935–37) as head of the US military mission. He retired in 1937, but was recalled in 1941 to head US forces in the Far East. He fought a delaying action against the Japanese in the Philippines, retreated to Australia in 1942, and became Supreme Commander in the Southwest Pacific. After a successful Allied campaign in 1943–44, MacArthur was made a five-star general. As Supreme Allied Commander, he formally accepted the Japanese surrender aboard the USS *Missouri* in Tokyo Bay (15 August 1945). From 1945–51, as commander of the Allied occupation force, he was responsible for Japan's demilitarization, democratization, and economic regeneration. He became UN commander in Korea (1950), leading the campaign against the invading Communist forces and twice taking the war across the 38th parallel into North Korea, but he was relieved of his duties in 1951 after a public disagreement with President Truman over the military conduct of the war.

Macmillan, Harold, 1st Earl of Stockton (1894–1986) British prime minister. Macmillan fought in World War I, and was seriously wounded. Elected to parliament as a Conservative in 1924, he was a noted opponent of appeasement policies in the 1930s. Churchill appointed him to various posts in the wartime government: minister of supply, colonial under secretary, minister resident at Allied headquarters in North Africa, minister for air. Out of office from 1945–50, he was made housing minister on the Conservatives' return to power in 1951 and was responsible for the construction of 300,000 houses in a year. He was defense minister (1954), foreign secretary (1955) and chancellor of the exchequer (1955–57). As prime minister (1957–63) he continued many of the postwar policies of social reform, and prosperity in the UK climbed. Abroad, he dismantled much of the British empire in Africa, and worked to improve relations with the US after the Suez crisis of 1956, fostering close relations with Presidents Eisenhower and Kennedy. He also pursued rapprochement with the Soviet Union. At home, economic difficulties and political scandal in the 1960s led to a decline in his government's popularity and, in ill-health, he retired in 1963. He was created an earl on his 90th birthday.

Madonna (Madonna Louise Ciccione) (1958–) US pop star and actress. She won a dance scholarship to the University of Michigan, and in 1978 joined the Alvin Ailey Dance Theater in New York. Her first album, *Madonna* (1983) won her instant fame. In 1985 she made her first and most successful movie, *Desperately Seeking Susan.* She played to massive audiences on a series of world concert tours, and was reputed to be the world's highest-earning woman, cultivating her own myth and projecting an aggressive and outrageous sexuality. Her message of social and religious iconoclasm was presented with a level of irony that was calculated to emphasize her toughness. Her collection of erotic photographs *Sex* (1992) bolstered her continuing controversial image, though her dominance of the pop charts began to wane.

Magritte, René (1898–1967) Belgian painter. After studying at the Royal Academy of Fine Arts in Brussels, Magritte became a wallpaper designer and commercial artist, but became more and more attracted by Surrealism. He held his first one-man show in 1927, which was badly received. He moved to Paris, where he became associated with the painter André Breton and others. In order to surprise and jar the viewer's consciousness he placed familiar but congruous objects in startling arrangements, such as a railway engine emerging from a fireplace, producing works of a strange and dreamlike quality.

Mahler, Gustav (1860–1911) Bohemian–Jewish-born composer and conductor. Mahler attended the Vienna Conservatory from 1875–78, and it was here that he met the composer Anton Bruckner (1824–96), whose music he later championed. His first notable

Nelson Mandela in 1992, two years after his release from imprisonment.

work, the cantata *Das Klagende Lied* was composed in 1880. In 1897 he was appointed director of the Vienna Court Opera, a post he held until 1907, when he went to New York as the conductor of the Metropolitan Opera, remaining there until his death. His orchestral works consist of ten symphonies (the Tenth left unfinished) and a sequence of song-cycles, of which *Das Lied von der Erde* (1907–09), a setting of Chinese poems in German translation, is the finest. The greatest of his symphonies are the Sixth (1903–05) and Ninth (1909–10), in which passion and poetry are balanced by a concise and chiseled structure. His work, though championed by Schoenberg and Webern among others, suffered long years of neglect after his death until, thanks in part to the huge success of Visconti's film *Death in Venice* (1971), which featured his Fifth Symphony, it began to receive more public performances.

Major, John (1943–) British prime minister (1990–). Major worked in banking before becoming a Conservative MP in 1979. He was first appointed to cabinet post as Treasury chief secretary in 1987. Margaret Thatcher promoted him foreign secretary in 1989 and chancellor of the exchequer later that same year – a meteoric rise that surprised many political commentators. He was elected leader of the Conservative party (November 1990) after Thatcher failed to win the necessary number of votes to secure her reelection. Major thus became Britain's youngest prime minister this century. Though widely regarded as Thatcher's natural heir, he quickly developed his own political line but failed to halt the declining popularity of his party. None the less, his government was reelected to power in 1992. His second term in office was marked by continuing economic crisis, while he struggled to unite a party and a nation that was bitterly and increasingly divided over the issue of European integration.

Malcolm X (1925–65) US Black militant leader. Born Malcolm Little, the son of a radical Baptist minister in Omaha, Nebraska, he converted to the Black Muslim sect (Nation of Islam) while in prison for theft from 1946–52. He broke with the Black Muslim movement after he had been suspended for describing the assassination of John F. Kennedy in 1963 as "the chickens coming home to roost". Following a trip to Mecca in 1964, he founded the Organization of Afro-American Unity and reaffirmed his conversion to orthodox Islam. The following year he was assassinated by a Black Muslim faction during a rally in New York. His intellectual influence increased after his death, and he became an ideological hero for many young Black Americans.

Mandela, Nelson (1918–) Black South African leader. In 1944 Mandela, a lawyer, joined the African National Congress (ANC). He became increasingly involved in organizing nonviolent resistance to the South African government's racialist policies, but when the ANC was banned after the Sharpeville massacre (1960) Mandela began to advocate armed struggle, helping to found Umkhonto We Sizwe (Spear of the Nation), the ANC's military wing. In 1961 he coordinated a three-day general strike and was imprisoned the following year for encouraging industrial unrest. Mandela was charged with treason in 1963 after the discovery of an arms cache. He made a four-and-a-half-hour speech at his trial in 1964, but was sentenced to life imprisonment. The South African authorities maintained that there would be no possibility of Mandela's release until he renounced the use of violence, which he steadfastly refused to do. In the course of his 26-year imprisonment, much of it spent in solitary confinement, he became an international symbol of Black resistance. His wife Winnie was also frequently subjected to restrictions on her personal freedom. In 1990, under the liberalizing regime of President F. W. de Klerk, the ban was lifted from the ANC. Mandela was at last released and, at the age of 71, made a dignified return to the political arena. His patience, courage and persistence over the years were rewarded when the legislation maintaining apartheid was dismantled at last in 1991. For their joint efforts in this respect, Mandela and de Klerk shared the Nobel peace prize in 1993. After the first free elections to be held in South Africa (April 1994), Mandela became its first Black head of state. Though his popularity stood higher than ever, he was increasingly estranged from his wife and they divorced in 1996.

Mao Zedong, revolutionary leader and founder of Communist China.

Mann, Thomas (1875–1955) German novelist. Born into a wealthy family, Mann's first novel, *Buddenbrooks* (1901), brought him instant success. It was followed by *Tonio Krüger* (1902), *Tristan* (1903), the elegant and haunting *Death in Venice* (1913) and *The Magic Mountain* (1924), for which he won the Nobel prize for literature in 1929. Following the rise of Nazism, Mann fled Germany in 1933, taking refuge in Switzerland, where he wrote the trilogy *Joseph and his Brothers*. In 1938 he emigrated to the US. He continued in his writings to examine the plight of Germany challenged by the irrationality of Nazism, first in *Lotte in Weimar* (1939) and then in his modern reworking of *Dr Faustus* (1947). In 1952 Mann returned to Europe and settled in Switzerland. The profound spiritual truths contained in his novels have assured his place as one of the great novelists of the century.

Mao Zedong (1893–1976) Chinese revolutionary leader and head of state. Mao fought with Sun Yat Sen's nationalist forces in the overthrow of the Manchu dynasty (1911). In 1921 he was a founder member of the Chinese Communist party (CCP), and later its leader. He led the Communists in a civil war against the nationalist forces of Jiang Jieshi (1927), and the following year founded a soviet republic in southeast China. From 1934–35 Mao led the Communists' Long March and their relocation in Shaanxi in northwest China. It was during this time that he wrote his chief works of political philosophy. The Communists finally achieved victory in 1949 and Mao dominated China for the next 27 years, becoming chairman both of the CCP and of the newly founded People's Republic of China. Mao laid emphasis on the peasantry as the driving force of the revolution in its fight against the rise of bureaucratic and technocratic elites. In 1958 he initiated the "Great

Leap Forward" to decentralize the economy and encourage continued economic growth. It was a failure, and Mao retired as chairman of the Chinese republic in 1959, remaining chairman of the CCP. Increasing ideological differences with the Soviet Union, and Khrushchev's lack of support in China's 1962 border war with India, damaged Sino–Soviet relations. Mao reasserted his power in the "Cultural Revolution" of the mid 1960s, a ruthless and violent attempt to halt ideological revisionism that threatened to disintegrate into civil war. Mao was the subject of a personality cult in his lifetime, but after his death his theories of mass revolutionary fervor as a spur to economic growth, and of a paramilitary way of life were replaced by an emphasis on managerial competence.

Marciano, Rocky (1923–69)
US boxer. Initially aspiring to a baseball career, Marciano took up boxing in the army. He had a powerful punch and immense stamina. Turning professional in 1947, he famously defeated the former champion Joe Louis in 1951 and won the world heavyweight championship a year later, retaining it for four years before retiring in 1956. In all he fought 49 bouts and successfully defended his title six times, scoring a total of 43 knockouts.

Marconi, Guglielmo (1874–1937)
Italian radio pioneer. While a student, Marconi's imagination was captured by an article discussing the possibility of using electromagnetic waves, discovered by Heinrich Hertz (1857–94) in 1888, for wireless communication. Within a year he had sent and received signals at distances up to 1.5 miles (2.4 km) and he took out his first patent in London in 1896, establishing the Marconi Wireless Telegraphy Company in London in 1899. His invention interested the British government, and soon experimental equipment was installed in naval vessels. In 1901 Marconi received the first Morse code radio signals sent across the Atlantic. He invented a magnetic detector (1902), a directional aerial (1905) and during World War I developed for the British government short-wave equipment for use over long distances. He shared the Nobel Prize for physics with K. F. Braun in 1909.

Marcos, Ferdinand (1917–89)
Philippine president. Elected to the Philippine House of Representatives in 1949 and to the Senate in 1959, Marcos became president in 1965 and gained reelection in 1969, thus becoming the first Philippine president to serve a second term. His regime maintained close ties with the US, but it

The media tycoon Robert Maxwell, whose empire collapsed in ruins after his death.

became increasingly unpopular at home and in 1972 Marcos imposed martial law. Opposition leaders were imprisoned and in 1973 a new constitution was introduced, granting the president semidictatorial powers. Marcos' disastrous economic policies increased unrest, and in 1981 the constitution was amended and martial law lifted. Marcos was reelected but did nothing to curb the excesses of his corrupt regime. He was held responsible for the murder of opposition leader Benigno Aquino who was shot on his return from exile in 1983. With opposition to his rule growing, Marcos was forced to call presidential elections in 1986 and was opposed by Aquino's widow, Corazón, who headed the popular "People's Power" campaign. Marcos was officially declared the winner but, accused of massive electoral fraud, lost the support of the army and fled to exile in Hawaii accompanied by his wife, Imelda.

Marley, Bob (1945–81) Jamaican singer and composer. Marley made his first record at 19 and a year later formed the Wailers. The group was the first to bring Jamaican reggae music, a combination of African, Caribbean and Black American soul rhythm, to a worldwide audience. A series of world tours added to Marley's enormous popularity. A devout Rastafarian, Marley's religious and political message reached millions through his music and he became a national hero, symbolizing the Black consciousness movement of the 1970s. He died of cancer.

Marx Brothers US comedy team: brothers Chico (1886–1961); Harpo (1888–1964); Groucho (1890–1977), Gummo (1893–1977) and Zeppo (1901–79). Their act was an almost surrealistic blend of slapstick, boisterous vitality, insult, anarchy and logic-chopping, in which each of the brothers (except Zeppo) had a separate comic persona. Gummo left the act in 1918 before the group's Broadway breakthrough in *I'll Say She Is* (1924), which was followed by *The Cocoanuts* (1925) and *Animal Crackers* (1928). The last two were filmed (1929–30) and ten more movies followed. Weak direction and weaker plots did not lessen their comic impact in classics such as *Duck Soup* (1933) and *A Night at the Opera* (1935). Zeppo and Chico had left the act by 1939, and it finally disbanded in 1949. Groucho subsequently pursued a successful solo career in movies and on TV.

Matisse, Henri (1869–1954) French painter and sculptor. Matisse gave up law in 1890 to study painting in Paris, first at the Académie Julian and then at the Ecole des Beaux Arts. His early work was influenced by that of the Impressionists and Neo-Impressionists, particularly the Divisionism of Seurat and Signy. He had his first one-man show in 1904. Works such as *Luxe, Calme and Volupté* (1904) and *Woman with the Hat* (1905) marked a new departure, with the use of simple forms and high-pitched color. In 1905 Matisse began exhibiting at the annual Salon d'Automne with a group of artists that included Derain, Vlaminck, Dufy and Roualt, known collectively as les Fauves (the Wild Beasts). During the next few years he traveled extensively in Europe and North Africa. In 1919 he designed stage sets for Diaghilev's Ballet Russe, but returned to sculpture and painting. Though an invalid in his last years, Matisse continued to work with the help of assistants, overseeing several mural projects and experimenting with large colored paper cutouts in abstract patterns, such as *The Snail* (1953).

Maxwell, Robert (1923–91) Czech-born British publisher and newspaper magnate. Maxwell joined the Czech resistance during World War II and later fought with the British army. He became a British citizen in 1946 and in 1951 founded Pergamon Press, which published scientific journals, using it as a base to build an extensive publishing and media empire. A Labor MP from 1964–70, he survived near-bankruptcy in the mid 1970s to become chairman of the Mirror group of newspapers (1984). A ruthless negotiator and wheeler-dealer, Maxwell's controversial business methods were for long the subject of rumor and speculation. After his mysterious death by drowning from his private yacht, it was discovered that he had been systematically defrauding two of his companies to save his vast empire from imminent financial collapse.

Golda Meir was prime minister of Israel during the Yom Kippur War (1973).

Mayer, Louis (1885–1957) Russian-born US movie mogul. Brought to North America at the age of three., Mayer started out in the scrap business, but in 1907 bought a rundown property in Massachusetts which he refurbished as a nickelodeon. Cashing in on the popularity of the movies, he soon owned New England's largest movie theater chain. He founded his own production company in 1918 and in 1924 merged with Metro and Goldwyn. A hardworking tyrant, Mayer's nose for popular taste and ability to spot potential stars such as Greta Garbo, Rudolf Valentino and Clark Gable made him the most powerful studio boss in Hollywood in the 1930s and 1940s.

McCarthy, Joseph (1908–57) US politician. Elected to the Senate as a Republican in 1946, McCarthy declared (1950) that 205 Communists had infiltrated the state department. He failed to name any, but nevertheless embarked on a highly publicized anticommunist crusade, becoming chairman of the powerful Permanent Subcommittee on Investigations in 1952. Though he interrogated hundreds of government employees, he failed to construct one reasonable case. Many people were victimized, however, and some forced out of their jobs. McCarthy then attacked major political figures, including Eisenhower, but his popularity declined after a televized 36-day hearing publicly exposed his oppressive cross-examination tactics. He was dismissed in 1954, and later officially censured by the Senate.

McLuhan, Marshall (1911–80) Canadian communications theorist. As Professor of English Literature at Toronto University, McLuhan became interested in the impact of the media on society and in 1963 was appointed director of the university's Center for Culture and Technology. He prophesied that printed books would become obsolete in the 20th century, killed off by television and electronic information technology, which would have the effect of creating a "global village". His ideas had great influence in the 1960s. His books include *Understanding the Media* (1964) and *The Medium is the Message* (1967).

McNamara, Robert (1916–) US businessman and politician. Hired as one of a young team to rejuvenate the Ford Motor Company in 1946, McNamara introduced rigorous cost-accounting methods and other successful management programs. Appointed the first non-Ford family member to be president of the company (1960), he resigned almost immediately to join President Kennedy's administration as secretary of defense, continuing in that role under President Johnson. He modernized the armed forces, restructured budget procedures and introduced cost-cutting. Initially a supporter of US military involvement in Vietnam, by 1966 he had came to question its escalation, and carried out a major investigation (later published as *The Pentagon Papers*), which concluded against continued bombing. In 1968 he resigned to become president of the World Bank.

McTaggart, David (1932–) Canadian conservationist. A successful business tycoon, McTaggart joined Greenpeace when it was founded in Vancouver in 1971 to campaign against US nuclear testing in Alaska. He was active in campaigns to monitor endangered species of whales and seals, and led protests against the dumping of chemical wastes at sea and the testing of atmospheric nuclear weapons. As chairman of Greenpeace International from 1979, McTaggart has helped guide its development into a major international pressure group.

Meir, Golda (1898–1978) Russian-born Israeli prime minister. Born Goldie Myerson and brought up in the US, Meir emigrated to Palestine in 1921, where she held various executive positions in the General Federation of Labor. An active Zionist, in 1946 she became head of the Jewish Agency's political department where she worked for the release of illegal immigrants and political prisoners. In 1948, after Israel's independence, Meir was made ambassador to Moscow, and in 1949 was elected to the Knesset (parliament) as a member of the Mapai party. From 1949–56 she was labor minister, organizing the building of houses and roads. As foreign minister (1956–66), she worked to develop good relations with nonaligned African countries. In 1966 she became general secretary of the Mapai party, and after the Six-Day War in 1967 was involved in the creation of the Labor party. She became

Yehudi Menuhin faces the cameras as a 14-year-old prodigy violinist.

prime minister in 1969, in which role she traveled widely in the attempt to negotiate peace in the Middle East. She headed the government during the Yom Kippur War of 1973 but resigned the next year, following criticism of Israel's state of battle-readiness.

Menuhin, Yehudi (1916–)
US-born British violinist. Raised in San Francisco, Menuhin was given his first violin at the age of three. He started lessons two years later, giving his first public solo performance at the age of seven. In 1924 the philanthropist Sidney Ehrman took on financial responsibility for Menuhin's career. In 1926 came his début with the San Francisco orchestra, and in the years that followed he appeared with many of the world's top orchestras and conductors, astounding critics with his mature musical understanding. At the age of 19, Menuhin withdrew from public performance for a time to perfect his technical knowledge. On returning to the concert platform, he became renowned as one of the great interpreters of Bartók and Elgar. In 1959 Menuhin moved to London and assumed the directorship of the Bath Festival (1959–68), becoming conductor of its orchestra, renamed the Menuhin Festival Orchestra. In 1963 he opened a school for musically gifted children in Surrey. Menuhin made many records as a solo performer and with other musicians, including jazz violinist Stéphane Grappelli and Indian sitarist Ravi Shankar, and was responsible for bringing many new and neglected composers to the public ear.

Menzies, Sir Robert (1894–1978)
Australian prime minister. Menzies studied law in Melbourne and practised as a barrister before becoming a member of the Victoria parliament (1928). He was elected to the federal parliament in 1934 and served as attorney general (1935–39) before assuming the premiership as leader of the United Australia Party (1939–41). Divisions

within the party led to his resignation, and his political career seemed in ruins. Yet in 1949 he was able to stage a political comeback that returned him to power as Australia's longest-serving prime minister (1949–66). At the head of the newly formed Liberal party, Menzies inaugurated a 16-year period of economic prosperity and industrial expansion, in the course of which he upheld Australia's strong position in the British Commonwealth, fostered immigration from Europe and gave political and military support to the British in Suez and to the US government in Vietnam and the Pacific.

Mies van der Rohe, Ludwig (1886–1969) German/US architect. Apprenticed as a stonecutter, Mies van der Rohe later became an architect and in 1911 set up his own practice. From 1920 he undertook ambitious skyscraper schemes, using the motto "Less is more" to produce good-quality, cheap mass housing. He was director of the influential Bauhaus school of architecture (1930–33) and in 1937 went to the US, becoming director of architecture at the Illinois Institute of Technology. His designs included the Seagram Building in New York and the National Gallery in Berlin. His architectural ideas, above all his use of simple forms, were highly influential.

Miller, Arthur (1915–) US playwright. His early experience of the Depression engendered in Miller a direct knowledge of poverty and a compassion that pervades all of his work. He rose to fame with *All My Sons* (1947), an Ibsenesque drama of family conflict, and with *Death of a Salesman* (1949), which won the Pulitzer prize and is generally regarded as his masterpiece. *The Crucible* (1953) compared McCarthyism to the Salem witchhunts of the 17th century. Other successes included *A View from the Bridge* (1955). Miller wrote the screenplay for *The Misfits* (1961) for his wife Marilyn Monroe; it was the last movie she made. The story of their marriage, which lasted from 1956–61, is told in *After the Fall* (1964). Miller's later plays generally met with less critical success than the earlier ones.

Miller, Glenn (1904–44) US jazz musician and bandleader. As a trombonist Miller played under many bandleaders including Ben Pollack, Tommy and Jimmy Dorsey and Ray Noble before forming his own ensemble in 1938. Its distinctive smooth, big-brass sound was instantly popular in hit singles such as "Chattanooga Choo Choo", "Moonlight Serenade" and "In the Mood". A radio series confirmed Miller's success, and the band appeared

François Mitterrand was president of France for an unprecedented 14 years.

in two movies, *Sun Valley Serenade* (1941) and *Orchestra Wives* (1942), winning it a worldwide audience. Miller's orchestra was disbanded in 1942 when he was drafted into the US army. He became head of the US Army Air Force band in Europe, broadcasting to US troops throughout the world. He died in service when the plane he was flying in disappeared over France.

Milosevic, Slobodan (1941–) president of the Serbian republic (1989–). Milosevic was the head of a major Belgrade bank before being drawn into the Serbian independence movement in the mid 1980s. A former supporter of President Tito, he became head of the Serbian Communist Party in 1987 and pledged himself to fighting for the union of the Serbian peoples of the six Yugoslavian republics in a Greater Serbia. In 1989 he was elected president of the Serbian republic and by 1992 had gained control of the Yugoslavian government and its armed forces after the secession of Croatia, Slovenia and Bosnia. He relentlessly pursued the Serbian cause, providing the backing for Serbian independence bids in Croatia and Bosnia whilst turning a blind eye to acts of ethnic cleansing, rape and torture by Serbian troops.

Mitterrand, François (1916–96) French president. A French resistance leader during World War II, Mitterrand was elected to the National Assembly in 1946, and from 1947–57 held cabinet posts in 11 different governments. He became the leader of the left-wing opposition to de Gaulle, unsuccessfully challenging him for the presidency in 1965. From 1971 he was first secretary of the Socialist party. He lost the 1974 presidential election to Valéry Giscard d'Estaing, but successfully built up his party's support and, in alliance with the Communists, defeated him to become president in 1981. As president, Mitterrand launched a program of industrial nationalization, introduced increased welfare payments and the minimum wage, and gave more power to local governments, but the world-wide recession later forced him to moderate his policies. In foreign policy, his tough but realistic attitude to the Soviet Union encouraged détente in the later 1980s. He was reelected to another 7-year term in 1988, but the last years of his presidency were overshadowed by ill-health. He died of cancer shortly after retiring from politics in 1995.

Miyake, Issey (1935–) Japanese fashion designer. After graduating from Tama University in Tokyo in 1964, Miyake studied fashion in Paris and worked for designers Laroche and Givenchy before going to New York. He returned to Tokyo to hold his first show there in 1971, with a second in Paris two years later. By now he had established his own bold and quirky style that made use of linear and geometric shapes wrapped and layered around the body. He continued to be an innovator, combining elements of West and East in his garments.

Modigliani, Amedeo (1884–1920) Italian artist. Modigliani studied painting in Rome, Florence and Venice before settling in Paris in 1906. He was influenced by Fauvism and Cubism, and in 1909 was introduced to sculpture by Constantin Brancusi. Part of the modern Paris school, his bohemian way of life contributed to his early death from tuberculosis. His most powerful work was produced in the last five years of his life, and it was only after his death that his unique, elongated portraits began to win recognition.

Molotov, Vyacheslav (1890–1986) Soviet politician. Molotov was a member of the military revolutionary committee during the Bolshevik revolution (1917). He joined the Communist party central committee in 1921, the Politburo in 1925 (when he also became chairman of the Moscow party committee) and in 1930 was selected as chairman of the Soviet of People's Commissars (effectively premier). As commissar for foreign affairs in 1939 he negotiated the nonaggression pact with Hitler. In 1941 Stalin replaced him as chairman of the council of ministers, and he then became first deputy chairman. Joining the state defense committee (war cabinet), he helped to form alliances with Britain and the US, and attended the Allied conferences at Tehran, Yalta, Potsdam, and San Francisco. Molotov retired as foreign minister in 1949, but served again in this capacity during 1953–56, when he became famous for making extensive use of the Soviet veto in the UN. In 1956 he was appointed state

Marilyn Monroe, exploited and then abandoned by the system that created her.

control minister, but took part in the attempted coup against Khrushchev in 1957 and was posted to Mongolia. He retired in 1962. During World War II his name was given to the Molotov cocktail – a crude bomb made of a bottle containing gasoline or other flammable liquid that he put into production as a wartime weapon.

Mondrian, Piet (1872–1944) Dutch painter. Mondrian's early works were somber landscapes until he moved to Paris (1909) where he became influenced by the Fauvists. He later turned to Symbolism, then Cubism, and from 1913 moved away from the use of perspective into compositions of black outlines filled in with blocks of primary color. In 1915 he cofounded the *de Stijl* movement, asserting that natural forms hid "reality". He worked in Paris and London before moving to New York in 1940, where he produced some of his finest paintings like *Broadway Boogie-Woogie* (1943). His work was a major influence on all abstract art.

Monroe, Marilyn (1926–62) US film actress. Born Norma Jean Baker in Los Angeles, she had an unhappy childhood in orphanages and foster homes. She married at 16, began modeling in 1945, and in 1946 was signed up with Fox as a bit-part actress of dumb-blonde roles. Movies such as *Niagara* (1952), *How To Marry A Millionaire* (1953), *Gentlemen Prefer Blondes* (1953) and *There's No Business Like Show Business* (1954) established her as the archetypal screen sex goddess, famous for her wide eyes and breathless voice. She married the baseball hero Joe DiMaggio (1954), and the playwright Arthur Miller (1956–61). Her later movies, such as *The Seven Year Itch* (1955), *The Prince and the Showgirl* (1957) and *Some Like it Hot* (1959) showed a delightful flair for light comedy and she had ambitions to be taken as a serious actress in *Bus Stop* (1956) and

The Misfits (1961). Her enormous popular success was at the cost of increasing unhappiness and self-doubt. Shortly after being fired from the set of her final, uncompleted movie for unpunctuality and failing to learn her lines she was found dead from an overdose of barbiturates. One of her last public appearances was to sing at John F. Kennedy's birthday celebrations in 1962, and after her death she was rumored to have had relationships with him and with his brother Robert.

Montessori, Maria (1870–1952) Italian educationalist. The first woman to qualify as a doctor of medicine in Italy (1894), Montessori taught at the University of Rome from 1900, becoming professor of anthropology in 1904. Her first "children's house" was opened in Rome in 1907. She sought to organize the child's environment and provide it with a variety of materials for educational development, emphasizing the importance of work rather than play, undertaken at the child's own pace. Self-education was a key factor in her strategy and teachers were to remain in the background. Montessori was an advocate of scientific observation and induction. The educational system that bears her name has had immense influence on nursery and infant education around the world.

Montgomery, Bernard (1st Viscount Montgomery of Alamein) (1887–1976) British field marshal. The son of an Anglican bishop, Montgomery served with distinction in World War I. In 1941 he was appointed to command the 8th Army in North Africa, which had suffered a series of defeats at the hands of the Axis forces, and swiftly built up morale. His victory at Alamein (1942) was regarded as one of the turning points of the war. He later commanded the ground forces throughout the Normandy landings (June 1944). Famous for his dress of beret and pullover, Montgomery was popular with his men, but his tactlessness often led to friction with Eisenhower, Allied supreme commander. He was deputy commander of NATO (1951–58) and wrote several books in retirement.

Moore, Henry (1898–1986) British sculptor. Born in Yorkshire, Moore studied art in Leeds and at the Royal College of Art in London, where he taught from 1926–32. He then moved to the Chelsea School of Art (1932–39) and at this time became recognized as Britain's leading avant-garde sculptor. He was greatly influenced by primitive art, as evidenced in one of his earliest sculptures, *Mother and Child* (1924–25). *Reclining Figure* (1929),

Robert Mugabe led the war against South Rhodesia to become Zimbabwe's president.

widely regarded as his early masterpiece, shows the influence of pre-Columbian Mexican art. Moore also explored Cubism and Surrealism. During World War II, working as an official war artist, he made a famous sequence of drawings of people in the air-raid shelters and of coal-miners. His international reputation mounted after winning the 1948 Venice Biennale sculpture prize and he came to be regarded as the world's greatest living sculptor. His major international commissions included reclining figures for the UNESCO building in Paris (1958) and the Lincoln Center in New York (1968). He later concentrated on drawing and etching.

Moro, Aldo (1916–78) Italian premier. A former law professor, Moro played a central role in Italy's politics in the 1960s and 1970s and was well-known as a conciliator. Secretary of the Christian Democrat party from 1959–63, he was active in creating a center-left coalition and on becoming prime minister in 1963 brought the Socialists into government for the first time in 16 years. Italy's economic weakness blocked his reformist aims, and he had difficulty in controlling the Socialists. He resigned in 1968 and became prime minister again in 1974, this time in a Republican coalition. On its collapse in 1976 Moro became president of the Christian Democrats. In March 1978 he was kidnapped by terrorists of the Red Brigade. The Italian government refused to comply with their demands for the release of political prisoners, and Moro was murdered after two months in captivity.

Morton, Jelly Roll (1885–1941) US jazz pianist, composer, arranger and vocalist. Born Ferdinand Joseph La Menthe, he is considered one of jazz's greatest pianists. Morton rose to success on the New Orleans music scene in the 1920s. Exploring the limits of the small jazz band, he is most famous for a series of sessions recordings with Morton's Red Hot Peppers made in

1926. By 1928 big bands like Louis Armstrong's were catching on and Jelly Roll came to be considered out-dated and old hat. Self-centered and boastful, he alienated many of his colleagues. He is best remembered for his classic stomps and blues such as "King Porter Stomp", "Black Bottom Stomp" and "Jelly Roll Blues".

Mountbatten, Louis (1st Earl Mountbatten of Burma) (1900–79) British admiral and viceroy of India. A great-grandson of Queen Victoria, he joined the Royal Navy as a cadet in 1913 and served at sea in World War I. In World War II Mountbatten commanded the 5th destroyer flotilla (1939–41). He was chief of combined operations (1942–43) and supreme allied commander Southeast Asia (1943–46), directing the liberation of Burma. Appointed the last British viceroy of India in 1947, he oversaw the subcontinent's partition and transition to independence and was later chief of the UK defense staff (1959–65). He was murdered by the IRA in 1979 while sailing near his holiday home in Co Sligo, Ireland.

Mubarak, Hosni (1928–) Egyptian president. Mubarak was a pilot and flying instructor in the Egyptian airforce who received advanced training in the Soviet Union before becoming airforce chief of staff (1969–72) and commander in chief (1972–75), emerging with personal credit from the Arab–Israeli war (1973). He served as vice president (1975–81), succeeding to the presidency after President Sadat's assassination. Despite a worsening economic crisis and pressure from Islamic fundamentalists he preserved political stability, maintaining close links with the West and remaining committed to peace negotiations with Israel.

Mugabe, Robert (1924–) Zimbabwean president. Mugabe was a schoolteacher before joining the Rhodesian nationalist movement in 1960. A Marxist, he helped found the Zimbabwe African National Union (ZANU) in 1963, and was imprisoned for subversion a year later. In 1965 Rhodesia's white elite made a unilateral declaration of independence from Britain. Mugabe became the leader of ZANU in 1974 while still in detention. Freed in 1975 he joined with Joshua Nkomo, leader of the Zimbabwe African People's Party (ZAPU), to form the Patriotic Front to wage guerrilla war against government forces. In 1980 he became Zimbabwe's first prime minister after ZANU defeated ZAPU in pre-independence elections. He succeeded in persuading the European

Benito Mussolini, Italian fascist leader, in a pose celebrating his seizure of power.

community to remain in Zimbabwe and introduced social reform. In 1987, after persuading parliament to unite the roles of head of state and head of government, he became executive president. ZANU and ZAPU were merged in 1988, making Zimbabwe effectively a single-party state.

Muldoon, Sir Robert (1921–92) New Zealand prime minister. Muldoon abandoned accountancy to enter parliament in 1960, rising to minister of finance in 1967. In 1974, as deputy prime minister, he successfully challenged prime minister Sir John Marshall for the party leadership. Succeeding him as prime minister in December 1975, he immediately instituted stiff financial measures and committed the country to public borrowing. He was defeated by the Labor party in a snap election in 1984.

Müller, Hermann (1890–1967) US geneticist. Müller began experiments into genetics in 1911 and later held academic positions in Moscow, Edinburgh and Indiana where he was professor in zoology (1945–67). From his studies of artificial mutations in the fruit fly he was able to demonstrate the potential cancer-causing dangers to humans of exposure to X-rays, and was awarded the Nobel prize for physiology or medicine in 1947.

Mulroney, Brian (1939–) Canadian prime minister. A successful businessman, Mulroney entered the Canadian parliament as leader of the Progressive Conservative Party in 1983. He became prime minister a year later after a landslide election victory. He signed a free trade agreement with the US and negotiated the Meech Lake Accord (1987), under which Quebec agreed to accept the 1982 Canadian Constitution in return for "distinct society" status. Reelected in 1988, he was unable to persuade all the provincial governments to ratify the Meech Lake Accord, and a new agreement was negotiated, the Charlottetown Accord. When this was rejected in a nationwide referendum in October 1992 Mulroney immediately announced his resignation, and in 1993 his party was decisively swept from power.

Munch, Edvard (1863–1944)
Norwegian painter. Munch's mother died of TB when he was in his teens, and one of his first paintings, after leaving art school, was *The Sick Child* (1885), depicting his sister, who also died of the disease. In 1885, on a trip to Paris, Munch saw Impressionist paintings and was influenced by Van Gogh and Gauguin. The bleak and claustrophobic dramas of the Swedish playwright August Strindberg also influenced his work. His neurotic, tortured mental state is reflected in the dark sexual turbulence of many of his paintings from the 1890s, including his best-known work, *The Scream* (1893). His later work, like *Horse Team* (1919), or *Starry Night* (1924) could be as bright as that of Van Gogh. Munch was the major forerunner of Expressionism and his work had particular influence in Germany.

Murdoch, Rupert (1931–)
Australian-born media tycoon. In 1952 Murdoch inherited a small Australian newspaper from his father. In a short time he turned it into a commercial success. He went on to acquire several more newspapers in Perth and Sydney, as well as a number of magazines and TV stations. Expanding his interests overseas, he bought the London *News of the World* and *Sun* (1969). Murdoch quadrupled the latter's circulation at the expense of other tabloids, taking Fleet Street into a series of ruthless circulation battles. After 1974 he turned his attention to the US, setting up a national weekly tabloid, *The Star*, and buying several daily newspapers and magazines. In 1981 he added the London *Times* to his circus of newspapers. His tough action against the print unions aroused much controversy and he was criticized for seeking to influence the editorial content of his newspapers too greatly. In the 1980s Murdoch purchased the 20th Century Fox film studios and six TV studios in the US, giving him control of one of the world's largest media and communications empires. He took US citizenship in 1985.

Mussolini, Benito (1883–1945)
Italian dictator. Expelled from the Socialist party in 1914 for advocating Italian intervention in World War I, Mussolini switched allegiances and created a militant antisocialist nationalist organization, the Fascists. Its

Egyptian president Gamal Nasser worked for Arab unity in the 1950s and 1960s.

blackshirted followers marched on Rome in 1922 and brought down the government. Mussolini became prime minister and by 1928 had turned Italy into a single-party state. Known as Il Duce (the leader), he used terror tactics and murder to suppress opposition, but through his program of public works, which had the intention of returning national pride to Italy, won the support of big business, the army and the church. In 1929 he agreed the Lateran Treaty with the papacy, establishing the Vatican State. His imperialist ambitions were realized in the invasion of Abyssinia (1935–36) and Albania (1939). In 1936 he formed an alliance with Hitler (the Rome–Berlin Axis), and he gave military aid to Franco in Spain. Entering World War II in 1940, Italy's armies suffered defeat after defeat. In July 1943 the Allies invaded Sicily and Mussolini was removed from power and imprisoned. The Germans intervened to set him up at the head of a puppet government in northern Italy. After the fall of Germany in April 1945 he was captured by Italian partisans and unceremoniously executed.

Nabokov, Vladimir (1899–1977) Russian-born US writer. Born into a wealthy, aristocratic St Petersburg family, Nabokov was a precocious child who read English before Russian or French. His family left Russia in 1919, and he studied at Cambridge. His first novels, all of them in Russian, were written in the 1930s. He moved to the US in 1940, earning distinction as a lepidopterist. His later novels, written in English, earned him praise for their linguistic ingenuity and intellectual brilliance, but it was the controversial success of *Lolita* (1953), the story of a man's erotic love for a young girl, that brought him public fame.

Namatjira, Albert (1902–59) Australian Aboriginal painter. A member of the Aranda tribe, Namatjira was born on a mission station near Alice

Springs. His artistic ability was spotted at an early age and in 1938, 41 of his watercolor landscape paintings were exhibited in Melbourne. Further exhibitions in the 1940s led to an enormous demand for his work, but Namatjira's artistic acclaim brought with it huge problems. As an Aboriginal, he did not possess Australian citizenship and his freedom was hedged around with restrictions. A special grant of Australian citizenship was made to Namatjira in 1957, but the following year he was imprisoned for illegally supplying alcohol to members of his people. A few months after his release he died suddenly of a heart attack. The art world remains divided over the quality of his work, but he is remembered for his unique, powerful images of the deserts of central Australia.

Nasser, Gamal (1918–70) Egyptian president. An officer in the Egyptian army, Nasser helped to found the Free Officers' movement during the 1940s which aimed at the removal of British rule. He fought in the Arab–Israeli war (1948), and masterminded the coup that overthrew King Farouk in 1952. Becoming prime minister in 1954, he almost immediately assumed effective presidential power. In 1956 he was elected president of a single-party state. Nasser's ambitious projects included land reform, industrialization and the construction of the Aswan High Dam on the Nile. He pursued a policy of nonalignment and gained international prominence at the Bandung conference of Afro-Asian states in 1955. In the same year, he became effective leader of the Arab League. After Britain and the US canceled aid for the Aswan Dam in 1956, Nasser expropriated the Suez Canal. Israel invaded the Sinai peninsula with Anglo-French support, and Nasser emerged from the ensuing international crisis with enhanced claims to leadership of the Arab world. In 1958, Egypt and Syria formed the United Arab Republic. Despite its nonaligned status, the UAR became increasingly dependent on the Soviet Union for financial and military aid. Following major defeat in the Six-Day War with Israel (1967) Nasser offered to resign but won a vote of confidence from the National Assembly. He had agreed to start peace negotiations with Israel shortly before his death.

Navratilova, Martina (1956–) Czech-born US tennis-player. A left-handed player of extraordinary physical power and skill, particularly in the serve-and-volley game, Navratilova was three-times winner of the Czechoslovak national singles title (1972–74) before defecting to the US (1975). She quickly

Paul Newman, one of Hollywood's most durable and popular actors.

impressed the western public, reaching the semi-finals of the women's singles at Wimbledon in 1976. She dominated women's tennis for nearly 20 years, winning the Wimbledon title a record nine times, as well as 54 other Grand Slam events. Her aggressive style and determination to win, combined with her strength and athleticism, marked her as one of the most formidable players of all time. She retired from competitive tennis in 1994.

Nehru, Jawaharlal (1889–1964) Indian political leader. Born into a Westernized high-caste Brahmin family, Nehru was educated in England and trained as a lawyer before returning to India in 1912. In 1919 he joined the nationalist Congress party and spent more than nine of the next 21 years in jail. In 1929, Nehru was elected president of Congress and played a major role in switching the party's demand from one for limited home rule to seeking India's total independence from Britain. He refused to support the Allies in World War II unless India was free, and in 1942 rejected the British offer of dominion status. In 1947 he agreed to the partition of the Indian subcontinent to create an independent Muslim state, Pakistan, and became independent India's first prime minister (1947–64). His policies combined a desire for a modern, secular, democratic socialist state with an assertion of Indian nationalism, exemplified by his determination to keep Kashmir within India, his forcible expulsion of the Portuguese from Goa in 1961, and his border dispute with China in 1962. He kept India in the British Commonwealth but adopted a neutralist role, making India into a major Asian power, and often acted as go-between in other nations' disputes.

Newman, Paul (1925–) US film actor, director and producer. A graduate of the Actors' Studio, Newman made several Broadway appearances in 1953–4, and won particular acclaim in *Picnic*. Hollywood snapped him up and he became a leading actor of his generation, noted for his intelligent performances, good looks and intense blue eyes. His best films include *The Hustler* (1961), *Hud* (1963), *Cool Hand Luke* (1967), *Butch Cassidy and the Sundance Kid* (1969), *The Sting* (1973) and *The Verdict* (1982). He interested himself in liberal causes and was a successful automobile racer. He was nominated seven times for an Academy Award before winning an Oscar for his performance in *The Color of Money* (1986).

Nicholas II (1868–1918) Russian tsar. Succeeding to the Russian throne in 1894, Nicholas was an autocratic and repressive ruler. He was forced in 1905 to create a parliament, or Duma, to meet revolutionary demands for constitutional monarchy, but it was limited to an ineffectual consultative role. On the outbreak of World War I, which Nicholas had tried his utmost to prevent, he appointed himself commander-in-chief of the Russian army. During his absence at the Front the country was effectively and disastrously ruled by the Tsarina Alexandra under the influence of her religious advisor Rasputin. Nicholas was forced to abdicate after the revolution of February 1917, and after the October Revolution of the same year he and his entire family were imprisoned in Yekaterinburg. They were murdered and their bodies disposed of by Red Guards in 1918.

Nicholson, Jack (1937–) US film actor. Before winning notice in *Easy Rider* (1969) Nicholson had starred in a string of undistinguished B-movies, writing and co-producing as well. Thereafter most of his films were highly successful and he excelled in sardonically humorous outsider roles. Credits include *Five Easy Pieces* (1970), *The Last Detail* (1973), *Chinatown* (1974), *One Flew Over the Cuckoo's Nest* (1975), *Terms of Endearment* (1983) and *The Witches of Eastwick* (1987). In 1994 Nicholson became the youngest recipient of the American Film Institute's Lifetime Achievement Awards.

Nicklaus, Jack (1940–) US golfer. A powerful, astute and apparently nerveless player, Nicklaus dominated world professional golf in the 1960s and 1970s, winning the Masters championship six times (1963, 1965, 1966, 1972, 1975 and 1986), the US Open four times (1962, 1967, 1972 and 1980), the PGA championship five times (1963, 1971, 1973, 1975 and 1980) and the British Open three times (1966, 1970 and 1978).

The ballet star Rudolf Nureyev rehearses with Natalia Makarova.

Nijinsky, Vaslav (1889–1950)
Russian dancer and choreographer. Nijinsky entered the Imperial Ballet in St Petersburg at the age of 17 and later joined the Ballet Russe, the company founded by the impresario Sergei Diaghilev (who became his lover) on its epoch-making visit to Paris in 1909. In 1911 he became *premier danseur* with the company, now permanently resident in Monte Carlo, astounding audiences with his agility, technical skills and expressive qualities. He danced the lead role in the first performance of Stravinsky's *Petrushka* and in *Le Spectre de la Rose,* both choreographed by Michel Fokine, but showed innovative choreographic power of his own in *L'Après-midi d'un faune*, *Jeux*, and *Le Sacre du printemps,* which caused a riot on its first performance in 1913. His career ended in 1919, after the onset of schizophrenia.

Nixon, Richard (1913–94)
US president. A Republican from California, Nixon entered the House of Representatives (1946–49) and became well-known for his aggressive line of questioning on the Un-American Activities Committee. He was elected to the Senate in 1950, and served as Eisenhower's vice-president (1953–60). He lost to John F. Kennedy in the 1960 presidential elections, but in 1968 made a successful comeback to defeat the Democratic candidate, Hubert Humphrey. Despite ordering the secret bombing of Cambodia in 1969–70, his foreign policy was committed to the gradual reduction of US military involvement in Vietnam. He reestablished relations with China, which he visited in 1972, and agreed the SALT I arms limitation treaty with the Soviet Union. He was reelected to a a second term in 1972 and by 1973 had withdrawn all US troops from Vietnam. His political career came to an end with the Watergate affair of 1973–4. Transcripts of conversations

between Nixon and his staff, made public by order of the Supreme Court, revealed that Nixon had tried to cover up a break-in to Democratic headquarters carried out by several of his close aides. Threatened with impeachment by Congress, he resigned in 1974, the first president ever to do so, and was succeeded by Gerald Ford, who granted him a full pardon.

Nolan, Sidney (1917–92) Australian painter. Nolan studied art in Melbourne and began to paint full-time in 1938. At first an Abstract painter, his work gradually become more representational, while retaining a haunting, atmospheric, abstract character. He made bold use of color, taking his themes from Australian myth and history. Two series of paintings based on the life of the outlaw Ned Kelly (1946–47; 1954–57) brought international fame. He traveled widely, and in 1953 settled in Europe. Later work included set designs for Covent Garden and the Sydney Opera House.

Norman, Greg (1955–) Australian golfer. A flamboyant character, renowned for his colorful taste in golfing hats, Norman became known as "The Great White Shark" after scoring a string of golfing successes beginning in 1976 with the Westlakes Classic. He won the Open titles in Hong Kong, France, Scandinavia, Canada and Australia (three times: 1980, 1985, 1987) and the UK (1986 and 1993).

Nuffield, 1st Viscount (William Morris), (1877–1963) British motor industrialist. The son of a farm laborer, Morris started work in a cycle repair shop in Oxford and set up his own business in 1904 to build bicycles and motorbikes. His first car was produced in 1912 and he went on to dominate the British car manufacturing industry. Much of his fortune was donated to charitable causes. He endowed Nuffield College, Oxford (1937) and in 1943 established the Nuffield Foundation for the encouragement of medical, scientific and social research.

Nureyev, Rudolf (1938–93) Russian-born ballet dancer. A soloist with the Leningrad-based Kirov ballet from 1958, Nureyev made world headlines when he defected to the West while on tour in Paris (1961). The next year he formed a legendary partnership with ballerina Margot Fonteyn at London's Royal Ballet. A dancer of enormous virtuosity and expression, Nureyev was matchless in classics such as *Giselle, Swan Lake* and *Les Sylpides* and also excelled in modern ballets and in modern dance, appearing in

Laurence Olivier starring in The Betsy (1977), one of his last screen roles.

works by every contemporary choreographer of note. From 1983–89 he was director of the Paris Opera Ballet, and in 1992 directed *La Bayardère* only months before his death.

Nyerere, Julius (1922–) Tanzanian politician. Nyerere qualified as a teacher and later studied economics at Edinburgh University. On his return to what was then Tanganyika he played a leading role in nationalist politics and became his country's first president on independence (1962). In 1964 he negotiated the union of Tanganyika with the island of Zanzibar to form the state of Tanzania. A deeply principled politician, Nyerere pursued a form of "self-reliant socialism" based on rural values. Every aspect of the economy was nationalized and cooperative *ujamaa* villages set up. Health care and literacy improved dramatically, but Tanzania's economy crashed in the 1970s. Nevertheless, Nyerere, who resigned in 1985, remained a much respected figure in African politics.

O'Keeffe, Georgia (1887–1986) US painter. In 1917 O'Keeffe, an early pioneer of Abstract painting, joined the photographer and art dealer Alfred Stieglitz's 291 Gallery group in New York. Stieglitz organized her first solo show in New York (1923) and they married in 1924. Her close-up flower paintings such as *Black Iris* (1926), which mimic sexual imagery, and architectural paintings such as *Ranchos Church Front* (1929) are figurative and precisionist in style. From 1929 she spent much time in New Mexico, settling there in 1946. In the 1940s she returned to Abstraction in works such as *Pelvis Series; Red with Yellow* (1945). Among her later works was a series of aerial views of the earth.

Olivetti, Adriano (1901–60) Italian industrialist. Trained as an industrial chemist, in 1938 Olivetti took over his father's small typewriter factory and turned it into one of the world's largest producers of office machinery. An ardent anticommunist, he nevertheless pursued a "Christian Socialist" industrial policy, providing employee benefits and allowing for a degree of worker participation in management.

Olivier, Laurence (1909–89)
British stage and screen actor. Olivier first attracted attention in a series of Shakespearean roles in London in the 1930s. His good looks took him to Hollywood to play romantic leads in *Wuthering Heights* (1939) opposite his then wife, Vivien Leigh, and *Rebecca* (1940). In 1944 he became co-director of London's Old Vic Company, and produced, directed and played in film versions of *Henry V* (1944), *Hamlet* (1948), *Richard III* (1955) and *Othello* (1965). One of the finest actors of his day, his virtuosity was never better seen than in his portrayal of the seedy vaudeville artist Archie Rice in John Osborne's *The Entertainer* (1957). He was director of Britain's National Theater (1963–73) and latterly appeared mainly on TV and in films.

Onassis, Aristotle (1906–75)
Greek shipping magnate. As a young man Onassis went to Buenos Aires in 1923 to seek his fortune and within ten years of arriving in South America had become a dollar millionaire. In 1932 he used $120,000 of his capital to buy up six Canadian freighters left idle by the Depression. These were to form the basis of the vast merchant fleet he built up over the next 20 years. In the 1950s he began acquiring huge oil supertankers and bulk carriers and from 1957–74 he owned and operated the Greek national airline, Olympic Airways. Onassis developed a reputation as an international socialite famous for his lavish gatherings of celebrities on board his yacht *Christina.* His much publicized affair with the opera singer Maria Callas was followed by marriage in 1968 to Jacqueline Kennedy, the widow of the assassinated US president.

O'Neill, Eugene (1888–1953)
US playwright. Son of an actor-manager, O'Neill was a sailor, then a journalist before beginning to write in 1912. His first play, written for his company, the Provincetown Players, rejected drab naturalism for a drama of poetry and passion. He won the first of three Pulitzer Prizes in 1920. During the prolific period that followed he wrote *Anna Christie* (1921), *All God's Chillun Got Wings* (1924) and *Desire Under the Elms* (1924). In *Mourning Becomes Electra* (1931) O'Neill reworked a theme from classical Greek tragedy. In 1936 he became the first US

Jesse Owens in the long jump at the 1936 Olympic Games in Berlin.

playwright to win a Nobel prize, and afterwards went on to write what many consider to be his finest plays: *The Iceman Cometh* (1939) and *Long Day's Journey into Night* (1940–1).

Oppenheimer, J. Robert
(1904–67) US physicist. Oppenheimer studied at Harvard, Cambridge and Göttingen Universities before becoming assistant professor of physics at the California Institute of Technology (1929). From 1942–45 he worked on the Manhattan atom bomb project and set up the Los Alamos laboratory where the first atomic bombs were made (1945). Resigning from the project, he argued for joint atomic energy control with the Soviet Union. He was chairman of the advisory committee of the US Atomic Energy Commission (1946–52) but in 1953 was declared a security risk because of his supposed left-wing sympathies and suspended from further secret nuclear research. He was director and professor of physics at the Institute for Advanced Study, Princeton (1947–66).

Orwell, George (Eric Blair)
(1903–50) British writer. Orwell's experiences of serving with the colonial police in Burma (1922–27) produced a revulsion against imperialism and he resigned while on leave in England. He lived rough for a while, writing about his experiences in *Down and Out in Paris and London* (1933). His anger against imperialism formed the subject of his first novel, *Burmese Days* (1934), and several other novels followed, including *Keep the Aspidistra Flying* (1936) and *Coming Up for Air* (1939). Always on the side of the individual against the organization, Orwell's political views shaped all his writing, and he voiced his skeptism of accepted socialist attitudes in *The Road to Wigan Pier* (1937). He fought in the Spanish Civil War, described in *Homage to Catalonia* (1938). After

the war he expressed his distrust of ideology in the two political satires that are his best-known work: *Animal Farm* (1946) and *1984* (1948), a terrifying vision of a state ruled by thought control and "newspeak".

Owens, Jesse (1913–80) US athlete. Owens is best remembered for winning four gold medals in the 1936 Berlin Olympics – for the 100- and 200-meter sprints, the long jump and the US 400-meter relay – to the fury of Adolf Hitler, who walked out of the stadium rather than be forced to congratulate a black athlete. But Owens most remarkable feat was on 25 May 1935 in Michigan, when he equaled the world record for the 100 yards and broke those for the 220 yards (200 meters), the 220-yard (200-meter) low hurdles and the long jump. In 1976 Owens was belatedly honored by the US government with the Presidential Medal of Freedom.

Palmer, Arnold (1929–) US golfer. The leading figure in world golf from the late 1950s to the mid 1960s, Palmer became a professional in 1954. He was the first to win the US Masters four times (1958, 1960, 1962, 1964) and to win $100,000 in prize money in a single year. Other titles included the US Open (1960) and the British Open (1961–62).

Papandreou, Andreas (1919–96) Greek prime minister. The son of George Papandreou, a prominent left-wing politician, he studied law at Athens University and was arrested and tortured for helping to publish a radical journal. Papandreou then followed an academic career in the US but returned to Greece in the early 1960s, and became increasingly involved in politics during his father's premiership (1963–65). Both he and his father were imprisoned by Greece's ruling military junta in 1967, and then allowed to leave the country. Returning to Greece after the junta's collapse (1974), he became head of the chief opposition party, the Panhellenic Socialist Movement (PASOK) and in 1981 was elected premier. Rumors of corruption and sexual scandal helped to bring about his electoral defeat in 1989 but he was reelected in October 1993. Serious illness forced him to resign shortly before his death in 1996.

Parker, Charlie ("Bird") (1920–55) US alto-saxophonist and composer. Born in Kansas City, Parker moved to New York in 1939, playing with some of the big bands while working out the musical ideas behind bebop. He formed an excellent five-piece in 1947, but after 1950 played gigs with pick-up groups or toured with band-

The Italian tenor Luciano Pavarotti relaxes after a performance.

leaders like Woody Herman and Stan Kenton. Parker's daring harmonic structures, explorations of rhythm and unique tone were a major influence on modern jazz but he died from heroin and alcohol addiction at the age of 34.

Parker, Dorothy (1893–1967) US writer, journalist and wit. Born in New Jersey, she started in journalism as a caption writer on *Vogue*, followed by a spell as drama critic of *Vanity Fair* (1917–20). With fellow writers Robert Benchley and James Thurber she established literary New York's legendary Algonquin luncheon club in the 1920s, which she made famous with her acerbic wit and quick one-liners: "Men never make passes at girls who wear glasses". From 1927 she wrote for *The New Yorker,* contributing book reviews, short stories and short, bitter poems of love and death. She also collaborated on several screenplays. Her personal life was unhappy: she was married three times, twice to the same man, and suffered a string of painful love affairs and suicide attempts. She left her estate to Martin Luther King.

Pasternak, Boris (1890–1960) Russian poet and novelist. Pasternak, born into a cultured Moscow family, worked in a factory during World War I and later in the ministry of employment. A lyric poet, he was associated with the Modernist poets Sergei Yesenin and Vladimir Mayakovsky. Several collections of verse and short stories were published in the 1920s, but Pasternak's work was officially criticized under Stalinism and for many years he found work translating Shakespeare and other classic Western writers into Russian. His literary masterpiece, *Dr Zhivago*, was published in the West in 1958. Its powerful account of an individual's struggle for integrity through the turmoil of war and revolution made it an instant bestseller, but it was banned in the Soviet Union and Pasternak was forced to decline the 1958 Nobel prize for literature.

Paul VI (Giovanni Battista Montini) (1897–1978) Italian pope. Ordained in 1920, Montini served in the Vatican diplomatic service until 1954. He was then appointed archbishop of Milan, where he became well-known for his liberal views. He was made a cardinal by Pope John XXIII in 1958. Elected pope in 1963, he continued the modernizing work of the Second Vatican Council but upheld the church's teaching on papal infallibility, priestly celibacy and contraception. He traveled more extensively than any pope before him.

Pauling, Linus (1901–) US chemist. One of the few people to have won two Nobel prizes, Pauling was awarded the first for work on chemical bonding and molecular structure (1954). A fierce critic of the nuclear deterrent, the second was given for his services to world peace (1962). He later opposed the Vietnam war and, always a controversial figure, championed Vitamin C as the means of combatting a wide range of non-nutritional disorders.

Pavarotti, Luciano (1935–) Italian tenor. Pavarotti had a musical upbringing and wanted to sing professionally, but became a teacher on the advice of his family. He later returned to his musical studies and in 1961 won an international singing competition, making his professional début in *La Bohème* the same year. He performed with La Scala's touring company (1963–64) and in 1965 toured Australia with Joan Sutherland. His New York début at the Metropolitan Opera House came in 1968. A superb bel canto singer, Pavarotti's voice was pure and simple even in the highest registers. He became widely popular throughout Europe and North America; his recordings sold massively, and his concert performances were always sold out. In the 1990s he enjoyed enormous worldwide fame, and commanded enormous fees, through a series of highly publicized outdoor concerts, in particular with Placido Domingo and José Carreras as the "Three Tenors".

Pavlov, Ivan Petrovich (1849–1936) Russian physiologist. Working at the St Petersburg Institute for Experimental Medicine, Pavlov conducted a long series of experiments into the physiology of the digestive system, winning a Nobel prize in 1904. But he is best known for the discovery of the conditioned reflex. He found that when dogs learnt to associate food with the ringing of a bell they began to salivate at the sound, even when food was absent. His finding helped inspire the development of behaviorist psychology.

Brazilian soccer star Pelé led his national team to three World Cup victories.

Pearson, Lester (1897–1972) Canadian diplomat and politician. After service in World War I, Pearson lectured in history at the University of Toronto before embarking on a successful diplomatic career in 1928. He played a leading role in establishing the United Nations in 1946 and subsequently served on many international commissions. His search for a diplomatic solution to the Suez crisis (1956) won him the Nobel peace prize the following year. He became leader of the Liberal party in 1958 and was Canadian prime minister (1963–68). Though a popular figure with the Canadian public, his premiership was troubled by the rising strength of the Quebec separatist movement and he resigned from politics in 1968.

Pelé (Edson Arantes do Nascimento) (1940–) Brazilian soccer player. The most celebrated player in the history of the game, Pelé made his international début at the age of 16. He led the Brazilian team to World Cup championship victories on three occasions (1958, 1962 and 1970) and during his career scored an astounding 1,220 goals. It was his brilliant ball control that won him admirers everywhere he played. After retiring from the Brazilian game in 1974 he signed a multidollar contract with New York Cosmos (1975–77), popularizing the sport in the US. Later he pursued a career as a sports commentator.

Peres, Shimon (1923–) Israeli politician. Peres' family settled in Palestine from Poland in 1934 and he was raised on a kibbutz. As a young man he was active in the Labor party youth movement. He completed his education in the US and in 1948 was appointed head of the navy in the new Israeli state, the first of several defense posts he was to hold. Elected to the Knesset in 1959, he was minister of defense from 1974–77. Following Yitzhak Rabin's sudden resignation, he became chairman of the Labor party and leader of the opposition (1977–84). As the result of a power-sharing agreement with Yitzhak Shamir, head of Likud (the Consolidation Party), Peres served as prime minister from 1984–86, when Shamir took over. The coalition was renewed after the general election of 1988 with Peres as deputy, but in 1990 it collapsed over Peres' support for American proposals to set up an Israeli–Palestinian peace conference. In 1992 Peres was replaced by Yitzhak Rabin as leader of the Labor party and took over the position of foreign minister. He resumed the leadership on Rabin's assassination in November 1995 but was defeated by Benjamin Netanyahu in national elections the following year.

Perez de Cuellar, Javier (1920–) Peruvian UN secretary general. De Cuellar embarked on a career in the Peruvian diplomatic service in 1944. He served as ambassador to Switzerland, the Soviet Union, Poland and Venezuela and as Peru's permanent representative to the UN from 1971–75 and 1979–81, when he headed peacemaking missions to Afghanistan and Pakistan. Elected UN secretary general in 1981, he acted as intermediary in the 1982 Anglo–Argentinian war and was a key figure in the Iran–Iraq peace talks of 1988. He attempted unsuccessfully to avert war between the UN allies and Iraq in 1991 and stood down as secretary general in 1992.

Perón, Juan (1895–1974) Argentinian politician. Perón helped organize a right-wing military coup in 1943 and became secretary for labor and social welfare, building up a popularist following among the working class which helped bring about his election as president in 1946. Perón was a firm advocate of economic independence, especially from the US and the UK. He accelerated the pace of industrialization, increased public spending, nationalized utilities and increased welfare payments. At first successful, he was reelected in 1951 thanks in part to the huge popularity of his wife Eva. But his policies ceased to work and amid soaring inflation Perón's style of government became increasingly authoritarian: political opponents were exiled or murdered, freedom of speech suppressed and civil liberties curtailed. Perón was deposed in a military revolt in 1955 and fled to Spain. The Perónist party remained an active force in Argentinian politics and won the national elections in 1973. Perón returned in triumph to Argentina to take office as president but died nine months later.

Pétain, Henri Philippe (1856–1951) French soldier and politician. A professional soldier, Pétain became a French national hero in

The most influential painter of the 20th century, Pablo Picasso in 1955.

1916 after his successful defense of Verdun. Promoted to marshal of France in 1918, his belief in the Maginot line was held as one of the reasons for France's military failure in 1940. In the aftermath of defeat he succeeded as head of state at the age of 84 and immediately sought terms from the Germans. He headed the collaborationist Vichy government (1940–44) and in 1945 was tried and convicted of treason, his death sentence being commuted to life imprisonment.

Piaf, Edith (1915–63) French singer. Abandoned by her mother at birth, Piaf started life as a child street singer and became a popular cabaret and music-hall performer in Paris. She was the intellectuals' darling, starring in Cocteau's film *Le Bel Indifférent* (1941). A tiny woman, with a powerful, strident voice, she packed an emotional punch fueled by her audience's knowledge of her tragic life. Her best known songs were "Je ne regrette rien" and "La vie en rose". She died prematurely after a life blighted by unhappiness and severe illness. Her funeral was attended by thousands of Parisians.

Picasso, Pablo (1881–1973) Spanish painter. The son of an art teacher, Picasso studied and worked in Barcelona and Madrid before moving to Paris in 1901 where he became part of a circle of writers and artists. His romantic, melancholy "Blue Period" (1901–04) was followed by the lighter, poignant "Rose Period" (1904–06). *Les Demoiselles d'Avignon* (1907) was a startling, iconoclastic piece, influenced by primitive art. From 1909–14 Picasso collaborated with Georges Braque, exploring Cubism in a series of pieces in which collage, wire, newspaper and string were used alongside paint. From 1917–24 he worked on designs for the Diaghilev ballets and moved into his "neoclassical period". By 1925 he had developed a relationship with the Surrealists, which manifested itself in his use of distorted bodies, as in *Three Dancers* (1925). A supporter of the Spanish Republic, from 1936–39 he was director of the Prado in Madrid. *Guernica* (1937), which many consider to be his masterpiece, was painted in protest against the bombing of a Basque village in the Civil War. Moving to Antibes in the south of France in 1946, he began to paint murals and ceramics. He became active in peace congresses and was, for a time, a rather unconvincing Communist. Without doubt the most influential figure in modern art, he worked in many different media and styles and produced an enormous body of very varied work.

Piccard, Auguste (1884–1962) Swiss physicist. In 1931, Piccard – a professor of physics – decided to make direct observations of the upper atmosphere from a manned hydrogen balloon and in 1932 achieved a record height of 16,940 meters (55,563 feet) in a pressurized cabin. Piccard then explored the ocean depths, and in 1953 descended 3,150 meters (10,330 feet) in a self-propelled bathyscaphe.

Pickford, Mary (1893–1979) US film actress. One of the most popular (and richest) stars during the silent movie era, Pickford had a radiant child-woman appeal, enhanced by her golden ringlets and unaffected style. She began her screen career in 1909, at the age of 16, with 11 years of stage acting already behind her. Dubbed "America's Sweetheart", she played little girls (and sometimes little boys) in movies like *Rebecca of Sunnybrook Farm*, *Poor Little Rich Girl*, *Daddy Longlegs*, *Pollyanna* and *Little Lord Fauntleroy*. Her fans insisted she kept to these roles and she was 28 before she was able to cut off her curls. In 1919 she founded United Artists with Charlie Chaplin, Douglas Fairbanks and D.W. Griffith, and in 1920 she married Fairbanks, to the public's delight. She retired in 1933.

Player, Gary (1935–) South African golfer. Player was small and slightly built and based his success on fitness, diet and technique rather than power and swing. One of the game's most durable players, he won the British Open three times (1958, 1968, 1974), the US Open once (1965), the US PGA title twice (1962, 1972), the US Masters twice (1961, 1974), the South African Open eight times, and the Australian Open six times.

Poitier, Sidney (1924–) US actor and director. Hollywood's "token" black star for almost two decades, Poitier was a charismatic personality

Cole Porter's witty and sophisticated lyrics still give pleasure today.

with an impressive acting talent. His first movie success came in *Cry, the Beloved Country* (1952) and major film credits include *The Blackboard Jungle* (1955), *The Defiant Ones* (1958), *Lilies of the Field* (1963), for which he won an Academy Award, *To Sir With Love*, *In The Heat of the Night* and *Guess Who's Coming to Dinner?* (all 1967). As a director Poitier's most notable movie was *Stir Crazy* (1980).

Pollock, Jackson (1912–56) US painter. Pollock became interested in the work of Carl Jung while working in New York in the 1940s. He admired primitive art and Picasso, and began to use mythic symbols in his paintings. But this did not provide the access he sought to the Jungian "unconscious", so in 1947 he began to work by splashing paint straight from the can onto canvas pinned to the floor, in a trance-like state in which his whole body was involved. The method became known as "Action Painting" and was attacked as well as imitated. But Pollock produced fine work such as *Full Fathom Five* (1947), and later masterpieces like *Ocean Greyness* (1953), which incorporated broad, accurate brushwork. A towering figure in the Abstract Expressionist movement, he was killed in a car crash at the age of 44.

Pol Pot (Saloth Sar) (1925–96) Cambodian political leader. A member of the resistance movement against French colonial rule, Pol Pot joined the underground Communist party in 1946. From 1963 he was the leading force behind the pro-Chinese communist Khmer Rouge guerrillas opposed to the governments of Prince Sihanouk and the US-sponsored Lon Nol, and took control of the country after Lon Nol's overthrow in 1975. Dedicated to the removal of all foreign influence from Cambodia (which he renamed Kampuchea) and the recreation in modern socialist guise of its past glories, with great brutality he instituted a highly collectivized agrarian regime, emptying cities, purging intellectuals, uprooting villagers and setting up huge work camps. Between one and three million people died from neglect and brutality in the notorious "killing fields". Ousted in 1979 by a Vietnamese invading force, he carried on guerrilla resistance from the Thai-Cambodian border. The government refused to negotiate while Pol Pot remained at the head of the Khmer Rouge, and in 1985 he was officially removed from leadership though continuing to exert political influence until his death.

Pompidou, Georges (1911–74) French president. As the aide of President de Gaulle, Pompidou helped draw up the constitution of the Fifth Republic in 1958–59, and to make plans for economic recovery. He was made a member of the Constitutional Council when de Gaulle became president in 1959, while continuing his outside banking activities. He was prime minister from 1962–68, but resigned after helping end the student–worker revolt. Elected president on de Gaulle's resignation in 1969, he strengthened the economy, maintained good relations with Arab nations, kept the French military independent of NATO, and reversed de Gaulle's veto on UK entry into the EC.

Porsche, Ferdinand (1875–1951) German automobile designer. In 1931 Porsche resigned from the Daimler Company in Stuttgart to establish his own automobile company. In 1934 he produced a design for Hitler's project, the Volkswagen ("People's Car"). This mass-produced car broke records on the postwar export market. After the war he developed and introduced the famous Porsche sports car with his son Ferdinand who carried on the company after his death.

Porter, Cole (1892–1964) US composer and lyricist. After studying at Yale University, where he composed 300 songs, Porter put on his first Broadway musical, *See America First,* in 1916. Thereafter military service and a playboy lifestyle across Europe kept him busy for a time, but after the musical comedy *Fifty Million Frenchmen* (1929) he became a major force on Broadway. Remembered for his witty, civilized songs and lyrics, his show credits include *The Gay Divorcee* (1932), *Kiss Me Kate* (1948), *Can-Can* (1953) and *Silk Stockings* (1955). He scored the movie *High Society* (1956).

Pound, Ezra (1885–1972) US poet. Pound was professor of Romance Languages in Indiana before leaving for Venice (1908). Here his first volume

The most famous GI in history. Elvis Presley in US Army uniform.

of poetry, *A Lume Spento*, was published. He met the poet W. B. Yeats and joined the Imagist movement, writing the first Imagist manifesto in 1914. He lived in Paris from 1921–24, where he wrote for *The Dial*, and then moved to Italy where he spent the next 20 years, working on his poem-sequence *The Cantos* (begun in 1915). During the war Pound made pro-Fascist broadcasts and in 1945 was arrested and imprisoned in Pisa. Here he wrote the very fine *Pisan Cantos*. Returning to the US he spent the next 12 years in a hospital for the insane but continued writing and translating. He was released in 1958 and returned to Italy in time for the publication of *Thrones* (1959), the final volume of *The Cantos*. After 1961 he fell virtually silent, producing only fragments. He had an immense influence on 20th-century literature.

Presley, Elvis (1935–77) US singer and actor. The son of a poor farmworker in Tupelo, Mississippi, Presley cut his first record as a present for his mother at the age of 18. Three years later, in 1956, he was the biggest rock 'n roll star in the world, selling 10 million records in a single year. His potent fusion of sex and music alarmed Middle America and he was attacked as a symbol of teenage rebellion. In 1958 he joined the US Army, after which he made a series of custom-built, more or less third-rate beach movies. His popularity declined, but he had a successful cabaret and concert comeback in the early 1970s before obesity and drug addiction led to his premature death.

Prokofiev, Sergei (1891–1953) Russian composer. Prokofiev, a precociously gifted musician, studied at the St Petersburg Conservatory (1904–14) under Rimsky-Korsakov. He first played his own work in public in 1908, galvanizing audience and critics, who denounced him as an *enfant terrible*. His First Piano Concerto (1912) nevertheless won the 1914 Rubinstein Prize.

His *Classical Symphony* (1917) made him world famous and he moved to the US where he wrote *The Love for Three Oranges* (1919) for the Chicago Opera. He returned to Europe in 1922 and settled in Paris until returning to the Soviet Union in 1936. Here he composed some of his most popular works, including *Romeo and Juliet* (1935–36), *Peter and the Wolf* (1936) and the score for Eisenstein's film *Alexander Nevsky* (1938), but in 1948 he was censured for writing "anti-democratic" music. From then on the erstwhile iconoclast toed the party line, though producing further fine work.

Proust, Marcel (1871–1922) French novelist. An asthmatic from boyhood, Proust was very close to his mother. He studied law and philosophy, and absorbed most of the world's classic works in all art forms. Increasing ill-health led to his withdrawal from society and after the death of his mother in 1905 he lived alone in a soundproofed apartment. After publishing a few stories and poems, he wrote his seven-part masterwork, *A la Recherche du temps perdu*. The first volume was rejected by two publishers, so in 1913 Proust paid for its publication. It was quite successful, and in 1919 he received the Prix Goncourt for Volume Two. The rest were published between 1921 and 1927. It is a nostalgic, self-analytic, comic autobiography, exploring sexuality, jealousy, the pain of love, disillusionment and psychological rebirth. The style is complex, with long, reverberating sentences. It is one of the century's literary masterpieces.

Puccini, Giacomo (1858–1924) Italian opera composer. Born in Lucca, Puccini was an organist and choirmaster before obtaining a scholarship to the Milan Conservatory (1880–83). His first operatic success came with *La Bohème* (1896), soon followed by *Tosca* (1900) and *Madame Butterfly* (1904), which have all remained popular favorites. Many consider the one-act opera *Gianni Schicci* (1918) and *Turandot*, unfinished at his death, his finest pieces. The last great opera composer in the Italian tradition, Puccini was innovative in his harmonies and orchestral scoring. His dramatic sense and melodic writing were unsurpassed.

Pulitzer, Joseph (1847–1911) Hungarian-born US newspaper editor and publisher. Pulitzer began his career on a German-language newspaper in 1868. By a dynamic series of purchases and mergers, he acquired St Louis's *Post-Dispatch* (1878) and New York's *The World* (1883) and founded the *Evening World* (1884).

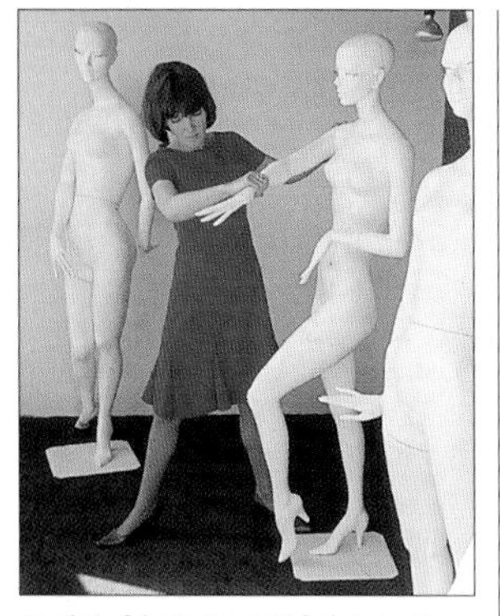

Symbol of the Sixties. British designer Mary Quant among the mannequins.

A crusading editor, he was sympathetic to labor interests and helped establish the Columbia school of journalism in New York. In his will he endowed the Pulitzer Prizes awarded for excellence in literature, music and journalism.

Qadhafi, Muammar (1942–) Libyan revolutionary and president. An army captain and leader of the Free Officers movement, Qadhafi led a military coup against King Idris in 1969 and proclaimed Libya a republic. In 1970 he closed down British and US military bases, deported ethnic Italians and Jews, and in 1973 nationalized foreign-owned sections of the oil industry. In 1977, as president, he installed a single-party system, blending his own interpretation of Islam with revolutionary socialism. He allied Libya with Egypt, and sought a pan-Arab federation of Libya, Egypt and Syria but later broke with Egypt over President Sadat's peace initiatives with Israel. Committed to the ending of colonial rule everywhere, Qadhafi allegedly supplied funds and weapons to liberation movements throughout the world, leading several countries to cease diplomatic relations. In 1986, after reports of Libyan involvement in several major European terrorist incidents, the US airforce bombed Qadhafi's headquarters in Tripoli. He was widely condemned for failing to hand over for trial those allegedly responsible for planting an explosive device aboard a Pan-Am airliner (1988).

Quant, Mary (1934–) British designer. The leader of the youth-oriented fashion movement of the 1960s, Quant studied fashion design at London's Goldsmiths' College and spent two years designing millinery before opening a boutique, Bazaar, in the King's Road, London (1955). By the mid 1960s her designs were being mass-produced and sold throughout Europe and the US. The miniskirt and hot pants were among her most famous creations.

Rabin, Yitzhak (1922–95) Israeli soldier and politician. Rabin served as a brigade commander in Israel's war of independence (1948) and quickly rose through the military hierarchy. Made chief of staff in 1964, he commanded Israel's armed forces during the Six Day War (1967). He served as ambassador to the US (1968–73), before succeeding Golda Meir as prime minister in 1974. Rabin demonstrated his tough stand on Arab terrorism by ordering the raid on Entebbe airport, Uganda, when Israeli and other hostages were rescued from a hijacked plane. Forced to resign in 1977 over a personal scandal involving dollar accounts he held in the US, Rabin was back in power again in 1992 as Labor prime minister, determined to bring about constructive peace talks to end Israel's long-standing conflict with its Arab population and neighbors. Despite fierce opposition within Israel, Rabin met and negotiated with PLO leader Yasir Arafat, signing a historic peace agreement on Israeli withdrawal from Jericho and the Gaza strip (1993), for which he shared the 1994 Nobel peace prize with Shimon Peres and Arafat. Despite mounting right-wing hostility, Rabin continued to work for peace, but was assassinated by a Jewish extremist after addressing a peace rally in Tel Aviv in November 1995.

Rachmaninov, Sergei (1873–1943) Russian composer and pianist. After study in St Petersburg and Moscow, Rachmaninov launched himself into a dazzling career as a conductor and virtuoso performer, playing many of his own compositions, particularly the Prelude in C Sharp Minor. He left Russia after the 1917 Revolution and settled in the US. The last great exponent of romanticism, much of his music has entered the classical repertoire. He is best remembered for his piano music, particularly the four piano concertos. His last major pieces were the *Rhapsody on a Theme of Paganini* (1934) and Symphony No 3 in A Minor (1936).

Ravel, Maurice (1875–1937) French composer. Ravel attended the Paris Conservatoire from 1899–1905. *Jeux d'Eau,* composed in 1901, antedated the innovative work of Debussy, who is often cited as an influence. Ravel repudiated this (though admiring Debussy), claiming Fauré and Satie as influences. *Shéhérazade* (1903), an oriental song-cycle, shows Ravel's characteristic clarity and precision. He composed prolifically until 1914, and in 1920 declined the Légion d'Honneur (resentful that he had never been awarded the Prix de Rome for which he competed on a number of

Ronald Reagan, one of the most popular presidents in US history.

occasions). In 1925 he produced the powerful opera, *L'Enfant et les Sortilèges*. His only popular success was *Boléro* (1928) which in many ways epitomized, almost parodied, his incisive musical style. He suffered a progressive nervous disease from 1932 and ceased composing during the last five years of his life.

Reagan, Ronald (1911–) US president. Reagan entered politics after a long, not particularly distinguished career as a screen actor. As Republican governor of California (1967–75), he increased taxes and cut state government spending. He ran a successful campaign for US president in 1980, standing on the platform of traditional American values and military strength. During two terms as president (1981–88) he raised military spending at the expense of nonmilitary expenditure, and lowered taxes, doubling the national debt in five years, but his Cold War policies later turned to détente, and his most notable achievement was the signing of the INF Treaty to dismantle nuclear weapons with the Soviet Union (1988). He survived an assassination attempt in 1981. The last years of his administration were overshadowed by the Iran–Contra scandal. This alleged that arms had been sold to Iran to obtain the release of US hostages in the Lebanon, and that some of the profits had been diverted to the right-wing Contra forces in Nicaragua. Toward the end of his last term Reagan began to show signs of weakening mental powers. After his retirement in 1988 he publicly admitted to the onset of Alzheimer's Disease.

Redford, Robert (1937–) US film actor and director. Redford's strong-jawed, blond looks helped make him one of the most popular Hollywood stars of the 1970s. After making his debut on Broadway in 1959 he won the lead in *Barefoot in the Park* (1963). His major movie success came with *Butch Cassidy and the Sundance Kid*

(1969), in which he starred with Paul Newman, repeating their success with *The Sting* (1973). Later credits include *The Great Gatsby* (1973), *The Way We Were* (1973) and *All the President's Men* (1976).

Renault, Louis (1877–1944) French automobile manufacturer. Renault Frères, set up by Louis and his brother Marcel, was by 1901 the eighth largest automobile company in the world, and the most important in France. Success was based on the manufacture of a cheap, reliable car, though after 1905 taxicabs were the company's best-selling vehicles. Known for his technical and organizational innovations, Louis Renault's transmission system was adopted by many smaller firms. The company manufactured military equipment, including aviation engines, during World War I, and its growth continued in the interwar period. In 1944 Renault was jailed as a collaborator for making military equipment for the Germans. He died in prison, and his company was nationalized.

Rivera, Diego (1886–1957) Mexican painter. Rivera studied art in Mexico and Madrid and toured Europe before settling in Paris in 1911 where, under Picasso's influence, he adopted Cubism. Returning to Mexico in 1921, he embraced its folk art and became active in the revolutionary movement. In 1923 he began to execute enormous murals, painted in a realistic manner with a strong political and historical narrative content. In 1929 he became director of Mexico's Central School of Fine Arts. His international reputation grew, and in the 1930s he also painted murals in the US. One of them, *Man at the Crossroads*, constructed for the Rockefeller Center, was a critical disaster and was later destroyed. Nevertheless, it is through these monumental works that Rivera has left an enduring mark on 20th-century painting.

Robbins, Frederick (1916–) US virologist. Robbins graduated in science at the University of Missouri in 1936 and went on to study medicine at Harvard. He held various posts associated with infectious diseases and pediatrics and during World War II he served with the virus and rickettsial disease section of the US army. Returning to medical research, he succeeded with J. F. Enders and T. H. Weller in growing cultures of the mumps virus (1948) and used the same technique to grow cultures of the polio virus in 1949. Robbins also did important work on hepatitis, Q fever and typhus. In 1954 he shared a Nobel prize with Enders and Weller.

The singer and actor Paul Robeson was hugely popular in the 1930s.

Robeson, Paul (1898–1976)
US singer and actor. The son of a slave, Robeson turned down a football career to read law but became an actor when he was unable to find work. His first big success came in Eugene O'Neill's *Emperor Jones* (1924), but it was the movie version of *Show Boat* (1936), in which he sang "Ol' Man River", that brought him world fame. Other movie credits include *Sanders of the River* (1935) and *King Solomon's Mines* (1937), and he won praise for his Othello in London and on Broadway (1930 and 1943). Ostracized for his left-wing sympathies in the 1950s, he lived mostly in Europe, and was a frequent visitor to the Communist bloc.

Rockefeller, John D. (1839–1937)
US oil tycoon and philanthropist. As head of the Standard Oil Company, Rockefeller employed ruthless methods to secure a virtual monopoly over the oil refining business in the late 19th century. A hated symbol of capitalism, Rockefeller confounded his critics by giving away large amounts of his wealth. Among his many benefactions in the early years of the century were the University of Chicago and the Rockefeller Institute for Medical Research. His philanthropic activities were perpetuated by his son John D. Rockefeller Jr (1874–1960), who presided over the creation of New York's Rockefeller Center (1939).

Rodgers, Richard (1902–79)
US musical-comedy composer. Rodgers met his future collaborator, the lyricist Lorenz Hart, at college when they put on a varsity show together in 1920. Their first professional success was a revue, and they went on to write sophisticated musical comedies including *Babes in Arms* (1937), *The Boys from Syracuse* (1938) and *Pal Joey* (1940). After Hart's death, Rodgers worked with Oscar Hammerstein on eight musicals including *Oklahoma!* (1943), *Carousel* (1945), *South Pacific* (1949), *The King and I* (1951) and *The Sound of Music* (1959).

Rogers, Richard (1933–) British architect. Rogers studied architecture in London and at Yale University, where he won several scholarships and met British architect Norman Foster. He worked with Foster from 1963–67 and then went into practice with his wife. From 1971 he worked with Renzo Piano. They shared a conviction that technology must be used to solve social and ecological problems, and attracted wide notice when they won a competition to design the famous Pompidou Center in Paris (1971–79). Rogers also designed the Lloyd's Bank building in London (1979–85).

Rolls, Charles (1877–1910) and **Royce, Sir Henry** (1863–1933) British motor manufacturers. Rolls, a keen balloonist and aviator, was already involved in classic car racing when he became a motor dealer in 1902. In 1904 he met the industrialist Henry Royce, who was engaged in manufacturing luxury cars, and they merged their operations in 1906 as Rolls Royce Limited. Their famous Silver Ghost model was introduced that year, but Rolls' contribution was cut short when he was killed in a flying accident in 1910, not long after he had entered the record books as the first person to fly the Channel both ways nonstop. Royce continued to pioneer other great classic cars such as the Phantom, the Silver Dawn and Silver Cloud, and during World War I he began to develop airplane engines. In the next war Rolls Royce engines powered Spitfires and Hurricanes, and eventually this became the most profitable part of the business, though Rolls Royce cars have never lost their international status.

Rommel, Erwin (1891–1944) German field marshal. A career soldier who served in World War I with distinction, Rommel was a brilliant cavalry general, tactician and exponent of armored warfare who owed much of his success to his practice of leading "from the front". He took over the Afrika Korps in Libya (1941) and scored a number of audacious victories over numerically superior British forces, but was defeated at El Alamein (1943) and ordered back to Germany. Increasingly disenchanted with Hitler's conduct of the war, he gave tacit support to the attempt to assassinate him in July 1944. Faced with trial, execution and dishonor, he chose suicide.

Roosevelt, Franklin D. (1882–1945) US president. A cousin of Theodore Roosevelt (US president, 1905–09), he was born into a wealthy, patrician New York family and married

Helena Rubinstein, the cosmetician who said "Any woman can be beautiful".

his cousin Eleanor Roosevelt in 1905. In 1921, while serving as assistant secretary to the navy, he was stricken with polio and suffered long-term paralysis of the lower body. With utmost determination, and helped by his wife who became a well-known political figure in her own right, he fought his way back to be elected governor of New York state in 1928. In 1932 Roosevelt was elected to the first of four consecutive presidential terms – a unique achievement. His "New Deal" program of economic and social reform included a Social Security Act (1935) that introduced unemployment and old age insurance and helped alleviate the effects of the Depression. He upheld US isolationist policy at the beginning of World War II while giving aid to the Allies through such measures as Land-Lease. In 1941 he famously defined the Four Freedoms he saw as essential to world peace: freedom of speech and of worship, and freedom from want and fear. But after the Japanese attack on Pearl Harbor (7 December 1941) isolationist sentiment vanished overnight and Roosevelt and the US public were united in a common purpose. As a wartime leader Roosevelt, unlike Churchill or Stalin, made few important strategic decisions, but he offered inspiring and visionary leadership and worked closely with Churchill to construct the Allies' peace aims. In failing health, he attended the Allied Conference at Yalta (February 1945), only weeks before his death.

Roosevelt, Theodore (1858–1919) US president. Roosevelt became a national hero during the Spanish–American War (1898) as leader of a volunteer regiment, the Rough Riders, in Cuba. The same year he became governor of New York and in 1900 was elected US vice-president. On President McKinley's assassination (1901) he assumed the presidency. He described his domestic policies as providing a "square deal" for all groups in the nation. Internationally, he based his policies on the principle of "speak softly and carry a big stick", asserting the right of the US to intervene militarily in the western hemisphere (an extension of the Monroe doctrine). He helped Panama gain its independence from Colombia (1903) and initiated construction of the Panama Canal. In 1906 he received a Nobel peace prize for his part in ending the Russo–Japanese war (1905). He stood down in 1908, but regarded his successor William Taft as too conservative, and put himself forward as an independent candidate in 1912, thereby splitting the Republican vote and allowing the election of Woodrow Wilson. At the time of his death he was contemplating running again for president.

Rubinstein, Helena (1870–1965) Polish-born cosmetician. She left Poland in 1902 to visit Australia, where she opened a beauty salon, offering free consultation and a cream of her own devising which she had taken with her. An instant success, she then traveled to Europe, opening salons in London (1908) and Paris (1912). In 1914 she moved to the US and set up salons in New York and elsewhere. By 1945 her empire extended throughout the world. Constantly improving and developing new lines in cosmetics, she was the first to introduce medicated skin-care products and cosmetics for men. Her art collection, housed in her New York apartment, included works by Picasso, Matisse and Dalí, and she gave generously to charitable causes.

Rushdie, Salman (1947–) Indian-born British novelist. Belonging to a wealthy Muslim family, Rushdie was educated in Britain. His first novel *Grimus* (1975) was followed by *Midnight's Children* (1981), which won the prestigious British Booker Prize. A rich, picaresque work, it related through the story of one family the history of partition in the Indian subcontinent. *Shame* (1983) also won critical acclaim. *The Satanic Verses* (1988) seemed set to have the same sort of reception as before, but a passage in the book, in which a group of prostitutes play at being the wives of the prophet Muhammad, came to the attention of fundamentalist Muslims, who denounced it as blasphemous. Riots occurred in a number of Islamic countries and the Iranian leader Ayatollah Khomeini pronounced a *fatwa* or sentence of death on Rushdie, who went into hiding. He continued to write and publish, making occasional unannounced appearances at literary functions. But a huge campaign by eminent literary figures and politicians failed to get the *fatwa* lifted.

The philosopher Bertrand Russell was a well-known supporter of radical causes.

Russell, Bertrand, 3rd Earl (1872–1970) British philosopher. Russell was born into a famous political and aristocratic family. Most of his original contributions to mathematics and philosophy were made in the period before World War I, when he was teaching at Cambridge University. A unifying theme throughout his work was that the scientific perspective on the world is on the whole the true one, and he sought to simplify the basic claims of human knowledge; in *The Principles of Mathematics* (1903) and the monumental *Principia Mathematica* (with Alfred Whitehead, 1910–13) he linked mathematics to logic. His passionate espousal of pacifism in World War I led to his dismissal from his Cambridge lectureship and to a period of imprisonment. A visit to the Soviet Union tempered his early enthusiasm for Communism. He succeeded his brother as the 3rd Earl Russell in 1931 and was four times married. A prolific writer and essayist on controversial matters, his libertarian stance on sexual morality, education and war led to his dismissal from the teaching post he held in the US in 1940 on the grounds that he was "an enemy of religion and morality", but Russell's later years saw him acclaimed with honors: the renewal of his Cambridge fellowship in 1944, an Order of Merit in 1949 and a Nobel prize for literature in 1950. But he continued to champion radical causes, helping to form the Campaign for Nuclear Disarmament and taking part in protest marches and acts of civil disobedience into his nineties. His three-volume autobiography (1967–69) is an absorbing account of his long and colorful life.

Ruth, Babe (George Herman) (1895–1948) US baseball player. The holder of a record 60 home runs in a 154-game major-league season (1927), Ruth became a professional in 1914. He pitched 29 consecutive scoreless innings for the Boston Red Sox in the 1916 and 1918 World Series. Sold as an outfielder to the New York Yankees for $125,000 in 1920, he stayed there until 1934. In 1930–31 he was the game's top earner with a salary of $80,000. He led the American League in home runs for 12 years, hitting a total of 714 in 22 major-league seasons.

Rutherford, Ernest (1871–1937) New Zealand-born British physicist. A scholarship in 1895 brought Rutherford to Cambridge to work under J. J. Thomson, carrying out research on the conduction of electricity by gases. He was appointed professor of physics at McGill University, Montreal (1898), where his investigations into the phenomenon of radioactivity discovered by A. H. Becquerel in 1896 established that two kinds of radiation were involved, which he designated alpha and beta. He received a Nobel prize in 1908 but was chagrined, as a dedicated physicist, to discover that it was the prize for chemistry. He was professor at Manchester University (1907–19) and then returned to Cambridge to head the famous Cavendish Laboratory (1919–37), where he attracted a succession of brilliant research workers who laid the foundation of modern atomic physics. His supreme achievement was the concept of the nuclear atom, paving the way for later research.

Sadat, Anwar el- (1918–81) Egyptian president. During World War II Sadat cooperated with the Germans and was imprisoned twice by the British. A member of Nasser's Free Officers movement, he took part in the military coup that deposed Egypt's King Farouk in 1952. One of four vice-presidents to Nasser (1964–66) and sole vice-president (1969–70), he succeeded to the presidency on Nasser's death and began a process of social and economic liberalization, expelling many Soviet advisors in 1972. In October 1973 he ordered a attack on the Israeli-occupied Sinai Peninsula, precipitating the disastrous fourth Arab–Israeli (Yom Kippur) War. In the aftermath of defeat Sadat restored relations with the US, worked to attract Western aid and investment and began to adopt a more conciliatory attitude toward Israel. In 1977 he made history by visiting Israel to present a peace plan in the Knesset, and following the Camp David talks (1978), which laid down principles for a lasting agreement in the Middle East, he and Israeli leader Menachim Begin were awarded the Nobel peace prize. Sadat responded with increasing harshness to political opposition within Egypt, particularly from those who attacked the treaty for its concessions to Israel, and was assassinated by Muslim extremists in 1981.

Saddam Hussein, dictatorial president of Iraq since 1979.

Saddam Hussein (1937–) Iraqi president. Of peasant stock, Saddam became involved in Iraqi nationalist politics as a student, joining the socialist Ba'ath party in 1957. In 1962 he was involved in an attempt to kill the Iraqi prime minister General Qassim and fled to Egypt. He returned to Iraq in 1963 after Qassim's downfall, and reorganized the Ba'ath party, playing a major role in the bloodless coup of 1968 that brought the Ba'ath party to power. He subsequently served on the Revolutionary Command Council until 1979, when he became Iraq's president and prime minister. He initiated a long and ultimately futile war with Iran (1980–88), in which more than one million people were killed, ordered a poison gas massacre of over 5,000 Kurdish Iraqis (1988), and in 1990 invaded Kuwait on the pretext that Kuwait had been manipulating oil prices to Iraq's detriment and stealing Iraqi oil. The international outrage this act provoked led to the Gulf War (January 1991) in which a massive air offensive was launched against Iraq by a multinational force under joint US and Saudi Arabian command. Iraq's forces were routed after setting oil wells ablaze and leaving the Gulf polluted with a massive oil slick. Most Western commentators predicted Saddam's early overthrow, but he maintained a stranglehold on power within Iraq, ruthlessly suppressing opposition from the Kurdish population in the north and from Shia Muslims in the south. He eliminated all potential political opponents, even from within his own family, and is known to have ordered the murder of two sons-in-law in 1996.

Sakharov, Andrei (1921–89) Soviet physicist and dissident. Sakharov was the youngest person ever admitted to the Soviet Academy of Sciences (1953) in recognition of his work on the development of the Soviet hydrogen bomb. In the 1960s he began to speak out against nuclear weapons, demanding an end to the arms race and better relations with the West. He campaigned for improved democracy in the USSR, cofounding the Human Rights Committee (1970). He received the Nobel peace prize (1975) but his freedom was increasingly restricted and in 1980 he was exiled to the "closed city" of Gorky. He and his wife Yelena Bonner undertook a series of protest hunger strikes. Released in 1986 on the orders of Mikhail Gorbachev, he continued his work for human rights and was elected to a seat in the Congress of People's Deputies (1989).

Salk, Jonas (1914–) US virologist. Salk began the search for a polio vaccine in the late 1940s. The vaccine, administered by injection, was released for general use in 1955, bringing the first hopes of ending this devastating disease. Mass vaccination programs followed and Salk's name became a household word. In the early 1960s his vaccine was replaced by an oral vaccine developed by A.B. Sabin, given on a lump of sugar. In 1963 he became director of the Salk Institute for Biological Studies in San Diego.

Sanger, Margaret (1883–1966) Founder of US birth control movement. As a nurse on New York's Lower East Side, Sanger encountered the poverty, illness and death associated with multiple pregnancies and began a lifelong campaign to supply women with birth control information and methods. Harassed by the authorities under the Comstock Law of 1873 which forbade dissemination of information about contraception through the mail, she was prosecuted for publication of her magazine, *Woman Rebel* (1914), and for distributing a pamphlet, *Family Limitation*. In 1916 she opened the first US birth control clinic in Brooklyn, and was arrested and sentenced to thirty days imprisonment. She founded the American Birth Control League (1921), organized the first World Population Conference (1927), was the first president of the International Planned Parenthood Federation (1953), and worked for birth control in many other countries, especially India and Japan.

Sartre, Jean-Paul (1905–80) French novelist, philosopher and playwright. Sartre studied philosophy at the Sorbonne University in Paris, where he met the feminist writer Simone de Beauvoir, his lifelong partner, and taught there until 1945. His first major work *Nausea* (1938) is a diary-novel describing a neurotic repulsion from objects. *Being and Nothingness* (1943) developed his existentialist ideas further, presenting the nature of

Helmut Schmidt, Social Democratic chancellor of West Germany from 1974–82.

human existence as essentially absurd and hopeless: the only escape is to confront the emptiness within oneself and accept this as freedom to construct one's own reality. Sartre believed that freedom included concern for and engagement in society, and *The Roads to Freedom* trilogy (1945–49), is an ethical exposition of these ideas in novel form. His plays, like *The Flies* (1943) and *The Camera* (1944), dramatize the passionate hostility bred of human alienation. In 1948 he founded the review *Les Temps Modernes* with de Beauvoir. His uncompromising radical position became more entrenched in the early 1950s as he embraced a form of Maoist Communism, causing him to break with many friends, including the novelist Albert Camus. His autobiography, *The Words* (1963), won him the Nobel prize for literature, which he declined. By now the respected patriarch of Parisian intellectual life, though still an *enfant terrible*, the later years of his life were spent writing a biography of Flaubert, on which he worked until he went blind.

Schmidt, Helmut (1918–) West German chancellor. After World War II military service (in which he won the Iron Cross) Schmidt studied economics at Hamburg University and joined the Social Democratic party (1946). First elected to the Bundestag in 1953, he served in Willy Brandt's government as defense minister (1969–72), and as finance minister (1972–74), consolidating what came to be known as Germany's "economic miracle". He succeeded Brandt as chancellor in 1974 and proved himself an energetic international statesman, helping to defuse tension with the Communist bloc. He enjoyed good relations with the US, and was a strong advocate of European cooperation. Economic problems at home led to the collapse of the SDP's coalition with the Free Democrats, and Schmidt resigned the chancellorship in 1982. He retired altogether from politics in 1987.

Schoenberg, Arnold (1874–1951) Austrian composer. Largely self-taught, Schoenberg began composing in 1883. His music became increasingly explorative, and in 1908 his search for the means of expression led him to adopt atonality, thereby initiating a musical revolution. From 1910 he taught at the Vienna Academy where Alban Berg and Anton von Webern were among his pupils and life-long disciples. The remarkable *Pierrot Lunaire* (1912) brought a degree of popularity, and in 1923 he made his first venture into dodecaphony, or 12-tone composition, with *Piano Suite*. The rise of Nazism led him to reconvert to Judaism and he wrote *Moses und Aaron* (1930–32). In 1933 he left Europe for the US, becoming a naturalized citizen in 1941. His music poses huge problems of performance and Schoenberg himself felt he had not solved the problems of harmony and harmonic direction created by his entry into the atonal world, but it had enormous influence on his contemporaries.

Schrödinger, Erwin (1887–1961) Austrian physicist. His great achievement was the Schrödinger Equation (1926) in which he expressed mathematically the simultaneous identification of atoms as both waves and particles, postulated by L. de Broglie in 1924. From this arose quantum mechanics. In 1927 Schrödinger succeeded Max Planck as professor of physics at the University of Berlin but left for Oxford after Hitler assumed power in 1933. From 1939–56 he was attached to the Institute of Advanced Studies, Dublin, and on retirement became Emeritus professor in Vienna.

Scorsese, Martin (1942–) US film director. A highly regarded filmmaker, Scorsese's most successful movies emphasize character and tough, gritty dialog rather than dramatic plot. His first major film was *Mean Streets* (1973); the jumpy camerawork, reinforcing his disturbing images of urban life, in *Taxi Driver* (1976) and *Raging Bull* (1979) was typical of his work. His more "commercial" movies include *Alice Doesn't Live Here Anymore* (1974), *New York, New York* (1977), *Goodfellas* (1990), (1993) and *Casino* (1995).

Sennett, Mack (1880–1960) Canadian-born movie actor, director and producer. Initially a comic actor, Sennett cofounded the Keystone Studios in 1912 and produced hundreds of slapstick comedies. Best-remembered for his "Keystone Kops" movies, Sennett's uninhibited one-reel farces defied convention. Sustained by

Soviet foreign minister Eduard Shevardnadze, in London for talks in 1987.

the energy of their visual gags, they were improvised, then brilliantly edited. Sennett had an ability to spot comic talent and is credited with discovering Charlie Chaplin. Among his other stars were Mabel Normand, "Fatty" Arbuckle, Gloria Swanson, W.C. Fields and Chester Conklin. Sennett's fortunes never recovered after the arrival of sound and he retired in 1935.

Shankar, Ravi (1920–) Indian sitar player. Shankar's brother Uday, regarded as one of the foremost Indian dancers of the century, founded a troupe in the 1930s that fused ancient and modern styles and brought Indian dance to Western audiences. Ravi Shankar began his musical career at the age of 10 in Uday's company and trained to play the sitar, a long-necked instrument belonging to the lute family. Later he founded the National Orchestra of India and was music director of All-India Radio. In 1956 he went on a world tour, winning enthusiastic acclaim for his performances of traditional ragas. He enjoyed particular fame in the 1960s when Indian music was taken up by a number of pop artists, including George Harrison of the Beatles, to whom Shankar taught the sitar. Shankar also had a long musical association with the violinist Yehudi Menuhin.

Shaw, George Bernard (1856–1950) Irish playwright. Born of Irish Protestant parents in Dublin, Shaw left school at 15 to work as a clerk. His mother, a singing-teacher who inspired in Shaw a love and knowledge of music, moved to London in 1873. Shaw followed her there two years later and set about forging a literary career for himself. He found work reviewing art, books, music and theater. At the same time he became a socialist, and was a cofounder in 1884 of the Fabian Society. Shaw's first play, *Widowers' Houses* (1892), was heavily influenced by the Norwegian playwright Henrik Ibsen. It was followed by the comedy *Arms and the Man* (1894), *Candida* (1897) and *Mrs Warren's Profession* (published 1898). At first more famous in Europe than at home, success in London came between 1904 and 1907 when the Royal Court theater staged 11 of his plays, including *John Bull's Other Island* (1904), *Major Barbara* (1905) and *The Doctor's Dilemma* (1906). Shaw was a master of English prose; his didacticism is balanced by his freshness and wit, and the integrity of his socio-political commitment. Perhaps his best-known play is *Pygmalion* (1913), later made into a stage and film musical as *My Fair Lady*, but in the first three decades of the century he wrote a stream of plays with strong moral and social messages, including *Heartbreak House* (1919), *Back to Methuselah* (1921) and *St Joan* (1923). The last, a superbly moving drama, won him the 1925 Nobel prize for literature. Shaw was also a prolific and witty essayist, pamphleteer, letter writer and broadcaster. A strict vegetarian and teetotaler until his death at 94, he bequeathed his estate to the reform of English spelling.

Shevardnadze, Eduard (1928–) Soviet (later Georgian) politician. His father and brother were prominent in the Georgian Communist party, and by 1957 he was the first secretary of the Georgian Komsomol, the Communist Youth League, and in 1959 became a member of Georgia's supreme soviet. Rising in the ranks of the MVD (civilian police), in 1965 he took charge of the Georgian ministry of public order, later the ministry of internal affairs, and led a major drive against crime. In 1972 he became first secretary of the Georgian Communist party, where he became well-known for his fight against corruption. In 1985 Mikhail Gorbachev promoted him to succeed Gromyko as foreign minister. Shevardnadze helped pave the way for the 1985 summit between Presidents Reagan and Gorbachev and laid the groundwork for the nuclear disarmament agreements with the US, notably the 1988 decision to scrap intermediate range ballistic missiles and the START treaty to reduce intercontinental ballistic missiles by 1990. He resigned from the foreign ministry in 1990 after disagreements with Gorbachev over the Kuwait crisis and in 1992 became president of Georgia, a country in deep economic and political crisis after months of damaging internal unrest.

Shostakovich, Dmitri (1906–75) Russian composer. Shostakovich attended the Petrograd Conservatory (1919–25), producing his First

The popular singer Frank Sinatra was famously nicknamed "Ol' Blue Eyes".

Symphony at his graduation and winning acclaim as pianist and composer. In 1936 his opera *Lady Macbeth of the Mtsensk District* (1930–32) was criticized in *Pravda* as a warning against modernism. His Fifth Symphony (1937) proved more ideologically acceptable to the party and he was reestablished as the leading Soviet composer. His Seventh Symphony, *The Leningrad* (1941), symbolizing the fight against Hitler, was massively popular. The Ninth Symphony (1945), a breezy, serene celebration of the war's end, was not so well received and in 1948 Shostakovich's music was denounced as "anti-democratic". Attacked and disgraced, he was forced to conform and proceeded to compose accessible, non-formalistic music, at the same time continuing to write pieces like the First Violin Concerto which were released only after Stalin's death. The Thirteenth Symphony, *Babi Yar* (1962) was criticized for its use of lyrics by the dissident poet Yevgeny Yevtushenko. Shostakovich was unique in the survival and triumph of his genius under the dictatorial conditions of the Communist regime. In addition to his 15 symphonies, he also wrote some fine string quartets.

Sibelius, Jean (1865–1957) Finnish composer. Sibelius switched from studying law to music in 1886, first in Helsinki and later in Berlin and Vienna. His choral *Kullervo Symphony* (1892) established him as a composer of Finnish themes: like the well-known *Swan of Tuonela* (1893), it draws on the Finnish epic poem *Kalevala*. The short symphonic poem *Finlandia* (1899–1900) was so imbued with nationalist feeling that it was adopted as the unofficial national anthem of Finland, then struggling to achieve its independence from Russia. A state pension enabled Sibelius to devote his time to composition and he produced a series of works including *Pohjola's*

Daughter (1906) and *Tapiola* (1925), a bleak, visionary tone-poem which is one of his greatest works. He explored the limits of tonality in the Fourth Symphony (1911), but drew back from atonality; his Seventh Symphony (1924) is among the most structurally perfect of all symphonies. Sibelius fell silent after 1925, and an unfinished Eighth Symphony was destroyed before his death.

Sinatra, Frank (1915–) US vocalist and film actor. Born in Hoboken, New Jersey, Sinatra was discovered by bandleader Harry James singing in a roadside café in 1939. He made his first recording with James and then moved to Tommy Dorsey's band (1940–42) before going solo. A spot on radio's "Hit Parade" series in 1943 brought stardom, and he was besieged by teenage female fans, known as bobbysoxers, wherever he appeared. His crooning, casual style in songs such as "Try a Little Tenderness" and "Night and Day" depended on impeccable musical phrasing. He soon began to appear in movies such as *Anchors Aweigh* (1945) and *On the Town* (1949) and received an Academy Award for his first dramatic role in *From Here to Eternity* (1952). He found even better form as a singer in *Guys and Dolls* (1955) and *Pal Joey* (1957). His colorful private life attracted gossip throughout his career: two of his four wives were Ava Gardner and Mia Farrow. In the early 1960s he was part of a well-publicized Hollywood "brat pack" that included Dean Martin and Peter Lawson. After announcing his retirement from show business in the early 1970s he made several memorable live come-backs.

Singer, Isaac Bashevis (1904–) Polish-born US Yiddish writer. Son of a Hasidic rabbi, Singer settled in New York in 1935 and wrote for a Yiddish newspaper. His stories and novels were written in Yiddish, and English translations only began to appear in the 1950s. His stories and novels, based on Polish–Jewish tradition and grounded in an affectionate realism, are a blend of faith, magic and mysticism. They include *The Family Moskrat* (1950), the story of a Jewish family in Warsaw where Singer grew up, *Satan in Goray* (1955), *Gimpel the Fool and Other Stories* (1957), and *The Magician of Lublin* (1960). He was awarded the Nobel prize for literature in 1978.

Smith, Bessie (1895–1937) US jazz vocalist. Born in Chattanooga, Tennessee, she quickly won fame as a blues singer and in 1923 moved to New York to record "Down-hearted Blues"

Soviet exile Alexander Solzhenitsyn meets the world's press in Zurich in 1974.

with Columbia: it sold 2 million copies. In 1925 she starred in a hugely successful summer touring show, *Harlem Frolics*, followed by a second show, *Mississippi Days*, in 1928, but her career declined as the Depression led audiences to seek more escapist music. Songs such as "Nobody Knows You When You're Down and Out" gained poignancy as heavy drinking and a frenetic lifestyle took their toll of her voice. She died in an auto accident.

Smith, Ian (1919–95) Southern Rhodesian prime minister. Born in the British colony of Southern Rhodesia (now Zimbabwe), Smith served with the RAF in World War II. In 1961 he founded the Rhodesian Front, dedicated to winning immediate independence for Southern Rhodesia without Black majority rule. Success in the 1962 elections brought him a cabinet post and in 1964 he became prime minister. Negotiations with the British government broke down and in 1965 Smith made a Unilateral Declaration of Independence (UDI). All further discussions failed, and the UN applied economic sanctions against Southern Rhodesia. In 1970 Smith declared an "apartheid-style" republic, provoking a long civil war waged by nationalist guerrillas supported by neighboring African states. In 1979 he was forced to include Africans in the government without, however, conceding effective majority rule. As pressure mounted he resigned as prime minister and was elected a member of the transitional government headed by Bishop Abel Muzorewa. He sat in the Zimbabwean parliament from 1980–87.

Smuts, Jan (1870–1950) South African soldier and politician. Of Dutch and French Huguenot descent, Smuts fought in the Boer war against the British in South Africa (1899–1902). Once peace was made, however, he played a mediating role, helping to persuade Britain to grant self-government to Transvaal and the Orange Free

State (1907). He worked actively to keep the Union of South Africa (created 1910) within the British empire, opposing Afrikaner calls for an independent republic and ensuring South Africa's entry into World War I. Smuts commanded the Allied troops in East Africa and was appointed to Lloyd George's war cabinet. He took part in the Versailles peace talks (1919) and helped to set up the League of Nations. He served twice as South African prime minister (1919–24 and 1939–48). In World War II he once more committed South African troops to the Allied cause, and was appointed field marshal in 1941. In 1945 he attended the San Francisco conference at which the United Nations Organization was founded. Committed throughout his political life to the creation of a South African nation that embraced both English-speakers and Afrikaners, he was largely indifferent to the welfare of Black South Africans.

Solzhenitsyn, Alexander (1918–) Russian writer. Born in Rostov, Solzhenitsyn graduated in mathematics and physics and fought in World War II. Denounced for criticizing Stalin in a letter, he spent 11 years from 1945–56 in labor camps and internal exile. *One Day in the Life of Ivan Denisovich* (1962), an account of a day in a labor camp, caused a sensation in Russia and abroad after its publication in the literary journal *Novy Mir*. He was criticized and his work banned. *The First Circle* (1968), dealing with the dilemma of scientists working for repressive governments, and *Cancer Ward* (1968) were both published abroad. The award of the 1970 Nobel prize for literature intensified the official campaign against him. Then followed *August 1914* (1971), the first volume of a projected trilogy about the events of the 1917 revolution, and *The Gulag Archipelago 1918–56* (three volumes, 1973–75), a chronicle of the network of prison labor camps based partly on personal testimonies held in his memory from his own incarceration. In 1974 Solzhenitsyn was arrested and exiled for "treason", settling first in Switzerland and then, from 1976, in the US. His Soviet citizenship was restored in 1990 after the collapse of Communism, and in 1994 he made a highly publicized return to Russia, undertaking a long journey of spiritual renewal from Vladivostok to Moscow, where he made his permanent home.

Spielberg, Steven (1947–) US film director and producer. A precocious filmmaking talent, Spielberg won a contract with Universal on leaving

Joseph Stalin, the 20th century's most ruthless totalitarian dictator.

college. He went on to make numerous box-office successes including *Jaws* (1975), *Close Encounters of the Third Kind* (1977), *Raiders of the Lost Ark* (1981), *E.T.* (1982), *The Color Purple* (1985) and *Jurassic Park* (1993). His long-nurtured project about the Holocaust, *Schindler's List* (1993) finally won him his first Academy Awards, for Best Director and Best Film.

Spock, Benjamin (1903–95)
US pediatrician and author. Spock graduated in medicine from Columbia University (1929) having trained in pediatrics and psychiatry. He practiced as a pediatrician in Manhattan (1933–47), and out of this experience wrote *The Commonsense Book of Baby and Child Care* (1946). Written in a relaxed, accessible style, it advocated a flexible and understanding approach to child care and became an immediate bestseller. It went through numerous editions and had an enormous impact on millions of parents. *A Baby's First Year* (1955, with J. Reinhart and W. Miller) followed. In the 1960s Spock become increasingly active in the anti-Vietnam war movement. He was tried for helping conscripts evade the draft but was subsequently acquitted. Critics said that his advice to parents had given rise to a generation of rebellious, permissive youth, and in the 1980s he himself admitted that some of the views in his books were misguided.

Springsteen, Bruce (1949–)
US rock singer. Born in Freehold, New Jersey, Springsteen's first album, *Greetings From Asbury Park, NJ* (1973), won praise from the critics who heralded him as the new Bob Dylan. A Boston music journalist famously wrote in 1974, "I saw rock and roll's future and its name was Bruce Springsteen". Commercial success came in 1975 with the release of

Born to Run. Known as "The Boss", Springsteen was admired for the driving rhythms, strong, full sound and enormous energy of his music, and for his meaty, socially concerned lyrics. Legal problems prevented him from recording further albums for three years, during which time he was able to perfect his live performance. By the mid 1980s he had become the most popular US singer since Elvis Presley with a world-wide cult following, and "Born in the USA" had the distinction of being quoted by both candidates in the 1984 US presidential elections.

Stalin, Joseph (Iosif Dzhugashvili) (1879–1953) Soviet political leader. Born in Georgia, Stalin was expelled from his theological seminary in 1898. In 1903 he joined the Bolsheviks but played only a minor role in the 1917 revolution. Afterwards he was appointed commissar for nationalities (1917–23) and a member of the politburo. In 1922 he was made general secretary of the party's central committee, a position of power he was able to exploit after Lenin's death (1924) to eliminate his political rivals and win control of the Comintern. Under a series of Five-Year Plans, Stalin massively accelerated the industrialization of the Soviet Union and collectivized agricultural production with brutal force. It is estimated that some 6 million peasants died as a result of these policies. Countless more Soviet citizens perished in the penal camps and purges of 1936–38 by which Stalin tightened his grip on power. In 1939 Stalin and Hitler signed a nonaggression pact, whereby the Soviet Union occupied eastern Poland and the Baltic states. After Germany attacked the Soviet Union without warning in 1941, Stalin appointed himself commander-in-chief and premier. As a military commander he was mediocre, even less than competent, relying on stubborn defensive tactics and the climate to whittle away the enemy's strength. As a war leader, he showed qualities of determination and clear-sightedness in his dealings with Churchill and Roosevelt to defend Soviet interests and acquire territorial gains. In the postwar years Soviet influence was brought to bear ever more severely on the countries of eastern Europe liberated by Soviet arms in 1945, creating a Communist Eastern bloc engaged in a cold war with the West. At home, he launched a fourth Five-Year Plan, increased political repression and tightened the hold of the Communist party. By his death in 1953, it is estimated that Stalin's long reign of terror had resulted in as many as 14 million deaths.

Meryl Streep was one of the most admired first-rank stars of the 1980s.

Stopes, Marie (1880–1958) British birth control pioneer. Stopes studied at London and Munich Universities before becoming in 1904 Britain's youngest doctor of science and first woman science lecturer at Manchester University, specializing in fossil botany. The distressing annulment of her first marriage in 1916 caused her to turn her attention to the desirability of sex education and birth control for married women in order to increase their pleasure in marriage. Her book *Married Love* (1918), which contained unprecedentedly direct information on intercourse and contraception, provoked a scandal on publication but sold many thousands of copies: it was banned in the US until 1931. In 1921 she founded a birth-control clinic in North London. Stopes' frankness and practicality were pivotal in changing attitudes toward women and sexuality but her later writings, many of them for children, became tinged with romantic fantasy and with views that verged on eugenics.

Strauss, Richard (1864–1949) German composer. One of the foremost conductors of his day, Strauss was appointed conductor of the Berlin Philharmonic Orchestra in 1894. He made his name as a composer with a series of tone poems, including the popular *Don Juan* (1889), *Till Eugenspiel* (1894–95), *Also Sprach Zarathustra* (1895–96) and *Ein Heldenleben* (1898). He wrote 15 operas, including *Salome* (1905) and *Elektra* (1909), which come close to embracing atonality. With *Der Rosenkavalier* (1909–10) he retreated into a Mozartian conservative manner, which made him popular and rich. These last two operas had libretti by the Austrian poet Hugo von Hofmannsthal, with whom he was to collaborate on several of his finest operas. In 1933 he was appointed to an official post by the Nazi government but resigned in 1935 after he was criticized for collaborating with the Austrian Jewish writer Stefan Zweig on the opera *Die schweigsame Frau*. He remained in Germany throughout the war, actively composing to the end of his life.

Stravinsky, Igor (1882–1971) Russian-born composer. Stravinsky was taught composition by Rimsky-Korsakov (1903–06) who influenced his early music. He leapt to fame with *The Firebird* (1910), written for Diaghilev's Ballet Russe, and followed it with *Petrushka* (1911) and *Rite of Spring* (1913) which was booed and hissed at its sensational first performance. Stravinsky later began composing in a neoclassical style in such pieces as *Pulcinella* (1920), a reworking of music attributed to Pergolesi. He rejoined the Orthodox Church in 1926 and wrote several Slavonic chorales. In 1940 he settled in the US, producing two major symphonies and his only full-length opera, *The Rake's Progress*. (1951), with libretto by W. H. Auden. In his later works he turned once again to experimental, 12-tone composition.

Streep, Meryl (1949–) US actress. Streep made her New York acting début in *The Playboy of Seville* (1969), and appeared in summer stock. Her first movie performance was in *Julia* (1972). In 1979 she added to her growing reputation with appearances in three films, including *Kramer vs. Kramer*, for which she won an Academy Award. Viewed by now as America's finest actress, she made movies in many different styles, particularly admired for her skill in foreign accents. Her most celebrated movies include *The French Lieutenant's Woman* (1980), *Sophie's Choice* (1982) and *Out of Africa* (1985).

Sullivan, Ed (1901–74) US TV presenter. Sullivan entered journalism as a sports reporter, joining New York's *Daily News* in 1932. He began writing the paper's Broadway column and gained a reputation for spotting new talent. CBS hired him to host the popular *Toast of the Town* (1948–55) and *The Ed Sullivan Show* (1955–71), which offered a mix of variety acts and well-known personalities. His terse, reserved style earned him the nickname "Great Stone Face".

Sun Myung Moon (1920–) South Korean businessman and religious leader. Sun Myung Moon claimed that his mission to rebuild the Kingdom of God on earth sprang from a vision he had at the age of 16, which gave him the key to righteousness and designated him as the Lord of the Second Advent.

Australian opera singer Joan Sutherland, unequaled for vocal power and wizardry.

In 1954 he founded the Unification Church. During the 1970s and 1980s large numbers of followers were recruited in the West, attracted by its mixture of theology, anticommunism and astrology, which was in tune with the search for alternative religions and philosophies among the disenchanted young. They submitted themselves to long sessions of prayer, chanting and singing and were conspicuous in public places selling candles, flowers and pamphlets. Critics accused his movement of brainwashing, and of breaking up families. Moon, meanwhile, extended his business empire though arms, agricultural machinery and pharmaceuticals manufacturing in Korea and Japan. Undeterred by a brief prison sentence in the US in 1984 for tax evasion, he continued to proselytize around the world, staging vast, open-air wedding ceremonies of thousands of specially-matched couples.

Sutherland, Joan (1926–)
Australian opera singer. Sutherland made her début in Sydney in 1947 and then studied at London's Royal College of Music before joining the Covent Garden Royal Opera in 1952. The power of her voice first suggested her career would lie in performing the great Wagnerian roles , but her husband and musical mentor, Richard Bonynge, encouraged her to work on vocal techniques that would allow her to take on the great bel canto roles of French and Italian opera. In 1959 she sang the title role in Donizetti's *Lucia di Lammermoor* for the first time. Her effortless coloratura technique and phenomenal high notes thrilled audiences and she went on to sing in all the major operas houses including Vienna (1959), La Scala (1961) and the New York Metropolitan (1961). In 1965 she toured Australia for the first time with her own opera company, and she chose the Sydney Opera House for her farewell performance in 1990.

Swanson, Gloria (1897–1983) US film actress. Swanson was discovered while she was working in a Chicago store and she worked as a film extra before playing in romantic comedies and tearjerkers for Mack Sennett. In 1919 she joined Cecil B. de Mille at Paramount, where she found stardom in bedroom farces such as *Male and Female* (1919) and *Manhandled* (1924). By the mid 1920s she had become America's favorite glamor queen, dominating the gossip columns. She made the transition to sound movies and set up her own production company, but the unfinished *Queen Kelly* (1928) drained its finances, and she retired in 1934. She made several comebacks, most memorably in *Sunset Boulevard* (1950). Her autobiography appeared in 1980.

Tambo, Oliver (1917–93) President of the African National Congress (ANC). Active in student politics, Tambo joined the ANC national executive in 1949 and, after qualifying as a lawyer, formed the first Black South African legal partnership with Nelson Mandela. Throughout the 1950s he was placed under frequent banning orders for his antiapartheid activities. By now deputy president of the ANC, he left South Africa for Botswana in 1960 on the directions of the National Executive who believed, correctly, that the ANC was about to be outlawed. For the best part of 30 years Tambo traveled the world as the ANC's expatriate leader, rallying support for the Black nationalist cause in South Africa. In 1965 he helped set up an ANC guerrilla training unit in Tanzania, which became its military HQ. In 1990, following Nelson Mandela's release from imprisonment, he was made honorary chairman of the ANC. He was already incapacitated by a stroke and died not long afterwards.

Taylor, Elizabeth (1932–) US film actress. Born in London of US parents, Taylor moved to California in 1939. As a successful child actress she played in two "Lassie" movies (1943, 1946) and *National Velvet* (1944). A striking beauty with startling violet eyes, she went on to star in movies such as *Giant* (1956), *Cat on a Hot Tin Roof* (1958) and *Butterfield 8* (1960), showing fine sensibility as an actress. In 1961 she began a well-publicized affair with her co-star in *Cleopatra*, Richard Burton, whom she twice married and divorced. They made several movies, including *Who's Afraid of Virginia Woolf?* (1966). Her growing health, weight and emotional problems attracted headlines throughout the 1980s. She married 8 times.

Mother Teresa's selfless care for the dying of Calcutta won worldwide admiration.

Te Kanawa, Kiri (1944–) New Zealand soprano. Te Kanawa won singing competitions at school and worked as a popular singer and recording artist in New Zealand and Australia before studying at the London Opera Center (1966). Stardom came suddenly with her Covent Garden début in the role of the Countess in Mozart's *The Marriage of Figaro* (1971), and a brilliant international career followed. Singing the full range of operatic soprano roles, she continued in high demand throughout the next two decades. Her frequent TV appearances and many recordings helped popularize opera, and she extended her range into other musical genres, making a famous recording of *West Side Story* with José Carreras under the baton of Leonard Bernstein. In 1981 she sang at the wedding of Prince Charles and Lady Diana Spencer, which was broadcast to over 600 million viewers.

Temple, Shirley (1928–) US film actress. Temple was the most popular child star ever – cute, dimpled and precocious, she could sing, dance and act. *Bright Eyes*, the first of her star vehicles, appeared in 1934. It featured "On the Good Ship Lollypop", the song for ever associated with her name. Her bright optimism was what Hollywood needed to distract audiences from the cares of the Depression, and for five years she proved a top box-office attraction, spawning an enormous spin-off industry of dolls and coloring books, but her period of screen stardom did not last long and she was a has-been by the time she was 12. She later found a second career in public life, becoming US representative to the UN in 1969 and later serving as ambassador to Ghana and Czechoslovakia.

Teresa, Mother (Agnes Bojaxhiu) (1910–) Albanian nun and founder of a charitable order. While at school she decided to be a missionary in India. She taught at a girls' convent school in Calcutta from

1929–46 but after receiving a call from God to live and work among the poor, moved to the slums of Calcutta. Here she established a congregation of nuns, The Missionaries of Charity (1950), to care for the poor, sick and dying, especially lepers, on the city streets. The order (which was recognized by the Vatican in 1965) spread throughout India, but her work did not become well-known in the West until the 1970s. Since then it has grown into a worldwide movement with 200 centers. Mother Teresa's book, *Gift from God,* appeared in 1975 and she has been the recipient of many international honors, including the Nobel peace prize (1979) and the US Presidential Medal of Freedom (1985).

Thant, U (1909–74) Burmese secretary general of the UN. A schoolteacher, Thant became a civil servant in the newly independent government of Burma in 1948. He was appointed a delegate to the UN in 1952 and became his country's permanent UN representative in 1957. He succeeded Dag Hammarskjöld as secretary general of the UN in 1961 and was reelected to the role for a further five years in 1966. Throughout his time in office he maintained a dignified neutral stance and was equal in his criticisms of actions that threatened world peace, whether from East or West. He played a crucial role during the Cuban missile crisis and conducted peace talks to end the civil war in the Congo (both 1962), organized a UN peace-keeping force in Cyprus (1964) and helped negotiate the armistice to end the Six-Day War (1967). Not long before his retirement in 1971 he succeeded in securing Communist China's admission to the UN Security Council.

Thatcher, Margaret (1925–) British prime minister. Thatcher studied chemistry at Oxford and worked as an industrial chemist before becoming a Conservative MP in 1959. She held a number of government and shadow posts, but was a surprising candidate for party leadership in 1975, defeating the former prime minister Edward Heath in a strongly fought campaign. In 1979 she became the first woman prime minister in British history. A right-wing Tory and firm monetarist, she took a strong line on law and order and defense, advocated ending government control of industry and introducing tax and public expenditure cuts, and sought to limit trade union power. Her policies were not popular at first and failed to bring about any fall in unemployment, but success in the Falklands/Malvinas war (1982) won her a landslide electoral victory the

President Tito, whose style of leadership gave Yugoslavia 30 years of stability.

following year. She persevered with policies to shed government spending commitments by extending privatization. In foreign affairs she developed a warm relationship with US president Reagan and a tough line with the USSR, where she was dubbed "The Iron Lady". She was reelected in 1987 to a third successive term, but could not prevent a sharp rise in inflation. Her introduction of a controversial poll tax increased public dissatisfaction and her stand against full European monetary union led to a split in her party. She resigned as prime minister on failing to secure the party leadership (1990). Made a life peer in 1992, she rarely attended the House of Lords.

Thomas, Dylan (1914–53) British poet. Born the son of a schoolmaster in Swansea, Wales, Thomas' first volume of verse was published when he was only 20. He won growing critical recognition during the 1940s, years in which he established a reputation as an *enfant terrible*, famous for his heavy-drinking, bohemian lifestyle which he shared with his wife Caitlin Macnamara, whom he married in 1936. He became known to a wider public in Britain and the US through his readings and broadcasts and with the publication of *Collected Poems, 1934–52* and his verse play for radio, *Under Milk Wood* (1954). Like most of his work, this drew heavily on his Welsh rural background and gave full rein to his verbal exuberance and lyricism. It remains the best-loved of his work. He died after a drinking bout in New York while on a lecture tour.

Thorpe, Jim (1886–1953) US athlete. Judged the greatest all-round athlete and footballer during the first half of the century, Thorpe was of American–Indian descent. He played semi-professional baseball in 1909–10, was chosen for the All-America football team in 1911–12 and won gold for the decathlon and pentathlon at the 1912 Olympics. Though relatively unsuccessful as a player in National League baseball (1913–19), he was one of the first stars of professional football from 1919–26. He also excelled in basketball, boxing, lacrosse, swimming and hockey, but declined into alcoholism and poverty in his later years.

Tito (Josip Broz) (1892–1980) Yugoslav president. Born in Croatia, Tito served with the Austrian army in World War I. He became a Communist while a prisoner-of-war in Russia, taking part in the 1917 revolution and the Russian Civil War. On his return to Yugoslavia he was imprisoned from 1928–34 for conspiring against the government. In 1934 he joined the central committee of the Yugoslav Communist party, adopting the party name "Tito", and was appointed party general secretary in 1937. He organized the partisan resistance movement against the occupying Axis forces after 1941, and managed to overcome all other rivals to win control of the government at the end of the war, establishing a federalized, socialist Yugoslav republic. State control of industry and agriculture was less rigid than in the other Eastern bloc countries, and in 1948 Tito became the first Communist leader to defy Stalin and break with Cominform over differences arising from Tito's moves to set up profit-sharing workers' councils. Attempts to find rapprochement with Khrushchev failed, and Tito also fell out of favor with the Chinese Communist leadership. During the 1960s and 1970s he became prominent among the members of the non-aligned movement. His strong leadership gave Yugoslavia 30 years of stability during which ethnic differences were submerged. In the decade preceding his death he established a collective leadership to succeed him, which lasted until the violent breakup of the Yugoslav Republic in 1991.

Tojo, Hideki (1884–1948) Japanese soldier and politician. As a leading member of the Japanese army's "control faction" in the 1930s, Tojo advocated expansion onto the Asian continent and served in Manchuria as chief of staff from 1937–40. He was minister of war (1940–41). Becoming premier in October 1941, he sought at the eleventh hour to avert what his policies had done so much to bring about: war with the US and the European colonial powers in Asia. By 1944 Tojo was chief of the general staff and assumed dictatorial control, but he could not prevent the fall of Saipan in summer 1944, which brought Tokyo into US bombing range. This led to his resignation. After the Japanese surrender he was tried for war crimes and hanged after bungling a suicide attempt.

President Harry S. Truman steered the US through seven eventful years of history.

Toyoda, Kiichiro (1894–1952) Japanese automobile pioneer. In 1933, after visiting automobile factories in the US, Toyoda established an automobile division within his father's loom business. He produced his first prototype vehicle in 1935 and in 1937 the business was incorporated as the Toyota Motor Company. Japan's lack of natural resources forced Toyoda to develop highly fuel-efficient engines. After the war, Toyota avoided the US- and European-dominated market of large and medium-sized car production, concentrating on smaller models. In 1949 the Japanese economy became severely depressed and the workforce was reduced to avoid bankruptcy. Toyoda (the president) and all his executive staff resigned. He died within two years, too soon to witness the company's stupendous recovery. In 1982 it became the Toyota Motor Corporation.

Trotsky, Leon (1879–1940) Russian revolutionary and Marxist thinker. Trotsky joined the Russian Social Democratic Labor party in 1896 and was banished to Siberia in 1900. He escaped abroad in 1902, and at the Second Party Congress in London (1903) sided with the Mensheviks against the Bolsheviks, criticizing Lenin as a potential dictator. Trotsky returned to Russia and was prominent in the 1905 revolution. Banished again, he escaped to Europe and tried to reunite the two wings of the party. He returned to Russia in 1917 after the February Revolution and joined the Bolsheviks. During the October Revolution, as chairman of the Petrograd soviet, he organized the seizure of power in St Petersburg. As commissar for foreign affairs (1917–18) he negotiated a peace treaty with Germany at Brest-Litovsk, but resigned before its conclusion. From 1918–25 he was war commissar and led the Red Army, which he founded, in the civil war of 1918–20, afterwards using its members as labor in Soviet Russia's economic reconstruction. A spell-binding orator,

Trotsky seemed the most likely successor to Lenin, but after his death in 1924 was outmaneuvered by Stalin and his comrades on the right, who argued for "socialism in one country" as against the "permanent revolution" advocated by the leftist group of Trotsky, Grigori Zinoviev and Lev Kamenev. In 1929 Trotsky was banished abroad, where he conducted a propaganda campaign against Stalin, who successfully represented Trotsky as a monster to the Soviet people. Trotsky made an unsuccessful attempt to create a Fourth International to fight fascism and replace the Comintern. He was assassinated in 1940 in Mexico City, probably by a Stalinist agent.

Trudeau, Pierre (1919–) Canadian prime minister. A law professor, Trudeau entered politics as a Liberal MP in 1965. Two years later he was made minister of justice. He gained the party leadership (against 20 other candidates) in 1968, and was shortly afterward elected prime minister on a huge popular vote. A young, dynamic and charismatic leader with a commitment to federalism, he threw his energies into confronting and dealing with the issue of Quebec separatism, and did not hesitate to suspend civil rights in Quebec after an outbreak of terrorism in 1970. He twice secured reelection, but his tough stand on domestic issues and a series of economic problems during the 1970s led to his party's defeat in 1979. Returned for a fourth term in 1980, he once again took on the problem of separatism, winning a referendum in Quebec rejecting calls for independence. He set about instituting reforms of Canada's constitution and the introduction of a bill of rights. These constitutional changes were passed in 1982, giving Canada full independence from the British parliament. He retired from politics in 1984.

Truman, Harry S. (1884–1972) US president. Elected as a Democrat to the US Senate in 1934, Truman rose to prominence as chairman of the Committee Investigating National Defense. He became vice-president in 1944, and succeeded to the presidency on Roosevelt's death in March 1945, in the last days of World War II. He at once prepared for the San Francisco conference at which the UN was founded, met with Stalin and Churchill at Potsdam, and gave the order to drop atomic bombs on Hiroshima and Nagasaki (August 1945). In the postwar period, Truman initiated a policy of Soviet containment. Declaring that a line must be drawn in Greece and Turkey against the advance of Communism (the Truman Doctrine, 1947),

Archbishop Tutu led the movement for nonviolent change in South Africa.

he lent massive aid to these countries. Surprisingly reelected in 1948, he approved the four-year Marshall Plan for the economic reconstruction of Western Europe and organized the Berlin airlift to defeat the Soviet blockade of the city. He committed the US to membership of NATO (1949) and approved the involvement of US troops in the Korean War (1950–53). Truman was less successful in his domestic policy: he failed to institute a radical program of legislation, known as the Fair Deal. He left office in 1953 after seven eventful years, his achievements disproving his critics who had earlier dismissed him as the "everyday American" who became president.

Trump, Donald (1946–) US property tycoon. In the 1970s and 1980s Trump transformed his family-owned real estate company into a business empire through buying and revamping hotel complexes and apartment blocks on the promise of huge tax incentives. He built the opulent Trump Tower (1982) as a monument to his tireless brand of self-promotion and in 1989 acquired the Eastern Airlines shuttle, renaming it after himself, but his business empire crashed in 1990. This was followed by a divorce settlement of $10 million to his wife Ivana in 1991.

Turing, Alan (1912–54) British mathematician. A pioneer in computing theory, Turing first addressed the possibility of a machine that could could answer mathematical problems in a research paper he wrote in 1936 while reader in mathematics at Manchester University: it essentially described a modern computer. During World War II he was employed at the Code and Cypher School at Bletchley Park, charged with finding a way of cracking the German "Enigma" codes, and it was here that Colossus, the world's first electronic digital computer, was built under his direction. Later (1945–48) he joined the National Physical Laboratory to develop the Automatic Computing Engine (ACE), putting his theoretical work into practice. He developed early programming techniques, but could find no one to back his ideas. A homosexual, he committed suicide after facing prosecution for indecency.

Turner, Ted (1936–) US TV news magnate. Turner inherited an advertising business from his father and bought a small Atlanta TV station while still in his twenties. By 1975 he had turned this into the first "super station" (WTBS), transmitting programs by satellite to cable networks throughout the US. Then followed CNN in 1980, the first 24-hour TV news station. Many observers doubted the public demand for such a service, but CNN's ability to provide instant hour-by-hour coverage of events such as the Irangate hearings and the Gulf War rapidly proved them wrong. By the 1990s CNN had become so important that public events around the world were timed to meet its schedules.

Turnbull, Malcolm (1954–) Australian lawyer. Turnbull attracted world media attention when he successfully defended the retired British MI5 official Peter Wright in the celebrated Spycatcher court case (1986–88) and became something of an Australian cult hero for the humiliating defeat he inflicted on the British establishment. Arrogant, pugnacious and wealthy, he was an outspoken and persuasive voice in the Australian republican movement.

Tutu, Desmond (1931–) South African archbishop. Tutu taught until 1957 when he trained for the Anglican ministry. He took an MA in theology in the UK in 1966, and on his return to South Africa became a lecturer in theology at Lesotho University. He was appointed dean of Johannesburg (1975) and bishop of Lesotho (1976–78) before returning to Johannesburg as the general secretary of the South African Council of Churches (SACC). An increasingly vociferous critic of the South African government, he was arrested in 1979 for organizing a march in protest against the detention of other churchmen. In 1981 his passport was confiscated on return from a well-publicized tour of the US and Europe meeting politicians and religious leaders. He received the Nobel peace prize in 1984 for his constant advocacy of nonviolent change in South Africa. Created the first black bishop of Johannesburg (1985), he continued to press international leaders for tough sanctions against the South African government but was no less outspoken in condemning black-

Lech Walesa, as president of Poland, addresses a Solidarity congress in 1990.

against-black violence. He was archbishop of Capetown and the titular head of the Anglican Church in South Africa (1986–96). An implacable advocate of nonviolent protest and a deeply spiritual man, few will forget his public joy when the first democratic elections were held in South Africa (1994), but he did not hold back from criticism of Mandela's government when he felt it necessary. He published *The Rainbow People of God: The Making of a Peaceful Revolution* (1994).

Valentino, Rudolph (1895–1926) Italian-born US film star. Arriving in the US in 1913, Valentino became a dancer in vaudeville. After four years as a Hollywood bit-part player, he won the lead in *The Four Horsemen of the Apocalypse* (1921) and instantly shot to stardom. His potent blend of exotic sensuality, mystery and illicit eroticism appealed irresistibly to female audiences in the US and around the world. His subsequent box-office hits were *The Sheik* (1921), *Blood and Sand* (1922) and *Monsieur Beaucaire* (1924). News of his death, from a ruptured ulcer, was met with unequaled hysteria from his inconsolable fans, several of whom committed suicide.

Varah, Chad (1911–) British carer. An Anglican clergyman working in the City of London in the 1950s, Varah became aware of the high numbers of desperately lonely and suicidal people. In November 1953 he set up an emergency telephone help line, originally staffed by just four people. The Samaritans' free counseling service, operating on 24-hour call, mushroomed over the years into a huge network. As Befrienders International, the movement had branches in more than 20 countries by the 1990s.

Veil, Simone (1927–) French politician. Born into a cultivated Jewish–French family, in 1944 Veil and her family were deported to Auschwitz. She survived to study law in Paris, and from 1959–65 was assistant public prosecutor in the ministry of justice. In 1970 she became the first female secretary general of the higher council of judges. In 1974 prime minister Jacques Chirac appointed her minister of health; reappointed in 1978, her responsibilities were extended to include the ministry for family affairs. On election to the European Assembly (1979), she resigned her government posts to serve as president of the first elected European Assembly (1979–82).

Vidor, King (1894–1982) US film director. Born in Texas, King directed a documentary feature *Hurricane in Galveston* in 1913. He moved to Hollywood and made a series of short films before *Peg o' My Heart* (1922) won him a long-term contract with MGM. Keenly interested in social subjects, he made his name with the anti-war film *The Big Parade* (1925). *The Crowd* (1928), *Hallelujah* (1929), *Street Scene* (1931) and *Our Daily Bread* (1934) had an equally humanistic, if sentimental, tone; in individual scenes he manipulated camera and sound brilliantly. He later turned to more commercial work, and *Duel in the Sun* (1946) and *War and Peace* (1956) represent the best from this period. In 1979 he received a special Academy Award for services to cinema.

Waldheim, Kurt (1918–) Austrian president and UN secretary general. After wartime military service Waldheim became a diplomat, working in a variety of posts abroad and in the foreign ministry at home. He became Austria's permanent representative to the UN (1964–68, 1970–71) and was Austrian foreign minister (1968–70). He failed in his first attempt to secure the Austrian presidency (1971) and was elected UN secretary general in 1972. In 1981 the Chinese blocked his reelection to the post. When, in 1986, Waldheim put himself forward once more for election as Austrian president, the World Jewish Congress asserted that as a Nazi transportation officer in Yugoslavia he had been actively involved in sending Jews to the death camps. He denied the charges and continued his campaign, and was elected with 54 percent of the vote. In 1994 a long-suppressed US Department of Justice report on his wartime activities confirmed the original accusations.

Walesa, Lech (1943–) Polish trade unionist and politician. An electrician in the Lenin shipyard in Gdansk, Walesa first came to prominence in 1980 when he led an unofficial strike in protest against a sharp rise in food prices. Industrial action escalated, and Walesa became head of an inter-factory

Andy Warhol, prime mover in the Pop Art movement of the 1960s.

strike committee which succeeded in having many of its demands met. Renamed Solidarity, the movement was outlawed in 1981 after the imposition of martial law by Poland's communist leaders, and Walesa was interned for a year. Conditions eased in 1983, and Walesa traveled abroad to accept the Nobel peace prize. A devout Roman Catholic, he was also received by the Pope, a fellow Pole. In 1989 Solidarity was legalized. It was allowed to contest the forthcoming elections, which saw the return of the Eastern bloc's first nonCommunist government. Walesa became president in 1990 but found himself without an answer to Poland's pressing economic problems. Defeated in the elections of 1995, he went back to his old job in the Gdansk shipyards. Despite a strong campaign, he was unable to prevent the yard's closure a year later.

Walker, Alice (1944–) US writer. Born in Georgia, Walker was active in the civil rights movement in the 1960s and was employed registering voters and as a social worker before becoming editor of *Ms Magazine*. An accomplished poet and critic as well as a fiction writer, she is best known for her third novel *The Color Purple* (1982), a moving tale of two sisters in the rural segregated South, which won a Pulitzer prize and was later successfully filmed by Steven Spielberg. A collection of her essays, *In Search of Our Mothers' Gardens: Womanist Prose* (1983) made a major contribution to Black feminist and gender studies.

Wallenberg, Raoul (1912–?) Swedish diplomat. Of Jewish descent and a member of a powerful Swedish banking family, Wallenberg was sent in 1944 by the Swedish government, with the support of the US War Refugee Board, to Nazi-occupied Hungary on a mission to rescue as many Jews as possible. He issued more than 13,000 visas to Jews on the pretext of invented connections abroad. As many as 5,000 Jews were sheltered in the Swedish compound in Budapest. When the Soviet army entered Budapest in January 1945 Wallenberg was taken into custody on charges of spying. He never returned, and the Soviet authorities denied all knowledge of his fate. They claimed later that he died in the Ljubyanka prison in Moscow in 1947, but there were consistent reports of his sighting by other prisoners until the 1950s and even as late as the 1970s. He was made an honorary citizen of the US (1981), Canada (1985) and Israel (1986).

Warhol, Andy (1930–87) US artist and filmmaker. Warhol worked in New York as an advertising illustrator, in 1957 winning the Art Director's Club medal. He was at the front of the Pop Art movement, producing works such as *Campbells Soup Cans 200* (1962), which became icons of the consumer society: his screen-prints of Marilyn Monroe (also 1962) revealed the star as another cleverly packaged commodity. He made underground movies, attempting to remove the element of creative choice by leaving a camera in one position for hours, as in *Sleep* (1963). Cultivating inconsequentiality and banality in whatever he did, Warhol's enduring achievement was to have turned these qualities into an art form. An eccentric figure in the avant-garde art scene, he made the classic statement on modern society when he claimed, in 1968, that "in the future everybody will be world famous for fifteen minutes".

Warner, Jack (1892–1978) Canadian-born film executive. Warner set up the Warner Bros studio with his two brothers in 1923. In 1927 they launched the first sound film, *The Jazz Singer*, starring Al Jolson, and throughout the 1930s produced a stream of gangster movies starring James Cagney, social dramas, biographies and Busby Berkeley musicals that reflected the mood of the Depression years. One of Warner's last box office successes was *My Fair Lady* (1964).

Watson, James Dewey (1928–) US molecular biologist. Watson worked as a virologist and geneticist in the University of Copenhagen (1950–51) before joining the Medical Research Council Unit at the Cavendish Laboratory, Cambridge (1951–53) where he worked closely with F. H. C. Crick on the structure of DNA. By then known to be the carrier of the genetic code, it was also being studied by Maurice Wilkins and Rosalie Franklin at King's College, London. Watson, Crick and Wilkins shared a Nobel prize in 1962 (Franklin was already dead) and

John Wayne played the tough but warm-hearted gunman in countless Westerns.

Watson's famous book describing the search for DNA's helical structure, *The Double Helix*, was published in 1968. He later returned to the US, to concentrate on cancer research.

Wayne, John (1907–79) US film actor. Many of Wayne's best roles were in John Ford movies – *Stagecoach* (1939), *Fort Apache* (1948), *She Wore a Yellow Ribbon* (1949), *The Quiet Man* (1952) and *The Searchers* (1956). He became an American folk hero: his strong, taciturn screen image was supported by his off-screen hawkish, patriotic statements. His performance in *True Grit* (1969) won him an Academy Award.

Weill, Kurt (1900–50) German composer. Weill's early works included chamber music and two symphonies, but it was the jazz-influenced rhythms of his scoring of Bertolt Brecht's *The Threepenny Opera* (1928), a brilliant updating of John Gay's *The Beggar's Opera*, that brought him fame. He continued to work with Brecht on socially concerned pieces, most notably *The Rise and Fall of the City of Mahagonny* (1930), a satire of get-rich-quick capitalism. A Jew, Weill fled Nazi Germany (1933) and eventually settled in the US, where he composed scores for musical comedies such as *Lady in the Dark* (1941). He was married to the singer Lotte Lenya, the greatest interpreter of his music.

Weissmuller, Johnny (1904–84) US swimmer and film actor. Weissmuller won a total of five gold medals in the 1924 and 1928 Olympics and set 67 world swimming records. He turned professional to model swimwear and was chosen by MGM to play Tarzan in 1932. Famous for his jungle-cries and chest-thumping, he made the role his own in at least 12 movies.

Weizmann, Chaim (1874–1952) Israeli statesman. Born in Russia, Weizmann trained as a chemist in Switzerland and took up a position at

Manchester University, becoming a British citizen in 1910. Dedicated since youth to the Zionist aims of Theodor Herzl, he cultivated the political connections he made through his work with the munitions industry and was instrumental in securing the British government's commitment to the Balfour Declaration (1917) in support of a Jewish national home in Palestine. He was president of the World Zionist Organization (1921–31, 1935–46), and first president of the new state of Israel (1948).

Welles, Orson (1915–85) US director, producer, screenwriter and actor. A prodigy actor, Welles toured and directed in Ireland as a teenager and founded the Mercury Theater with John Houseman in 1937. He first acquired public fame in 1938 when his radio dramatization of H. G. Wells' *The War of the Worlds* caused a panic among New Yorkers who believed that an invasion from Mars was really happening. Still only 25, he made his début as a film director with *Citizen Kane* (1941), a Hollywood classic about the rise to power of a newspaper magnate, obviously modeled on William Randolph Hearst. Though many of its photographic effects were not original, Welles used them to startling and dramatic effect and clearly had a brilliant organizing vision, but much of his later work was hampered by studio interference or financial problems. As an actor Welles is best remembered for his brooding screen presence in *Jane Eyre* (1944) and his portrayal of Harry Lime in *The Third Man* (1949).

Wells, H. G. (1861–1946) British novelist. Born into genteel poverty in Kent, Wells became a draper's assistant on leaving school but later took up work as a pupil-teacher and succeeded in winning a scholarship to London University, where he studied biology. He supported himself by lecturing and journalism and set about establishing a literary career. His scientific fantasies, such as *The Time Machine* (1895) and *The War of the Worlds* (1898) created a new literary genre. A prolific writer and a socialist, he also wrote a series of comic novels including *Kipps* (1905) and *The History of Mr Polly* (1910), and addressed contemporary issues such as female emancipation, free love, progressive education and "world government" in his numerous books, novels and articles. His private life was frequently the subject of scandal: he was twice married and had numerous affairs with "new" women including the writer Rebecca West. Wells originally held that science could create a perfect world but later came to believe

Australia's prime minister Gough Whitlam caused a constitutional crisis in 1974.

that human civilization was likely to destroy itself. He outlined his socialist, internationalist and Utopian solutions to the ills of modern society in passionately argued books such as *The Shape of Things to Come* (1933).

West, Mae (1892–1981) US actress. An entertainer at five, West wrote, produced and directed her first Broadway stage play, *Sex*, in 1926. Jailed for obscenity, she went on to direct several more of her own plays before joining Paramount. A shrewd woman with a talent for innuendo and double entendre, her blowsy persona made her both a sex star and a parody of that image. Her witticisms became folklore, and in 1935 she was the highest-paid woman in the US. Her films include *She Done Him Wrong* and *I'm No Angel* (both 1933). During World War II Allied soldiers famously nicknamed their inflatable life jackets after her. She returned to the stage in the 1940s and made a rare movie appearance in Gore Vidal's *Myra Breckinridge* (1970).

White, Patrick (1912–90) Australian novelist. White was sent to school in England and read modern languages at Cambridge, then settled in London where he wrote *Happy Valley* (1939) and *The Living and the Dead* (1941), novels that were untypical of his later work. During World War II he served as an RAF intelligence officer in Greece. Returning to Australia, he began to win a reputation with a series of novels on Australian themes: *The Tree of Man* (1955), *Voss* (1957), the story of an epic attempt to cross the continent, and *Riders of the Chariot* (1961). His writing, which is infused with symbolism, is often savagely satirical, attacking social conformity in highly wrought and resonant prose. An interest in Jung and myth led him to write *The Solid Mandala* (1966). With *The Eye of the Storm* (1973) he became the first Australian to win the Nobel prize for literature.

Whitlam, Gough (1916–) Australian prime minister. Elected to parliament in 1952 and leader of the Labor party since 1967, Whitlam came to power as Australia's first Labor prime minister for 23 years in 1972. He introduced constitutional changes, scrapping the honors system and ending conscription, and addressed the issue of Aboriginal land rights. His radical measures led frequently to conflict within his own party. He continued to press home his economic policies as Australia went into recession, even reclaiming national ownership of resources sold overseas, and his support in parliament collapsed (1974). The governor-general, Sir John Kerr, took the unprecedented step of dismissing Whitlam's government and appointing a caretaker prime minister. In the ensuing general election Labor was defeated though Whitlam held on to the party leadership, only to be forced to resign a year later.

Wiesenthal, Simon (1908–) Austrian war crimes investigator. Born in Poland, Wiesenthal practiced as an architect but was sent as a Jew to a Nazi forced labor camp (1941–43). He escaped but was soon recaptured and spent the rest of the war in Mauthausen concentration camp. More than 80 members of his family died in the Holocaust. Indelibly scarred by his experiences, Weisenthal devoted the rest of his life to bringing Nazi war criminals to justice, working for the US Army's War Crimes unit until its closure in 1947, and then setting up his own organization in Austria. In 1960 he obtained proof that Adolf Eichmann, chief of the Gestapo's anti-Jewish operations, was in hiding in Argentina and obtained his capture and trial in Israel in 1961. He searched painstakingly though piles of records and interviewed camp-survivors to track down hundreds of former Nazis, determined to show that the victims of the camps were not forgotten.

Williams, Tennessee (Thomas Lanier) (1911–1983) US dramatist. Born in Columbus, Mississippi, the son of an itinerant salesman, Williams had his first Broadway hit with *The Glass Menagerie* (1945), a bitter-sweet comedy based on his own family. He immediately won recognition as an important talent. *A Streetcar Named Desire* (1951), with its unforgettable portrayal of combustible sexuality, secured his first Pulitzer prize, followed by *Cat on a Hot Tin Roof* (1955), a satire on Southern mendacity and greed. Several other plays followed and he also published collections of verse, but much of his later work fell into self-parody.

The novelist and critic Virginia Woolf was at the center of British intellectual life.

Williams, William Carlos (1883–1963) US poet. Williams, who was a medical practitioner in his hometown of Rutherford, New Jersey, was encouraged to write experimental poetry by Ezra Pound. In his finest work, *Paterson* (5 volumes, 1946–58), he uses the metaphor of his hometown to explore the soul of America and of modern man. He also produced a great deal of prose including historical essays, a novel-trilogy, short stories and a play, *A Dream of Love* (1948). His autobiography appeared in 1951, and his final collection *Pictures from Brueghel and Other Poems* (1962) won him the 1963 Pulitzer prize.

Wilson, Harold (1916–95) British prime minister. A former lecturer in economics at Oxford University, Wilson became a Labor MP in 1945 and in 1947 was made president of the Board of Trade, resigning in 1951 in protest over the introduction of medical prescription charges. He was elected party leader in 1963 and, promoting Labor as the party of technology and efficiency, secured electoral victory in 1964 and became prime minister. He was reelected with a greatly increased majority in 1966, but soon met with economic problems and in 1967 was forced to devalue the pound. He had to abandon plans to introduce trade union reform and though the economy began to recover and Wilson's popularity revived, Labor failed to win the 1970 election. He regained the premiership in 1974, in the midst of a miners' strike. Inflation continued to rise sharply, and in 1976 Wilson resigned as premier and party leader. He was created Baron Wilson of Rievaulx (1983) and retired from public life.

Wilson, (Thomas) Woodrow (1856–1924) US president. The son of a Presbyterian minister from Virginia, Wilson rose to prominence as the reforming Democratic governor of New Jersey and in 1913 became president running against President Taft and

Theodore Roosevelt on a split Republican ticket. He immediately embarked upon a program of radical domestic legislation, to achieve what he had described as the New Freedom. Wilson adopted a neutral stance on the outbreak of World War I, but Germany's submarine warfare, particularly the sinking of the ocean liner *Lusitania,* helped bring the US into the war in April 1917. In 1918 he listed his Fourteen Points necessary to a lasting peace and attended the Paris Peace Conference (1919), where he played a role in establishing the League of Nations. A signatory to the Treaty of Versailles, he was awarded the 1919 Nobel peace prize.

Winfrey, Oprah (1954–) US broadcaster. Born in the Southern state of Tennessee, Winfrey had an unhappy childhood and was sent to a detention home at the age of 13. Overcoming all obstacles, she became the the first woman to own and produce her own talk show and the first Black person to own a large television studio. Her show owed its enormous worldwide success to her ability to coax, wheedle or bully her studio audience into answering hard-hitting and sometimes sensational questions on issue-raising topics. By the 1990s she was one of the top-earning TV personalities in the world.

Wittgenstein, Ludwig (1889–1951) Austrian-born British philosopher. The son of wealthy and cultured parents, he trained in mechanical engineering and aeronautics in Germany and Britain. His pursuit of basic principles led him to mathematics and philosophy, and he studied under Bertrand Russell (1911–13), who described him as extraordinarily brilliant. His *Tractatus Logico-Philosophicus* (1922), written during wartime military service, consists of seven propositions on thought and language, including the observation that language, as our only means of articulating thought, cannot in the end account for itself. These ideas have been enormously influential. He abandoned philosophy in pursuit of a simple life but returned to Cambridge as a lecturer in 1929. He took British citizenship in 1938 and in 1939 became professor of philosophy, resigning the post (which he had called a "living death") in 1947.

Woolf, Virginia (1882–1941) British novelist and critic. Woolf was the central figure in the Bloomsbury group of British intellectuals in the years before, during and after World War I. Her mother died while she was young and she had a traumatic adolescence, leading to a series of breakdowns: she was subject all her life to fits of intense

The poet William Butler Yeats was the voice of Ireland's literary and cultural revival.

depression and mental illness, Woolf devoted her life to literature, both as a critic and reviewer and as an innovative novelist. In *Jacob's Room* (1922), *Mrs Dalloway* (1925), *To The Lighthouse* (1927) and *Orlando* (1928), which spans four centuries in the central character's life and encompasses a change of sex, she developed a poetic, near-musical technique to explore the current beneath the surface in individual lives and relationships. Her work is extraordinary in its sensitivity and its representation of the natural flow of consciousness: her tour de force is *The Waves* (1931). Her works of criticism include *The Common Reader* (1925) and *A Room of One's Own* (1929). Fearing the onset of madness, she drowned herself. Several volumes of letters and journals have been published since her death, adding to her reputation as a writer.

Wright, Frank Lloyd (1869–1959) US architect. Wright set up his own architectural practice in Chicago in the 1890s, becoming known for his long, low suburban "prairie houses", such as Robie House (1909). A pioneer in open planning and the application of modern technology to architecture, he was influenced by Art Nouveau and Japanese styles and believed we should live closer to nature, in scattered buildings. Among his best-known houses are Taliesin, the home he designed for himself in Wisconsin (1911), Falling Water, near Pittsburgh (1936) and Taliesin West (1938), his home and school near Phoenix, Arizona. Public buildings include the Tokyo Imperial Hotel (1916–20), the Broadacre City Project (1938), which featured dispersed "organic" office buildings, the Johnson Watt Tower (1950) and New York's Guggenheim Museum (1957), built around a spiraling central ramp.

Wright, Orville (1871–1948) and **Wilbur** (1867–1912) US aviation pioneers. Talented and self-taught mechanics, the Wright brothers set up a bicycle business to finance their early aviation experiments. In 1903 they made the first powered airplane flight at Kitty Hawk, North Carolina. It lasted less than a minute and covered a distance of about a quarter of a mile. Two years later "Flyer III" undertook a flight of 24 miles lasting over half an hour. Their success enabled them to give up the bicycle business and devote themselves fulltime to aircraft production. Wilbur died from typhoid in 1912, and Orville sold his interests in the company in 1915.

Yamamoto, Isoroku (1884–1943) Japanese admiral. Yamamoto was wounded in the Russo–Japanese war (1904–05), and was later educated at Harvard (1917–19). His naval career included a spell as Japanese naval attaché in Washington (1926–28). Virtually a lone voice in opposing Japan's entry into World War II, as commander in chief of the combined fleet (1939–43) he was responsible for planning and directing the attack on Pearl Harbor (December 1941). Afterwards he remarked: "I fear we have only wakened a sleeping giant, and his reaction will be terrible." Six months later his forces were defeated at the battle of Midway (June 1942). He was killed when his plane was shot down over the Solomon Islands.

Yamauchi, Hiroshi (1927–) Japanese electronics tycoon. Yamauchi took over control of his grandfather's Nintendo company, specializing in hand-produced Japanese playing cards, in 1949. In the 1960s he began developing portable video games. The Nintendo Entertainment Systems was launched in the US in 1985. By the end of the decade Nintendo had 80 per cent of the US video games market, and its profits exceeded even those of the Nippon Steel Corporation and Hitachi, Japan's industrial giants.

Yeats, William Butler (1865–1939) Irish poet. Regarded by many as the finest poet in English of the early 20th century, Yeats took up writing poetry seriously as an art student at the Metropolitan School of Art, Dublin. His verse, which drew on Celtic myth and legend, was a major creative voice in the "Celtic twilight", the literary revival of Irish nationalism. In 1889 he met Maud Gonne, for whom he had an unrequited passion. With Lady Gregory, he set up the Irish Literary Theater, Dublin (1899), which became, in 1904, the Abbey Theater. In 1922 Yeats entered the Irish Senate and in 1923 he was awarded the Nobel prize for literature. As well as the Gaelic folk tradition, he was influenced by Japanese and Chinese philosophy and

Boris Yeltsin, who brought about the end of Communism in Russia.

art. His poems, particularly in his late flowering period, are noted for their intensity of feeling and lyrical beauty of language. Among the best-known of them are "The Lake Island of Innisfree", "Easter 1916" and "Sailing to Byzantium".

Yeltsin, Boris (1931–) Russian politician. A construction engineer, he joined the Communist party in 1961, becoming known over the years as a reformer. In 1986 he became first secretary of the Moscow City party committee, and took on the task of purging the system of corruption. Entering the politburo in 1986, he rocked the establishment by making a speech blaming himself for inertia and hypocrisy under Brezhnev. In 1987, impatient with the pace of perestroika, he angrily proffered his resignation and was relegated to a provincial post. He staged a comeback in 1989, winning a landslide victory to become Moscow City deputy in the new legislature. Yeltsin became an ever greater thorn in Gorbachev's side, making frequent calls on him to resign. The two men made an uneasy alliance to tackle the Soviet Union's snowballing domestic problems, but after the attempted coup against Gorbachev (1991), Yeltsin, now president of the Russian Federation, suspended the Communist party, forcing Gorbachev's retirement. In 1993 he used firepower to remove conservative hard liners from the Russian parliament building. Dogged by his failure to solve the crisis in Chechenya and cure Russia's worsening economic problems, his style of government became increasingly erratic. He was accused of drunkenness and suffered two heart attacks in 1995, but came back to win reelection as president in July 1996 despite further rumors of ill-health.

Zapata, Emiliano (1879–1919) Mexican revolutionary. A peasant of almost pure Indian stock and with little formal education, Zapata adopted the slogan "Land and Liberty" to seize control in his home state of Morelos. He drove out the rich landowners, divided the lands of their estates among the peasants, and established schools, social services, and agricultural credit organizations. His reforms were reproduced in the 1917 Mexican constitution introduced by Alvaro Obregón and implemented under subsequent governments. Though his methods were controversial, Zapata became a national hero of the Mexican revolution. He was killed in an ambush by government troops.

Zhou Enlai (1898–1976) Chinese politician. Zhou became a member of the Chinese Communist party in Paris in 1921, and on his return to China joined the nationalist Guomindang movement led by Jiang Jieshi. Barely escaping Jiang's antiCommunist purges (1929), he joined Mao Zedong in building up the Red Army and organizing the Long March (1934–35). He became the Communist party's chief negotiator with the Guomindang, and in 1936 saved Jiang from execution by his own generals by securing his promise to make war against the Japanese his first priority. In 1949 he became the first prime minister and foreign minister of the People's Republic of China. He was prominent in securing the Sino–Soviet alliance (1950), negotiated concessions for Korean and Indochinese Communists at the 1954 Geneva peace conference, and attended the Bandung Conference of Afro-Asian neutral countries (1955). A stabilizing influence during the Cultural Revolution (1966–69), Zhou helped curb the worst excesses of the Red Guards and later paved the way for President Nixon's visit to China (1972).

Zhukov, Georgi (1896–1974) Russian soldier. Zhukov, the son of a peasant, began his military career as a conscript in the tsarist army. Joining the Red Army in 1918, he assumed command of a cavalry regiment in the civil war (1918–20). He made himself expert in armored warfare and defeated the Japanese 6th Army in Mongolia (1939). During World War II he became known as the "undefeatable general". He led the defense of Leningrad (1941), commanded the Moscow front later that same year, launched the counter-offensive to relieve Stalingrad (1942), and commanded the Red Army's advance across Poland to Berlin (1944–45). As minister of defense (1955–57) he took Khrushchev's part in the power struggles within the Kremlin, but was later dismissed for "political mistakes" and for encouraging a personality cult.

PICTURE CREDITS

Abbreviations

AOL	Andromeda Oxford Limited
HG	Hulton Getty
P	Popperfoto
RF	Rex Features

2 P; 4 Pioneers of Soviet Photography; 6-10 P; 12-14 HG; 16 RF; 18 HG; 20 Sipa Press/RF; 22 J. Dezort/RF; 24 RF; 26 P; 28 RF; 30 Ginies/Sipa Press/RF; 32 HG; 34-36 P; 38 Len Hutton/HG; 40 HG; 42 RF; 44 United Artists/Kobal Collection; 46 P; 48 RF; 50-56 HG; 58 P; 60 Alexander Baxhaum/RF; 62 HG; 64 Nils Jorgensen/RF; 66 HG; 68 P; 70-72 HG; 74 P; 76 RF; 78 P; 80 HG; 82 Novosti/RF; 84 P; 86 HG; 88 Tim Rooke/RF; 90 RF; 92 P; 94 Richard Bowditch/LGI Photo Agency/RF; 96 HG; 98 RF; 100 Matteini/RF; 102 P; 104 AOL; 106 Sipa Press/RF; 108 Hatami/RF; 110-112 HG; 114 P; 116 RF; 118 HG; 120 Dave Hogan/RF; 122-124 HG; 126 RF; 128 HG; 130 P; 132 RF; 134-138 HG; 140 P; 142 RF; 144 HG; 146 Stills/RF; 148 P; 150 RF; 152 Sipa Press/RF; 154-156 HG; 158-160 RF; 162 Trippett/Sipa Press/RF; 164 P; 166 HG; 168 P; 170 M'Sadek/Sipa Press/RF; 172-174 HG; 176 P; 178-180 HG; 182 Weber/Sipa Press/RF; 184 RF; 186 P; 188-190 HG; 192 RF; 194 Sipa Press/RF; 196-198 RF; 200-204 HG; 206 Robert Trippett/Sipa Press/RF

Jacket Pictures: 1-2 HG; 3 P; 4 Clive Brunskill/P